# Hugo von Hofmannsthal and His Time

D0839849

## HERMANN BROCH

# Hugo von Hofmannsthal
## AND HIS TIME
### The European Imagination,
### 1860–1920

Translated, Edited, and with an Introduction by
## Michael P. Steinberg

The University of Chicago Press
Chicago and London

This translation is based on the Suhrkamp Verlag edition of Hermann Broch's
works in the volume entitled *Schriften zur Literatur I: Kritik*, © Suhrkamp
Verlag Frankfurt am Main 1975. *Hofmannsthal und seine Zeit* appears on pages
111–284 and 300–334 of that volume.

The University of Chicago Press, Chicago 60637
The University of Chicago Press, Ltd., London

*Library of Congress Cataloging in Publication Data*
Broch, Hermann, 1886–1951.
    Hugo von Hofmannsthal and his time.

    Based on the author's works in the volume entitled
Schriften zur Literatur I: Kritik.
    Bibliography: p.
    Includes index.
    1. German literature—20th century—History and
criticism—Addresses, essays, lectures.  2. Literature—
History and criticism—Addresses, essays, lectures.
3. Criticism—Addresses, essays, lectures.  I. Steinberg,
Michael P.  II. Title.
PT403.B7413  1984        830′.9′00912        84-76
ISBN 0-226-07514-1
ISBN 0-226-07516-8 (pbk.)

# CONTENTS

# Contents

# ACKNOWLEDGMENTS

The translation of *Hofmannsthal und seine Zeit*, somewhat like the original work, was a project that seemed to expand continuously. Many people have helped along the way, and both process and product owe much to them.

My first thanks go to Arno J. Mayer for pointing me in the direction of Broch, and to Carl E. Schorske and John W. Boyer for providing the crucial early encouragement. Raymond Geuss and Christine Schnusenberg read an early draft of the translation and made many valuable suggestions. Leonard Krieger, Arnaldo Momigliano, and Paul Ricoeur read the introduction and corrected errors and ambiguities. Kenneth J. Northcott, fresh from translating Arnold Hauser's *Sociology of Art*, read a late draft of the translation with a scrupulous eye and with unfailing sensitivity and generosity; I owe him my largest debt of gratitude. I would also like to express my gratitude to Christa Sammons of the Hermann Broch Archive at Yale University and to Hermann Friedrich Broch de Rothermann for his many insights into nuances of his father's work. Finally, I wish to thank my fellow students in the Committee on Social Thought of the University of Chicago. Their constant interest in the largest movements and the smallest details of this project were a noble expression of what is so special about that department. My relationships with Broch and with my wife Carol have been chronologically parallel almost to the day; her patience and sustenance during the reign of this *ménage à trois* have been immeasurable.

Whatever part of this volume I may consider mine is dedicated to my most immediate link with the generation of Hermann Broch and its concerns—the memories of my grandparents, Norbert and Rose Burger, Max and Hilde Steinberg.

MICHAEL P. STEINBERG

# TRANSLATOR'S INTRODUCTION

# Hermann Broch

*Hofmannsthal and His Time*

When Hermann Broch died in New Haven in 1951, he left behind an assortment of unfinished manuscripts that testified to his overworked, reasonably productive, and underpublished final years. His troublesome health and near desperate financial straits were not eased by his refusal to continue writing novels, a vocation that had brought him profound success, first with *The Sleepwalkers (Die Schlafwandler)* between 1931 and 1932, and even more with *The Death of Virgil (Der Tod des Vergil)* in 1945. The events of World War II and his own exile had convinced him of the ethical duty to understand society and politics through rational, empirical analysis, and hence ethically to apply all new knowledge to the programmed establishment of democratic society. Thus, to the displeasure of his publishers, Broch since *The Death of Virgil* had devoted himself almost single-mindedly to his protracted and never-completed study, *Mass Psychology (Massenwahntheorie)*, which amounted to almost 600 pages of fragments when it was published unabridged for the first time in 1979.

*Hofmannsthal and His Time (Hofmannsthal und seine Zeit)*, written in this final period between 1947 and 1950, stands next to *The Sleepwalkers* as a major synthetic examination of the "end" of the European world—its politics, its art, and, above all, its values. The essay represents the completion of a circle in Broch's writing career. He had started in his native Vienna as an essayist, a cultural critic much in the mode of Karl Kraus, whom he continued to admire, and had turned to the novel with great deliberation, in the interest of gaining a kind of knowledge of reality which he considered achievable only through the immersion of the self (the author) into the

1

world he wishes to understand. *The Sleepwalkers* is a product of that immersion. Its goal is the understanding of the dissolution of the European system of values. As fiction, it reflects Broch's conviction that philosophy had lost the ability to address such a question, that positivism in particular had marked the philosophical abandonment of the search for values. His eventual turn away from literature was again in the interest of knowledge, but it was also the result of his later conviction that the observer must stand back from the world he examines and construct a logical study of the particulars of reality instead of a metaphorical study of a holistic, symbolic reality.

"Confession is nothing, knowledge is all." This statement (from the third chapter of *Hofmannsthal and His Time*) describes the object-centered ethic and aesthetic of Hofmannsthal, and could clearly be taken as the unswerving watchword of Broch's entire intellectual career. The form that that knowledge takes, as well as the path most appropriate to reach it, is what changes during the course of that career. These deliberate variations in the path to knowledge form an essential parallel between Broch and his subject Hofmannsthal, whose career proceeded from genre to genre in every bit as deliberate a way. Their original identities were certainly not equal—Broch was never educated to be the aesthete Hofmannsthal was—but their intellectual developments were changing responses both to the political and cultural apocalypse and to the demand for reconstruction that defined their times. In that response, each moved from a concern with the purely aesthetic to a concern with the political. In a path more subtle than Broch's but not without parallel to it, Hofmannsthal the aesthete and lyric poet became Hofmannsthal the essayist and builder of the post–World War I Salzburg Festival, which he viewed as a didactic symbol of a reconstructed Austria.

Hugo von Hofmannsthal (1874–1929) and Hermann Broch, born in Vienna in 1886, were both members of the final generation of Habsburg Austria which faced the collapse of the dual monarchy and the empire, an experience whose ramifications were broad enough to represent for the entire generation a true apocalypse of the Western world. The unparalleled political collapse and transformation of the Austro-Hungarian Empire after 1918 into "the republic that no one wanted" completed an internal dissolution that had intensified over decades if not centuries, a dissolution that was immanent in the disharmony between the Habsburg state and its national and cultural components. The state was an artificial entity held together by neither language nor culture nor economy. In all respects it was a Tower of Babel, whose political and cultural fragmentation had been extended by its intellectuals into all spheres of rationality. As rational communication and the sense of society it implies were considered more and more elusive if not

2

totally false, languages of art—in other words, style—as well as language itself were condemned as both meaningless and false. Hence the popular notion of Vienna as the crucible of modernity, the little world, in Friedrich Hebbel's phrase, where the big world holds its rehearsal. The roster of intellectuals who came from this world and who challenged it with new modes of thought and art has by now become almost a guest list for an imaginary salon that intellectual historians might dream about. It includes Klimt, Schiele, Kokoschka in art; Loos and Otto Wagner in architecture; Mahler and the "Vienna School" of Schönberg, Berg, and Webern in music; the logical positivists of the "Vienna Circle" and its most famous adjunct, Wittgenstein, in philosophy; Hofmannsthal, Rilke, Musil, George, Schnitzler, Kraus, and Broch in literature; and, of course, Freud. The ease with which these thinkers can be referred to as a cohesive group should not obscure the difficulty of understanding the dynamics of that cohesion. Broch's groundbreaking understanding and judgment of those dynamics and their relation to European cultural trends in general is perhaps the fundamental accomplishment of *Hofmannsthal and His Time*.

There are no doubt vast biographical and intellectual similarities between Broch and Hofmannsthal, but in a way they are more evident to us today than they were to Broch, and it therefore seems a clear exaggeration to call the essay a "symbolic autobiography." Broch was born into a Jewish family of textile manufacturers of Moravian descent (on his father's side). He was destined to enter the family business and did so, remaining active in it until 1927. Hofmannsthal was born a Catholic into a family of Jewish-Moravian-textile business descent (again all on the paternal side: Broch himself provides details of the genealogy). Yet his grandfather had been the last family member to be active in the business, and his lawyer-father raised him as an aesthete (an education whose details and implications are, again, masterfully recounted in the essay).

As far as intellectual affinity is concerned, the determination to find a discourse that would be an ethically viable and epistemologically valid response to the modern apocalypse, as well as the resulting pattern of acceptance and rejection of art (as opposed to essayistic writing), form a similarity between the two men powerful enough to diffuse all differences. These are the terms with which Broch always identified his intellectual and ethical task, yet it was only in the very process of writing on Hofmannsthal that he began to identify and respect the same task and determination in the latter. This fact cannot be overlooked. Broch the admirer of Kraus had adopted Kraus's somewhat misguided hostility to the "aesthete" Hofmannsthal. Broch's evaluation of Hofmannsthal remains ambiguous, but develops constantly throughout the text, and contributes to the intensity and urgency of the text.

It is the relation between ethics and aesthetics, between the ethical quest for knowledge and the world view of the aesthete, that is the theme of *Hofmannsthal and His Time* and the criterion on which both Hofmannsthal and his time are judged. Broch traces the path of the aesthete par excellence as he becomes the most eloquent spokesman for the rejection of aestheticism.

"My book," Broch wrote of the Hofmannsthal essay in October 1948, "is actually an intellectual history of Europe, 1860–1920."[1] That is indeed its true identity. The choice of Hofmannsthal and the extension of biography into a paradigmatic critical history of an entire epoch were developments beyond the intentions and in many ways "against the will" of the author.

In 1947, John D. Barrett, president of the Bollingen Society, asked Broch to edit a volume of the translated prose writings of Hofmannsthal and to provide an introduction. Broch agreed reluctantly; he had no great sympathy for Hofmannsthal and was hesitant to interrupt his work on the *Mass Psychology* project on which he had been concentrating since 1941. He had hoped that the work already completed on that project would gain him a position with the Institute for Advanced Study at Princeton, where he had been living since 1939; but that fell through, and he accepted the Hofmannsthal offer as the most secure prospect of "financing 1948."[2]

Broch's new contact with Hofmannsthal soon changed his opinion of him. "The Hofmannsthal starts to take shape," he wrote to his close friend Erich Kahler in September 1947. "Just as a homosexual relationship develops slowly between the chambermaid and the lady, so I feel toward H.; with a sense of slight perversity I overcome my revulsion."[3] And in October: "The Hofmannsthal is a far greater task than I had imagined, and the setback it has forced in my own work brings me to absolute despair: when one has only a few years of work left to him, one can no longer delay on one's so-called life's work."

The final transformation of both the work and the author's attitude to it was clear by January 1948, when Broch wrote to his German publisher Daniel Brody, "I can only portray Hofmannsthal, this homunculus, if I portray alongside him the entire epoch, and that is a damnable task."[4] The increasing inappropriateness of the essay for an introduction to the Bollingen volume was clear: the context was too broad, the portrait of Hofmannsthal too equivocal. The book, Broch wrote, "is in fact not a book about Hofmannsthal at all, but shows rather how a highly talented man, who out of weakness succumbed too much to the conditions of his time, became a bad poet."[5] Yet when he analyzed one of Hofmannsthal's early lyric poems in the second chapter of the essay, Broch found himself convinced by its dreamlike quality.

In January 1951 Broch finally wrote to Barrett that the "critical biography of Hofmannsthal . . . is an entirely separate matter and should come out as an additional volume to the whole edition."[6] The publishing history that ensued, all posthumous, is complicated. The section on Hofmannsthal's prose writings, the content of the third chapter of this volume, was translated into English and published in 1952 as the introduction to the Bollingen volume, as originally planned.[7] The initial two chapters were first published, with the prose writings section as the third chapter, in the Rhein Verlag's 1955 edition of the essays (the sixth volume of a projected ten-volume complete works), edited by Hannah Arendt. Two subsequent editions—Piper-Munich in 1964 and Suhrkamp-Frankfurt in 1974—included the first two and the first three chapters respectively. It is not altogether clear why Arendt set the precedent of omitting the fourth chapter, "The Tower of Babel." Broch had sent her carbon copies of the first three chapters but never of the fourth, which was written last, and it is likely that she relied on her own copies rather than on the full manuscript which had been stored after Broch's death in the Beinecke Library of Yale University.[8] That fourth chapter was not published until 1975, in a Suhrkamp edition that complicated matters further by including it as the third chapter and displacing the prose writings chapter to an appendix. It is clear from Broch's manuscripts that he intended the work to be published in its entirety as four chapters, with the prose writings section as the third and the "Tower of Babel" as the fourth. The current volume offers the first English translation of the first, second, and fourth chapters and a new translation of the third, and it is the first edition in any language to present the work in its entirety as four chapters. As the first complete English translation of any one of Broch's nonfictional works, it should play some part in carrying westward the considerable Broch renaissance already evident in Germany and in France.

*Hofmannsthal and His Time* no doubt does justice to Thomas Mann's remark that "my books cannot be read, only reread." It is a cavernous and subtle work; my advice to the reader is to read enough at the first sitting to sense the spontaneous passion and rhythm which, for all the digressions, never abandon the text. These are the qualities beyond accuracy that I have worked hardest to preserve. I have tried almost without exception to preserve the integrity of the sentences, following the example of Jean Starr Untermeyer, translator of *The Death of Virgil*, who saw the key to Broch's style in the principle of "one thought—one moment—one sentence."[9] Where an English word or phrase is awkward or a rendering of a German coinage or phrase without an exact English equivalent, I have included the German word or expression in brackets. Several fundamental translation choices are given brief comments in the notes.

Those notes are deliberately sparse. I have worked on the premise that there is little more annoying or condescending to a reader than an overannotated text. On the whole I have provided notes only for those names in the narrow Austrian context that are obscure enough to merit more complete identification as an aid for further reference. The fact that Broch did not provide a single footnote made me all the more wary of adding too many of my own.

This text is built on themes, categories, and a vocabulary deeply rooted in Broch's thought. It therefore seemed to me that the most helpful introduction to the essay would focus on the historian rather than on the history, and describe the "style of thought"—a Brochian term—of which *Hofmannsthal and His Time* is a late and noble example. What follows, then, is not a biography or summary of Broch's works but a chronological analysis of some of the works, ideas, and concerns most fundamental to the essay itself.

## Early Writings on Aesthetics and the Turn to Kant

As he himself put it, Broch was "destined even before birth to become a spinner, weaver, and cotton mixer." He received professional training for the textile business at the Vienna Institute for Weaving Technology (*Webschule*) and at the well-known *Technikum* of Mulhouse in Alsace (then Germany, now France), where he graduated in 1906 with the degree of textile engineer. In 1908 he and a colleague invented and patented a cotton-mixing machine; it was in the same year that he began to write short, fragmentary essays of cultural criticism.

These early attempts at aesthetic and cultural criticism helped form Broch's later philosophy of an integrated ethics and aesthetics. The definition of the aesthetic realm as an ethical component of a society developed in two steps: first, the definition of art as a form of knowledge, and, second, the concept of ethical art. This trajectory starts with the "notebooks" called "Culture 1908–1909,"[10] finds its ethical component in the turn to Kant around 1913, and matures in the later writings, perhaps more than anywhere else in *Hofmannsthal and His Time*. Art as a unique system of knowledge of the object world rather than as one of confession or expression of the subject world is the hallmark of that ethical understanding. The establishment of this foundation led Broch himself to turn to art—in his case to the novel. The section of this introduction devoted to *The Sleepwalkers* will discuss his idea of *Dichtung*—poetic writing—as a form of knowledge.

The early writings—most of which were never published during his lifetime—reveal a steady adherence to the Schopenhauerian tradition of pessimism as well as to the apocalyptic tone and message of Broch's contemporary Karl Kraus. Broch himself recalled in 1942 that it had been in

Kraus's feuilleton *Die Fackel* (The Torch) that he had found the "spiritual courage and spiritual implacability" he had been seeking as a young man.[11] In a 1909 issue of *Die Fackel*, for example, Kraus published an article called "Apocalypse," in which he wrote, "It is my religion to believe that the manometer is at 99. Gases from the world-brain-sewer swarm everywhere; culture can no longer breathe, and in the end a dead humanity lies beside its creations, whose discovery had cost so much spirit that no more is left over to help."[12] Similarly, in 1908 Broch prophesied "the end of white man's civilization," of "white man's thought," in other words, of "rationalism"—all pejorative terms.[13]

The one spiritual realm that could survive the breakdown of "rationalism" was the realm of art; it was therefore doubly important to Broch, as to Kraus, that an apocalyptic age not bring about the disintegration of art. The possibility of aesthetic survival, which eventually disappeared into Broch's expanding pessimism, survived nevertheless as a product of his reading of Schopenhauer, the prime source of his adherence to the idea of *Geist* versus *ratio*.[14] Schopenhauer was the evangelist of chaos versus cosmos, of the rejection of the Idealist faith in reason and Christianity. His "clear thinking," Broch wrote in "Culture 1909," "defines the aesthetic: the feeling of beauty is joy."[15]

In this Schopenhauerian mode, Broch formed his first notion of the Platonic totality, a notion that would later grow to become the ethical ideal for a restored society. Here it is purely aesthetic. Following Schopenhauer, he writes that the "perception of beauty is the knowledge of the Platonic Idea, yet it leads to the very opposite result: beauty as affirmation, as the greatest stimulation of the will." Following this notion of aesthetics, Broch identifies musical rhythm as the prime example of the imposition of the will, of "manifest energy."[16] He proposes that the three-beat rhythm is the purest aesthetic manifestation of the will, and furthermore that it contains a unity of essence and ornament that is the goal of all art. To shun ornament altogether—the mistaken policy, Broch writes, of the "apostles of purposiveness" and their leader Adolf Loos—is obtuse; "their objection that human beings should no longer tattoo themselves is childish and a confusion of human, climatic, hygienic grounds with aesthetic ones: people still wear rings, women still accentuate their necklines with pearls, and Herr Loos still parts his hair, instead of shaving his head, and adorns himself with a tie."[17] Ornamentation, Broch repeats, is the criterion of expression—expression of the will—of every artistic style. Every viable art has its organic—not imposed—ornamentation.

"Culture 1908" appeared the same year as Loos's essay *Ornament and Crime*,[18] a polemic that linked historical copying in architecture with an overall degeneracy of purpose, identifying false, imposed ornamentation as the signal of decadence and the corruption of aesthetic sensibility. The dishonesty of architectural "copying"—the theme that opens *Hofmannsthal and His Time*—and inorganic ornamentation on the one hand, and the impossibility of Loos's alternative of unornamented art on the other, preoccupied Broch for a good three years. In 1910 he defended Loos's controversial department store on Vienna's Michaelerplatz, a structure void of any ornament, whose starkness was a direct affront to the neo-Baroque imperial palace across the street. Broch applauded the honesty expressed in the refusal to paste anachronistic ornaments onto a modern facade, but in a 1911 essay called "Ornament, or the Case of Loos," he concluded that, as an aesthetic, this refusal was impossible. "The Loos ideas are pedagogically valuable, but otherwise impossible, because they are so true," he wrote. "Ornament," he continued, "was the musical expression of the breed and of the spirit of *all* art, quintessence of culture, symbol of life, clearer and terser than all reason."[19] Broch thus declared a total aesthetic apocalypse. He accepted the Loosian idea of the impossibility of ornament, yet added to it that the absence of ornament means muteness, expressive impotence, and cultural void.

Broch pursued the idea further in his more ambitious essay of 1912 called "Notes to a Systematic Aesthetic." In it he reduced Loos's theory to "an affirmation, a most conscious affirmation of the inability of the modern to create ornament."[20] Ornament, he wrote, is a correlative of style, and "culture and style are entirely unified." Stylistic parallels among different art forms, between those of space (visual arts) and time (music), for example, can be discussed in terms of ornament. A Baroque urn and a Baroque musical composition share a system of ornamentation, a similar symmetry and repetition of motives (a motive being a curved handle or a single musical phrase). Thus, "the ornament can count as the predominant characteristic of the style and is applied as such. It is an abbreviation of the style, its trademark or (to extend the fruitful mathematical parallel) its differential."[21] The extension of ornament into style and eventually into culture itself forms the kernel of Broch's theory of style as it is expounded in *The Sleepwalkers* and *Hofmannsthal and His Time*. Style is the means by which a culture finds and exhibits its coherence, and a culture that can create no ornamentation and hence no style has lost all ability to talk about itself, to express its coherence. "Culture," Friedrich Nietzsche had written in 1873, "is above all unity of artistic style in all the manifestations of a people's life."[22] Broch applies this idea to a state of historical decline and uses stylistic incoherence as a signal of cultural disintegration.

As an essay, the "Notes to a Systematic Aesthetic" are hardly clear or straightforward. Broch submitted it to Ludwig von Ficker's Innsbruck-based journal *Die Brenner*, and it was rejected. The essay "cannot boast of any clarity," Broch himself wrote in 1913.[23] All the same, two important strands can be detected in it. The first is the burgeoning theory of style; the second also stems from the discussion of style, yet provides the means for the transcendence of that discussion from the realm of the purely aesthetic to that of the ethical. It is, precisely, the replacement of Schopenhauer with Kant.

Schopenhauer, who considered himself the first direct descendant of Kant, collapsed Kant's dualism of subjective knowledge and objective world into a purely subjective realm. Within that subjective realm the real, noumenal world resides in the will, and the phenomenal or knowable world is manifest in the representation of the will. Kant's noumenal and phenomenal become the will and the representation of the will. Thus for Schopenhauer the will *is* the "thing-in-itself," or the noumenal, an assertion that Broch flatly rejects in the "Notes." Kant's dualism rests on an ethical foundation: the impossibility of knowing the noumenal world dictates the necessity of ethical action based on reason. Ethical action is governed by the existence of the objective world; responsibility to that objective world prevents the subject from acting on the sole authority of his will.

In its briefly stated but crucial acceptance of Kant, the "Notes to a Systematic Aesthetic" represents a turning point in Broch's early writings, the initiation of a shift in both concern and language that will form the basis of his entire career. The turn to Kant in 1913 initiates the concern with ethics; the very word "ethics" does not appear at all in any of the writings before that date. As aesthetic tracts and rejections of both revivalist, eclectic art and the aesthetic theory that combats it, the "Notes" portend Broch's grounding of aesthetic theory in ethical principles. *The Sleepwalkers* expounds and embodies that connection; its theme is the ethical fall of a civilization, and in its form it is an ethical statement concretized as a work of art. A work of art that extends the understanding of ethical principles Broch comes to define as "ethical art." That notion matures further in the fourth chapter of *Hofmannsthal and His Time*, through the idea that a work of art can only achieve the status of ethical art by presenting an internally, i.e. aesthetically, consistent and truthful picture of ethical realities. Art must not polemicize about an ethical reality but find and reflect it, not express knowledge but find it in a way of which it alone is capable. This idea of art is grounded in the confrontation of a subjective epistemology and an objective ethics; Broch was able to arrive at this combination through his understanding of Kant.

The pretext for Broch's first public treatment of Kant came in a 1913 attack on H. Stewart Chamberlain's book *Immanuel Kant*. In that review, ironically entitled "Ethics," Broch rejected both Schopenhauer and the ethical relativism of the scientific positivists. (The latter had been at the height of their reign at the University of Vienna during Broch's short first stint there in 1906.) As Paul Michael Lützeler has written, it is in this essay that Broch drew from Kant the philosophical position that enabled him to defend relativism as the cardinal point of a subject-oriented epistemology, yet at the same time to reject the antiethical political ramifications of relativism, which Broch labeled "Machiavellianism." Kant's position of the "relativistic world view" (*weltanschaulicher Relativismus*) in the "Transcendental Dialectic" of the *Critique of Pure Reason* provided Broch with an argument against dogmatism.[24] Broch's understanding of Kant's position as a rejection of dogmatism led him in turn to accuse both Nietzsche and Schopenhauer of misunderstanding Kant, of falsely reconciling Kant's relativism with the "arbitrary" dominion of the Will. Hence this repetition of a statement made in the Notes: "In nothing else was Kant as misunderstood, and no one contributed more to such misunderstanding than Schopenhauer . . . what did Schopenhauer make of the 'thing-in-itself'? The Will!"[25]

Broch was now faced with the dilemma of how it was possible for "Machiavellianism" *not* to follow from epistemological relativism. He found the answer in Kant, asserting that the Ethics and not the Critiques formed the core of Kant's work. (Presumably he meant the Second Critique rather than the First and Third.) The categorical imperative became for Broch a "sociological law," the basis for the critique of Machiavellianism as well as the foundation of Broch's idea of a "new humanity."[26] It was thus possible to defend an individual epistemology as a bulwark against dogmatism and, at the same time, to reject the ultimate relativism of an individual ethics or value system.

The ethical led Broch to the political and to a brief infatuation with Austro-Marxism, the movement forwarded by Max Adler with the goal of integrating Marx and Kant. Adler had written in 1904 that "the Kantian ethic is . . . a great sociological knowledge, and its much abused categorical imperative is merely the precise expression of the same: that ethical life with its command of duty is not an individual value but, on the contrary, represents the unimpeachable form of the social relations of active men. The categorical imperative is nothing other than the form of social cohesion."[27] Adler's opposition of "ethicality" [*Sittlichkeit*][28] to "individual value" became a cornerstone of Broch's own theory of value. His sympathy for Austro-Marxism and its goal of reconciling Marx with Kant, however, focused more on Kant than on Marx, and never extended into practical politics. He wrote of a "pure politics" as an extension of the "autonomy of the spiritual . . . the concretization of purely ethical demand" and hence concluded that "pure politics is democracy." He hesitated to extend his discussion into a practical political program out of fear of a "politics of interests" in the form of a "dogmatization of the ethical." That trend he saw in bourgeois capitalism (and its characteristic pursuit of "enjoyment") as well as in socialism ("the proletarians of today are the bourgeois of tomorrow," he wrote in 1918).[29] At this point in his career, ethics and politics both remained in the realm of the ideal.

## Toward a History and Philosophy of Value

It is clear that the tradition of apocalyptic cultural criticism that Broch's early writings followed could not continue as his sole guide. The turn to Kant and the rejection of Schopenhauer formed the first step in Broch's deviation from a discourse whose political ramifications soon eclipsed its philosophical intentions. In both Germany and Austria the "pathology of cultural criticism," in Fritz Stern's phrase, engendered a powerful combination of mystical German utopianism and practical German nationalism, antiliberalism, and anti-Semitism.[30] The writings of Paul de Lagarde, perhaps the most influential cultural critic in late nineteenth-century Germany, contained all these elements. Similarly, the thought of Schopenhauer and his devotee Richard Wagner could be appropriated easily enough into practical politics. In Austria, the rise of the Germanic Ideology can be charted through the intentions and membership of the Vienna-based Deutscher Klub. What had begun as a student fraternity founded on a cult of Nietzsche and Dionysus developed in the early 1880s into a powerful mouthpiece of German nationalism, under the leadership of Georg von Schönerer, Hitler's "teacher."[31]

Nietzsche was no doubt the patron saint of the Germanic Ideology; whether his writings actually shared anything with that ideology continues to be a subject of long and intricate debate. Nietzsche was certainly no democrat, and he was no doubt an antiliberal cultural critic par excellence. Yet he was just as much an antinationalist and, if not a philo-Semite, an anti-anti-Semite. His refusal to espouse any programmatic ideology separated him from his contemporaries and assured the survival of his critical voice far beyond the end of the Germanic Ideology.

Broch wrote little about Nietzsche, yet his debt to him is great and evident, his construal of him radically different from that of the various cults. Broch seized on the solitude of Nietzsche, separated him from his contemporaries, and found in his thought a philosophy of values that could serve as a foundation for his own. He knew very well that, within the boundaries of the Nietzschean tradition, to talk of values as autonomous entities rather than as components of a single, universally ascribed ethic was to admit an impoverished state of spirit and ethics, since the existence of many values and value systems implies a pluralistic system of ethics within a given culture or society. A culture that operates under a universally ascribed ethic needs no recourse to the subordinate discourse of values—group values or individual values—within it. That is the Platonic ideal of the "totality," whose dissolution Nietzsche considered the bane of modernity. For Nietzsche as for Broch, the dissolution of values (as components of a universal ethic) and that of art go hand in hand.

What are the possible responses to the dissolution of values? To suggest a program that would restore the lost totality is to advocate a cultural conservatism of the kind Nietzsche scorned: the conservatism of the Germanic Ideology. Though his own proposals of heroic formations of a new society are vague and ultimately irresponsible, they strove toward novelty rather than toward restoration, and toward a society built on cosmopolitan rather than on nationalist foundations. Although Broch ultimately rejected Nietzsche's heroic ideals and envisaged in their place a democratic ideal, he accepted the degree of historicism inherent in Nietzsche's anticonservatism. In this context, Nietzsche and Broch stand between the Germanic Ideology and the tradition of German historicism associated with Ranke, Rickert, and Dilthey. To put the issues somewhat schematically, the Germanic Ideology holds that there was once a totality, that it is a German ideal, and that it can be restored; for Nietzsche and Broch there was once a totality, it was not German, and it cannot be restored through any imposed, external program. For the pure historicists, there never was a totality; hence there is obviously no talk of restoration.

In this context, Broch posited his burgeoning philosophy of values against a major consideration of historicism. Ultimately, he rejected historicism as a source for a philosophy of values, but accepted it as a prime source for his philosophy of knowledge. For this reason, his two essays on historicism, "The Concept of the Human Sciences" of 1917, and "On the Understanding of Our Time: Paradigmatic Sketches Toward a Theory of History," written between 1917 and 1919, are of paramount importance.[32]

Historicism is an elusive term that encompasses two essential meanings. First, it identifies a theory of knowledge proposing that man attains knowledge of himself through a knowledge of his own history (an assertion that Nietzsche rejected and Broch accepted), and that the knowledge associated with the historical or human sciences is thus quite different from that associated with the natural sciences. This is the idea of the human sciences as proposed by Wilhelm Dilthey. The goal of the historian, according to Dilthey and Heinrich Rickert, is to identify the values of a historical epoch prior to and different from his own. Hence the second meaning of the term historicism: the assumption that different epochs have different value systems, that history molds and changes values beyond the control of any constant or ideal "totality." Thus the historicist discussion of values presupposes a plurality of value systems, at least in time, if not in space. According to that model of time, no "totality" could ever have existed, and "each epoch is immediate to God," in Ranke's celebrated phrase.

Nietzsche and Broch stand apart from the pure historicists in their assertion that there did at one time exist a totality, which has since been lost. For Nietzsche that totality was ancient Greece; for Broch, medieval Christianity as exemplified and unified in Gothic architecture. This assertion of a lost totality places Nietzsche and Broch on a different footing from that of the historicists in a crucial aspect: it implies a negative evaluation of all epochs subsequent to the loss of totality. In their identities as cultural critics, Nietzsche and Broch do not merely examine modernity; they condemn it. Thus they do not accept the claim of impartial investigation of the human sciences. Although that investigative context was irrelevant to Nietzsche, it loomed large in Broch's path. Thus, though his acceptance of a Nietzschean historicism enabled Broch to reject the cultural criticism of the Germanic Ideology, his rejection of the "value neutrality" of the historicist tradition separated him from a basic tenet of historicism.[33]

This is not the case with the historicist theory of knowledge as expounded by Dilthey, who provided Broch with the foundations of his own epistemology. Dilthey's idea of *Verstehen* as the epistemological foundation of the human sciences helped form, or rather reform, Broch's own idea of *Geist*. The first source of Broch's idea of *Geist* as opposed to *ratio*, as discussed above, had been Schopenhauer, but it was through Dilthey's thought that he modified it to fit his Kantian, object-directed and ethically motivated perspective. Broch's use of Dilthey to develop his Kantian perspective is entirely logical, as it was Dilthey who had expressly extended Kant's epistemology from the natural sciences to the historical sciences. The resulting idea of *Verstehen* has been defined as "not merely rational consciousness, but the sum total of feeling, volition, and thought," a definition that would serve Broch's *Geist* equally well.[34]

Broch's essay "On the Concept of the Human Sciences" is an appreciation of Dilthey despite his—according to Broch—positivistic goal of absolute knowledge, in which Broch could never believe. The epistemological foundation Broch attributes to Dilthey founded as well his own eventual vacillations between history and philosophy on one side and creative writing (*Dichtung*) on the other. Once the human sciences are separated from the natural sciences in the knowledge they embody, their consanguinity with art increases. Dilthey's emphasis on subjective understanding as the foundation of the human sciences led Broch to see a unity of human science and art. The domains of history and art both involve the element of *mastery*, he writes in this essay; mastery, defined as the unity of subjectivity and technique, is associated with the accomplishment of the historian and the artist but would be an inappropriate quality to attribute to a natural scientist or mathematician. An epithet like "grand master of mathematics," Broch suggests, gives the impression of a clown. Mastery entails subjectivity and individuality: "the gift of historical genius is no more transferable than that of artistic genius, and no one can continue work on the torso of his creation." The essay closes with the warning that the Diltheyan emphasis on subjectivity should not lead to a devaluation of the ontological, objective content of the human sciences. This is a fairly standard injunction in the context of the human sciences; it is more interesting for the fact that Broch constantly evokes the same criterion in the context of art: confession is nothing, knowledge is everything. It is no doubt the Diltheyan idea of knowledge that Broch has in mind.

This essay on the human sciences is followed, both chronologically and thematically, by a much larger one that is truly a forerunner of the Hofmannsthal study. Entitled "On the Understanding of Our Time: Paradigmatic Sketches Toward a Theory of History," it was written between 1917 and 1919. Its four sections are subtitled: "The value reality of the epoch," "Construction of historical reality," "Logical dissolution [*Auflösung*] of reality," and "Artistic style as the style of the epoch." The fourth section is the longest, and the entire essay is an introduction to Broch's mature theory of style as the all-encompassing measure of an epoch.

The essay opens with a paragraph that Broch would later use as the opening of the "Dissolution of Values" treatise, one of the narrative strands of the third book of *The Sleepwalkers*: "Is this distorted life of ours still real? is this cancerous reality still alive? the melodramatic gesture of our mass movement towards death ends in a shrug of the shoulders,—men die and do not know why; without a hold on reality they fall into nothingness; yet they are surrounded and slain by a reality that is their own, since they comprehend its causality."[35]

The First World War brought a particular necessity to the understanding of the contemporary situation and its causes, and provided an urgent field of application to the modes of knowledge of the human sciences. The understanding of reality had become more than ever an ethical demand. For Broch as for many of his generation, the war was the apocalypse of a culture which had been disintegrating for decades, if not centuries. At the core of that process was the disintegration of values: for Broch, the dissolution of the "totality" represented by the unity of style (Gothic style as indicator of a unified Gothic epoch, for example).

Broch's historical method is thus based on the juxtaposition of ethics and aesthetics as the components by which an epoch is judged. Ethical reality is made manifest through aesthetic representation. Broch's own motivation is ethical—the ethical demand of understanding the ethical—or unethical—

makeup of an epoch. He presupposes that every epoch can and ought to be judged as a totality, or as a failed totality. That totality must result from a universality of style, and style is made manifest most obviously in architecture, but just as crucially in the visual arts, music, and literature, and finally in the very "style of thought." As a result of this formulation, Broch's analysis of an epoch leads him to a discussion of its art, as art acquires a position as the absolute indicator of the ethical makeup of an epoch. He takes very seriously the implications of the term "evaluation" (*Bewertung*): to evaluate a work or style of art is to unite the scale of beautiful and ugly with that of good and evil—an ethical scale. The values of art are ethical: "The aesthetic is the absolute in historical value reality, just as the ethical is the absolute in the historical setting of values." Hence the ethical context for the chapter "Artistic Style as the Style of the Epoch."

The ethical goal of art, as of historiography, is the understanding of reality. Art is ethical if it exhibits a process of thought that attempts an original understanding. Only such an attempt makes a work ethical, and only an ethical work can be beautiful. A work or style that is void of this thought process but that claims nonetheless to be beautiful is unethical: it is kitsch. To judge a work kitsch is to judge it on ethical grounds. To judge a work beautiful is to judge it ethical; ethical and aesthetic demands are united: "the aesthetic realm of an epoch . . . functions solely as the logical locus of ethical—in this case artistic—demands, whose evolution emerges as the center of investigation."

In the investigation of modernity, the phenomenon demanding attention is "modern art." Broch speaks of the "modern" as the necessary reaction of a French-centered Europe against the age of absolute kitsch, as a general evolution in response to new demands which were at once ethical and aesthetic. Painting more than any other art form emerges as the main exponent of these demands, forming the spectrum of the "modern" that begins with impressionism and ends with expressionism. The search for the modern is the search for a new understanding of reality, and that is to be achieved through a new understanding of the medium—in this case, the "image."

In response to the representation of nature in the painting of Millet and Courbet, impressionism "understood itself before anything else as honesty, as the turn away from all narrative, as the centering of *l'art pour l'art* in the 'concerns of surface and color,' as neutralization of the object." The failure of impressionism was its inability to live up to its misdirected theoretical goal of "scientific" representation of nature. As a result of that failure, it degenerated into mere technique, into such rational game playing as pointillism. The road out from this sterility, then, was the ethical demand for a new understanding of the medium. Two alternatives presented themselves,

Broch writes, and "they were called Van Gogh and Cézanne, both aiming toward the unconditional and absolute, in the knowledge that only in the unconditional and absolute can the totality and unity of the work of art be anticipated."

Van Gogh was the fulfillment of the demands of naturalism.[36] In other words, no technique separated him from his portrayal of nature; he was "pure intuition" and hence immediate to his objects. His chaotic and inconsistent representation of objects was void of any interpretation or imposed order. He showed the chaos of experience and did not, so to speak, "make a picture of it"; in other words, he offered no artificial order or artificial beauty. Yet his mission exceeded the boundaries of visual art; the reality he strove to portray was one that could not be understood visually. This is most evident in the psychological reality of a "naturalism that strove to a radical ontology of experience and the world."

Cézanne, on the other hand, was the master of the "objectless image." His portraits, unlike those of Van Gogh, are almost unhuman; he "loves the object insofar as he desecrates and abolishes it," Broch writes. Cézanne thus creates *nature morte* out of *nature vivante*, yet at the same time grants nature a new, strictly "painterly" life. For Van Gogh it was the immediacy to the object rather than the object itself that counted; for Cézanne, the object had become meaningless altogether. In the end, therefore, through a radical confrontation with their medium, both painters continued the nineteenth-century process of neutralizing the object. All content was the same; everything was "paintable."

Nevertheless, the confrontation with the medium of the kind exemplified by Van Gogh and Cézanne is an honest and ethical aesthetic process. The ethical goal of art is knowledge; knowledge is achieved through coherence, and coherence in art is the creation of a thought process out of the language of the medium, rather than out of "quotations" from external sources. The latter produces kitsch: "The art of 1869 was kitsch in itself, and kitsch is not to be defined as an aesthetic, but rather as an ethical category of radical evil, like every art that functions not for the sake of the work but rather creates its validity through values adopted from foreign value-domains. A style of painting that uses naturalistic pieces of wood is kitsch; music in which cowbells ring is kitsch." Kitsch is any style based on "eclectic effect."

Hence the final paradox of Broch's quite subtle idea of ethical art—a paradox treated at length in the final chapter of *Hofmannsthal and His Time*. The ethical goal of art is knowledge of the world, of reality. Yet in order for a work or style to achieve that goal, it must remain formally autonomous; it must stick to the formal language of its medium. Thus, once the aesthetic and ethical goals of art are united, the notion of *l'art pour l'art* is meaningless.

16

For their pursuit of understanding by way of a revolution of the medium, the painting of Van Gogh and Cézanne, the architecture of Adolf Loos, and the music of Bruckner and Hugo Wolf (contrasting, naturally, to that of Wagner, but also, oddly enough, to that of Brahms) form for Broch high achievements of ethical art. The ultimate failure of impressionism and postimpressionism, the destruction of the object, echoes, in Broch's mind, the ultimate failure of the architecture of Loos. Modern art and architecture, if they are to be honest, have no ornament, and are therefore mute, because modernity has "dissolved the object . . . and only the object can be of aesthetic value."

## The Turn to Art and *The Sleepwalkers*

By the time Broch turned thirty-five, in 1921, he had defined his lifelong field of investigation as that of the dissolution of values, the trademark of modernity. By what method and through what genre this reality was to be understood remained the unanswered questions. The search for the most honest and fruitful genre occupied him for the rest of his life, and engendered his double identity of philosopher and artist. His vacillating allegiance to the conflicting modes of knowledge of philosophy and art inspired his theory of knowledge, which alongside his philosophy of values is consistently regarded as the cornerstone of his thought.

Between 1922 and 1931 Broch published nothing.[37] In 1925, while still active in the family textile business, he reenrolled at the University of Vienna and for the next four years followed lectures in mathematics and philosophy. Among his teachers were Rudolf Carnap and Moritz Schlick, founder in 1928 of the Ernst Mach Society, later known as the Vienna Circle. Schlick called the group's philosophy "consistent empiricism"; logical positivism became its American label.

It did not take long for these Viennese philosophers to excite Broch's antipositivist convictions. Indeed, it was the dominant position of logical positivism which, more than anything else, caused Broch to abandon philosophy and turn to literature. He found the philosophical approach of his contemporaries to be a closed "individual system," directed by internal logic with no concern for broader issues of ethics and values. As Ernestine Schlant has written, "The logical positivists of the Vienna Circle relegated the search for values to metaphysics, and in turn refused to acknowledge metaphysics as a legitimate field of historical inquiry . . . Positivism became for Broch synonymous with the autonomy of any system which pursued its goals without reference to a common value center."[38]

Broch sought a form of discourse with the ability to confront the totality of the world, one that would provide a "world picture." He found that form in the modern novel, to whose evolution he contributed, and he wrote of his theory of the novel in a 1933 essay entitled "The World Picture of the Novel."[39] The modern world is unique for its loss of a world picture, he wrote; only fragmentary pictures and value systems remain: a commercial one, a military one, a scientific one, and an artistic one in the form of kitsch. In this state of dissolved values, every member or group within a society sees the world from the point of view of his immediate concerns. The ethical imperative of modern existence, then, is the creation of a total value system adequate to its epoch in the same way that the Gothic style and correspond-ing value system was adequate to its epoch. The ethical mission of the novel is to rise to its unique ability to create a world picture.

The novel's task, according to Broch, is not simply to mirror reality; reality is available without author and without reader. Nor is it to provide facts about reality; a narrative that aims to capture a totality by capturing a totality of facts is a decayed kind of "reportage." The mere assemblage of facts, he writes, becomes an absurdity, not unlike the antics of American tourists whose Baedekers reveal that their sole purpose is to gather facts. "Reportage in its most radical consequence is the breakthrough of the dogmatic in the shape of reality . . . the dogmatism of hypernaturalism."[40] The proper naturalistic goal of the novel is the truthful elaboration of human experience: an exploration into realms of which it alone is capable. In its ability to understand the dynamics of experience, the novel must "transcend into spheres of dreamlike higher reality." Creative or poetic writing (*Dichtung*) is always a "desire for knowledge," and the novel has the ability to attain knowledge to the extent of creating a total picture of the world. The aesthetic goal of the novel is unity and coherence, and the ethical purpose of that coherence is the total picture it provides. The novel presents a picture of totality that is of course symbolic rather than duplica-tive of an actual total picture. In doing so, it approaches its highest goal— that of mythos. "The endless, never attained goal of science to gain a totality of knowledge, the endless wish, never fulfilled in reality, of the individual value system to reach an absoluteness and a union of all rational and irrational elements of life—all this finds in the cosmogony and in the unity-creating syntax of poetic writing, not a real, but indeed a symbolic fulfillment."[41]

Artistic knowledge, which strives toward this totality, stands opposite scientific knowledge, which classifies and divides its world picture into autonomous fragments of both value and knowledge. This dichotomy evokes once again the epistemological distinctions between natural and human sciences made by the German value philosophers of the turn of the

18

century. Broch carries further the dichotomy, however, in a 1933 essay entitled "Philosophical and Poetic Knowledge." The nineteenth century remains for him at once the "heroic age of all natural science" and the "age of the dissolution of values."[42] Thus, in his own world picture, Broch stands in the legacy of Nietzsche, who wrote in *Beyond Good and Evil* that "it is perhaps just dawning on five or six minds that physics too is only an interpretation and exegesis of the world—and *not* a world-explanation."[43]

In 1941 Broch wrote of his turn to creative writing, or *Dichtung:* "*Dichtung* is legitimized by the metaphysical evidence which fills man and to which *Dichtung* penetrates when all other rational means of thought prove to be insufficient for this task: *Dichtung* has always been cognitive impatience, and a perfectly legitimate impatience at that."[44] Similarly, while writing *The Sleepwalkers* he wrote to his publisher of "the autonomous and inviolable private claim of the poetic to those deepest irrational layers, to that truly panicked region of experience . . . in which, steered only by primal affects, childlike attitudes, memories, erotic desires, man is driven on, animal-like and beyond time."[45]

Broch also wrote of a second reason for his turn to literature: "the immediate ethical impact . . . Ethical effectiveness is to a large extent due to enlightenment; and for such activities the work of literature is a far better means than science."[46] This conviction Broch was ultimately to lose; the symbolic nature of poetic knowledge of reality later appeared to him cognitively and hence ethically severed from actual reality, so that after the Second World War he returned to the scientific study of political reality.

Like the painting of Van Gogh and Cézanne, the modern novel was to achieve new knowledge of reality through a new understanding of its own medium. It stands to reason that Joyce was Broch's paragon, and that Broch became one of the first to acclaim *Ulysses* as the modern novel par excellence. The modern novel, he wrote in his 1936 essay "James Joyce and the Present," "must emerge from a precise state of consciousness, from a precise state of logic, in short from a precise technique of thought, from a logic that is bound to the time in question and that hence leads automatically to its themes and its peculiar content."[47] It is not enough to provide a discussion of modern concerns. Thus, "when, for example, Gide uses a novel as a frame for psychoanalytic or other scientific excurses, modernity is not attained. It could have been attained only if the spirit of scientific thinking—as it presents itself through a specifically rational and causal character—[had] penetrated the entire remaining poetic narrative."[48] *Ulysses*, on the other hand, is truly a psychoanalytic novel because the narrative form itself duplicates the psychoanalytic process: Molly's soliloquoy, Broch suggests, duplicates the therapeutic technique of free association. Granted,

Joyce ultimately rejects psychoanalysis; the parallel between it and his own style is strictly one of method. Joyce's style thus aims at a duplication of the style of thought of his age.

The correspondence of a changing use of language and narrative voice to the object world it describes elevates the position of narrative art as an instrument for understanding the world. Variation of narrative voice and style is a technique unavailable to philosophical or expository prose. Unlike a univocal expository work, which can only comment from a fixed position on the world it observes, literary narrative can change its voice to incorporate the many points of view and voices within the totality it describes, and hence truly understand its object world from within. Drama, for its lack of narrative voice, has always been closer to this goal; Goethe more than anyone else portended for Broch the technique of a deliberate juxtaposition of voices.[49]

The final identity of this technique is what Broch calls the "relativity of language." (It must be asserted that with this metaphor he abandons his dichotomy of scientific versus poetic knowledge.) The theory of relativity, he writes, discovered that the point of view of the observer is conditioned by his field of observation. The classical novel used language as a fixed instrument, since it construed its field of observation as a fixed entity. The more complicated method of Joyce stems from the knowledge that "one cannot simply place the object into the cone of observation and simply describe it; rather, the subject of representation, in other words the 'narrator as idea,' and likewise the language with which he describes the object of representation, must be incorporated as the means of representation." The goal is the union of object and method of representation.[50]

These ideas inspired Broch's first major success and perhaps his greatest achievement, his novel *The Sleepwalkers*. Its composition required total commitment; after defining his task in 1927 Broch sold the textile business and devoted himself to nothing but the novel. In 1928 he envisaged a novel composed of a series of short stories; this plan was abandoned—eventually to be revived for the novel *The Guiltless* (*Die Schuldlosen*)—and what fragments of these stories there were, were lost. The novel remained a triptych, however, with each book focused on a personality and a style of thought that exemplified each of three stages on the European path to apocalypse: 1888, Pasenow or Romanticism; 1903, Esch or Anarchism; 1918, Huguenau or Realism.[51]

Although Broch thought and often stated that the end of the nineteenth century was the end of a millennium, he never lost hope that a new civilization would arise. The historical epoch of *The Sleepwalkers* is that of "no longer but not yet," a period beyond the end of the viability of the old "totality" of civilization and its values, yet before any premonitions of a new millennium. It is thus a period of half-consciousness, a state of mind and ethics expressed through the metaphor of sleepwalking. It describes an altered consciousness rather than a dulled one, a consciousness in which reality dissipates into the dreamlike but in which the dreamlike possesses the ultimate ability to produce a coherent vision of a new reality. In its reality and in the narrative style that describes it, each period in the sequence of 1888–1903–1918 is more and more dreamlike. "The saturation with dreamlike elements becomes all the more visible," Broch wrote, "the more powerless the old value traditions become. 'Dreamy' romanticism gives less room to the dreamlike than a period of actual value chaos, in which even the dreamlike is turned untamed upon itself, itself becoming absolutely real."[52] The dream consciousness of sleepwalking can be both an unethical and an ethical response to the value chaos of the epoch: unethical in the form of abdication of reality and its lost values, ethical as the search for a new and higher reality. The narrative itself, in its dreamlike quality, falls into the second category. It follows its protagonists into a dreamworld and its surreal components; two of the protagonists (Pasenow and Esch as opposed to Huguenau) and the narrative itself are motivated by what Broch called "the longing for awakening." Yet neither these two protagonists nor the narrative succeed, ultimately, in forming a coherent vision of the new. For Broch this failure was ultimately to signify the ethical and epistemological failure of art as a form of knowledge.

The narrative style is molded by its objects. The first book is the story of the Pasenows, a Prussian *Junker* family living out an obsolete feudal existance and clinging to its obsolete values. Broch called his narrative a "harmless tale of regular tempo and nearly unbroken naturalistic coloring . . . still clinging to the style of the old family novel."[53] The style and rhythm of the second book, the story of the professional and erotic adventures of a bookkeeper, Esch, a Luxemburger living in various Rhineland towns, "moves with an explosiveness," Broch wrote, in keeping with its restless protagonist. In the third book, the brutal tale of Huguenau, a deserter who uses and destroys members of the population of an imaginary German border town, all narrative traditions are broken. The story is told in fragments and with no consistent narrative voice. Intertwined in the narrative is the treatise called "The Dissolution of Values," itself told from a nebulous point of view, commenting on the chaos and apocalypse that literally "surround" it.

The novel's problem, Broch wrote, is precisely the dissolution of the European value system that had been delimited by a common faith. Pasenow is conscious of the breakdown, Esch feels its imminence, Huguenau no longer operates within the reaches of the old system at all. Pasenow seeks refuge in traditional religiosity, Esch in an "erotic mysticism"—both of these "half-solutions which bring no liberation from the dreamlike, but which rather drive the ethical into the sphere of darkness and instinct, the archetype of tragic guilt. The avenger of this guilt, ostensibly supported by the crisis of 1918, necessary in the 'value-free,' realistic man (symbolized by an almost sinful type, who naively lives out his childhood dreams, in real life, to their conclusions): Huguenau, for whom the possibility of a return- ing ethos is explained in the epilogue, in the view toward Platonic freedom, on which alone everything depends." Esch's profession of bookkeeping becomes a metaphor for an "individual value system," and Huguenau becomes a nightmarish vision of a true "value-free" man. Hovering beside and above these three figures is the character of Eduard von Bertrand, "symbol of the entire structure" and "the single hero of the entire novel," the modern man caught within but not defined by materialism, "the passive main character of the entire novel, archetype of the 'rational man,' in many ways the predecessor of the realist, yet not value-freed but, rather, value- negating, ethical opposite (and opposite as well in novelistic technique) of the sin of the unawakened man destroyed by the sin of the rational man."[54] Bertrand is the foil to both Pasenow and Esch, both of whom are "moral types, if subjected to different moral dogmas. Moral dogmas, all the same, that are dying out in this time of the decay of values and that are being reduced to 'romanticism.' Bertrand, on the contrary, is the specifically aesthetic man; he knows of the ethical dissolution of values and attempts to rescue his life from an advanced moral (not ethical) autonomy."[55] In all of Broch's thought, the ethical as the creation of a new value system is distinct from the moral as a dogmatic and, hence, stale value system.

## *The Death of Virgil* and the Turn Away from Art

Despite the increasingly dreamlike nature of both narrative style and content, the goal of *The Sleepwalkers* is a truthful understanding of a historical reality. It is also a historical novel in the most fundamental sense of history: that of motion. Its epoch and its characters are in constant motion, both in time and, interestingly enough, in space: westward from the heart of Prussia to the frailest edge of German territory. Sleepwalking as a state of altered or dream consciousness is a state of motion. The twofold meaning of this state reflects Broch's characteristic device of destroying accepted polarities, in this case that of rational and irrational. The dream- like is irrational in its abdication of reality, yet rational in its inherent search for a new, ethical consciousness. In this sense, sleepwalking like *Dichtung* itself is the liminal state between aestheticism and ethicality.[56]

Although the idea of artistic creation as a suspension of reality and as actual somnambulism is in the heritage of the symbolist poets, the ethical demand that art and its somnambulism be directed toward a search for new values is at once Broch's contribution to and denial of that aestheticist tradition. While writing *Hofmannsthal and His Time*, Broch discerned in Hofmannsthal's lyric poetry and prose writings the same ethical motivation and the same use of the dreamlike, and hence changed his opinion of a poet he had always disdained. Between these two works stands the novel for which Broch is most remembered, *The Death of Virgil*. If *The Sleepwalkers* rested on an idea of artistic knowledge beyond cognition which would understand a historical totality, *The Death of Virgil* retreats to a discussion of the possibility of that knowledge. The ultimate desire for a knowledge beyond cognition is for a knowledge beyond consciousness, in other words a knowledge of death. Inevitably, therefore, *The Death of Virgil* becomes an indictment of art for its failure to achieve true knowledge beyond cognition.

The ethical goal of artistic knowledge is the understanding of realms of life beyond the grasp of rational, scientific thought. The title of Broch's 1933 novel *The Unknown Quantity* (*Die Unbekannte Grösse*) refers to that realm. "*The Unknown Quantity*," Broch wrote, "was meant to uncover the irrational background of a life directed toward purely rational cognition and wanted to demonstrate how a breakthrough from the irrational (the death of the [protagonist's] brother and his first love) reconnects the consciousness which had become independent, how it reconnects it with its origins in the soul, so that that particular unity of cognition can emerge which must be viewed as the basis of all religiosity."[57] Yet Broch considered this short novel inadequate to its task; *The Death of Virgil* readdressed the same subject.

This is Broch's *Ulysses*, a novel describing the last twenty-four hours of the poet Virgil's life, following him into trances and delirium in which he reevaluates his identity as an artist and redefines the meaning of his art. Whereas *The Sleepwalkers* attempted to understand apocalypse and cultural death, *The Death of Virgil* is an attempt—whose impossibility is *a priori*—to understand the state of mind of actual, physical, personal death. The novel ends at the moment of Virgil's death, at his moment of entry into "the world beyond language."[58] The impenetrability of that world implies that art no more than any other form of thought can transcend the boundaries of human consciousness. If art cannot understand death, it cannot achieve understanding of a true totality. The artist who recognizes this inability recognizes the limits—or the failure—of art. Hence, the climax of the novel comes in Virgil's resolution to burn the *Aeneid*, which he now sees as a failure, and his subsequent arrival at a resignation that causes him to allow the *Aeneid* to survive, incomplete, as a testament of partial, and not total, understanding.

The private journey the novel portrays by no means eclipses the political situation that defined the experiences of both Broch and his Virgil. It was a historical, political affinity that first drew Broch to his subject. In 1935 he was invited to give a lecture over the Vienna radio network on the theme of "literature and the end of culture." "It did not take much reflection," he later wrote, "to recognize the parallels between the first century before Christ and our own—civil war, dictatorship, and a dying away of the old religious forms; indeed, even to the extent of the phenomenon of emigration there were marked parallels."[59] "Virgil lived in a time," he wrote in another letter, "which can in many ways be compared to ours, a time filled with blood and horror and death, yet all the same a time of upheaval and renewal, a time in which the hereafter announced its arrival."[60]

In 1939, shortly after his own emigration to the United States, Broch described his novel in a letter to the Guggenheim Foundation:

> Virgil, standing on the threshold between two ages, exemplified the ethic poet par excellence; he summed up antiquity, as he antici-pated Christianity. As age overtook him, he was more and more overwhelmed by the antithesis of creative form and pure cognition, until, near the end of his days, he had determined to destroy the *Aeneid*. Just before his death Augustus persuaded him to desist from this decision. My book describes Virgil's last night on earth. I have tried to capture that fleeting moment of life which is the moment of death. The work follows untrodden paths of thought and concept, unfolding a four-dimensional sequence of lyrical im-ages designed to create a synthesis of that border region in which the rational and the irrational, reality and unreality blend into one.[61]

Yet at the same time that he was being drawn to this private, dreamlike narrative, Broch embarked on the preparation of a "Resolution for the League of Nations," a proposed redefinition of the league's ethical purpose as the preservation of human rights and dignity against the "legalized injustices" of national governments. In connection with this project he corresponded with Einstein, Thomas Mann, Jacques Maritain, and Stefan Zweig. On the basis of that correspondence, which had been exposed by a local mailman eager to ingratiate himself with the new authorities, he was arrested on 13 March 1938, the day of the Anschluss. After two weeks in jail, Broch embarked on a frantic quest for a visa. James Joyce, after some coaxing, mailed him a French visa, which he never received; finally Stephen Hudson sent him an English one, and Broch left for London in September.[62] After a summer in Scotland with Willa and Edwin Muir, the translators of *The Sleepwalkers*, he sailed for America, settling in Princeton (and finally in New Haven). His combination of objective interest and personal involvement in politics encouraged an interest in empirical political study as well as in the Virgil narrative. Although he had polemicized against ivory-tower intellectualism in his League of Nations Resolution, he continued to pursue this most hermetic and esoteric novel. He later spoke of the seeming contradition: "The book was valid so long as I had not thought about publication, which means before my emigration and the year afterward. The menace Hitler made death very real—some of the passages were written in jail. I was not only certain that I would no longer publish anything, but I also wanted to familiarize myself with the experience of death . . . a necessity for everyone who can no longer find the traditional consolation in religious tradition. I concentrated almost exclusively on the experience of death, worked myself completely into dreamlike states of trance, and wrote everything down almost automatically."[63]

It is probably not possible and certainly not advisable to summarize the 500-page trance that is *The Death of Virgil*. Instead, I want merely to sketch the components of its narrative and thematic climax, and the final resolution that Broch/Virgil reaches. Virgil, engulfed by the flames of the underworld and convinced that his art has been a misguided pursuit of beauty at the sacrifice of truth, decides to burn the *Aeneid*. He considers his failure the failure to transcend the boundaries between art, reality, love, and beauty. "Virgil does not yet realize," Ernestine Schlant has commented "that despite the most committed 'titanic' efforts, the cognitive boundaries can only be expanded, never broken open in the here and now. Neither the creation of art nor any other cognitive act can break through temporal confinement."[64] He cannot shake the belief that "genuine art bursts through boundaries, bursts through and treads new and hitherto unknown realms of the soul, of conception, of expression, bursting through into the original, into the immediate, into the real."[65]

Virgil's argument for burning the *Aeneid*, as he presents it to Caesar, is that he "wrote it not only for the reader but primarily for myself."[66] He alone, therefore, can judge his work against the "standards . . . of artistic perfection, that gracious compulsion of work which permitted no choice and reached beyond all that was human and earthly." "I was impatient for knowledge,"[67] he continues, " . . . and that is why I wanted to write down everything . . . for this, alas, is what poetry is, the craving for truth; this is its desire and it is unable to penetrate beyond it."[68] Virgil then concedes that he now understands the goal of his poetry to be the understanding not of life but of death: "I have only hemmed in death by metaphor [*Gleichnis*]. . . . Metaphor is not the same as knowledge, metaphor follows knowledge though sometimes it precedes it, rather like an inadmissible and incomplete forecast brought into being by words alone, in which case metaphor becomes nothing but a dark screen standing in front of truth and concealing it instead of shining out from its midst."[69]

The period before death is the "no longer but not yet" of consciousness that corresponds to the space between two historical epochs. The inability to form a coherent vision of the new is paralleled by the inability to attain knowledge of death. Thus the unacknowledged failure of *The Sleepwalkers* to attain knowledge becomes the acknowledged failure, indeed the very theme, of *The Death of Virgil*. The *Aeneid* is dedicated to Caesar; Virgil finally allows it to survive, imperfect and incomplete, as a gesture of friendship rather than as a testament of knowledge.

Notwithstanding the fundamental epistemological impossibility for the novel to be complete, Broch never considered it finished, even according to the measure of the realm of the possible. He was nearly obsessed by the fact that Joyce had spent seventeen years on *Finnegans Wake*; on one hand he felt the need to revise the *Virgil* manuscript continually, and did so between 1939 and 1945. On the other hand he wrote repeatedly that "the ivory tower had become immoral," that the political events of the time vitiated the legitimacy of artistic response.[70] The grounds for the turn away from art were thus in part political, but fundamentally epistemological.

The state of resignation reached by Broch/Virgil at the conclusion of the novel is the realization that although the goals of thought must be open, there is no such thing as an open *system* of thought, that thought and knowledge cannot transcend the temporal confines of consciousness. The multifaceted symbol of the ring, which pervades the book, points to this philosophical premise. In the moments before death, Virgil perceives his life and the universe as a totality, a closed ring, and a coherent system. This is his final illusion; earth and stars seem to unite. But the vision disintegrates: earthly life—plant life—seems to grow wild, extending beyond its bounds and eclipsing every star, including the sun. Consciousness, attempting to overstep its bounds, turns light into darkness. Finally this darkness becomes the breakdown of consciousness itself: "In the course of this un-nightly boundless nocturnality he felt everything which had been firm and able to be retained dissolving, felt the ground slipping beneath his feet, dropping into forgetfulness and infinity."[71]

The major reversal of Broch's aesthetic theory presented in *The Death of Virgil* is the renunciation of the epistemological claim of art—and thought itself—to grasp the totality of life. If the ethical goal of understanding is to be maintained, then art can no longer present itself as the bearer of such understanding, for the criterion of aesthetic value is unity and completeness, and the vision of the world it can present can at most be symbolic or incomplete.

The work to which Broch dedicated his final years, the *Mass Psychology*, is an almost intentionally fragmentary, unsystematic, and "open" investigation of the social conditions that promote totalitarianism. It claims first to diagnose the social and psychological bases of the mass hysteria that produced Nazi Germany, and, second, to outline a program for the reconstruction of an ethical, "open" democratic society on a foundation of human rights. The empirical, scientific structure of the *Mass Psychology* is as far removed as one could imagine from the dreamlike, symbol-laden and symbolic realm of *The Death of Virgil*. In fact, in an autobiographical sketch that accompanies the *Mass Psychology*, Broch belittles not only "art as knowledge" but the entire creative side of his own career. All the same, his abiding interest, he wrote in 1945, was in "the same problems as in the Virgil: here too, I am concerned with the processes which lead the human being to the loss and regaining of his *vérités fondamentales*, in short, his religious attitudes."[72]

Within the context of the ethical goal of a free, democratic society, Broch refrains from proposing any utopian vision whatsoever—the new and therefore unknown cannot be honestly described from the point of view of a state of consciousness that does not know it. An open (in other words self-transcendent) system of thought is epistemologically impossible, and a closed system that claims openness is dishonest and unethical. The grounds for the refusal to delineate a utopia are therefore at once epistemological and ethical. Broch's idea of the new is thus in the most literal sense anticonservative, and opposed to the tradition of German utopian cultural criticism.

Yet it is not a truly liberal vision either. Though he refuses to describe the ideal society, he never relinquishes the conviction that a necessary component of it must be a new, universally ascribed ethic. The Platonic totality must be restored, although it cannot be conceived of in advance. Broch will not dictate the values of the new system, but neither will he allow the possibility that an ethical society can lack a coherent value system. This conviction opposes the tradition of Anglo-American pluralistic liberalism from John Stuart Mill to John Dewey to Isaiah Berlin, a tradition that defines the ideal, open society by a pluralism of values.[73] Broch's vision is at once antiutopian (hence antidogmatic) and antipluralistic, and hence a unique—if unrecognized—contribution to modern social theory.

The *Mass Psychology* no doubt demands a major interpretive analysis, but that is far beyond the scope of this introduction. For its attempted synthesis of the social theoretical models of Marx and Freud, it merits comparison with contemporaneous writings of the Frankfurt School critical theorists, with whom, as far as I know, Broch had no contact.

Broch's work on the *Mass Psychology* between 1941 and 1951 was interrupted twice: by the novel *The Guiltless* and by *Hofmannsthal and His Time*. Since American publishers retained interest in him almost exclusively as a novelist, he was persuaded by prospects of desperately needed financial remuneration to reformulate some of his ideas in the form of another novel.

*The Guiltless*, published in 1950, deals, in Broch's words, "with conditions and types prevalent in the pre-Hitler period. The figures chosen are thoroughly 'apolitical'; what political ideas they have are vague and nebulous. None of them is directly 'guilty' of the Hitler catastrophe. . . . Nevertheless it is precisely from such a state of mind and soul that Nazism derived its energies. For political indifference is ethical indifference, hence closely related to ethical perversity. In short, most of the politically guiltless bear a considerable share of ethical guilt." It is a novel of eleven stories, of which six were old and five were newly written.[74] The ethical nucleus of the book is the confession of Andreas, a character who appears in several of the stories: "Original sin and original responsibility are related, and the question: where is they brother?—is addressed to us all, even if we know nothing of the crime. We are born into responsibility, and this alone, the magical place of our birth and our being, is decisive."[75]

A comment Broch made in 1949 with regard to *The Guiltless* seems to betray the anti-aesthetic stance of his final decade: "Science is unable to provide totalities; these it must leave to art, including the novel. Thus the function of art as the creator of totality has taken on a hitherto undreamed-of urgency and scope."[76] *Hofmannsthal and His Time*, although a work of history and not art, testifies to the fact that Broch had not given up his goal of portraying the totality of an epoch. His only explicitly historical work, it truly is a synthetic and "total"—if neither exhaustive nor dogmatic—cultural history of fin-de-siècle Europe. For Broch, as for most historians who use the term, "fin-de-siècle" is an apocalyptic rather than a strictly chronological term. The theme of decline that transverses the work forms a recapitulation of Broch's intellectual career and its two main components: the philosophy of value and the philosophy of knowledge. In evaluating the career and the "dreamlike" poetic and prose writings of Hugo von Hofmannsthal, he examines an embodiment of the ethical-aesthetic search for knowledge in a world defined by the dissolution of values and style. As critics of the world that produced them, both Hofmannsthal and Broch strove for an ethical response to the demands of that world through varying modes of expression: the philosophical essay, the political essay and tract, and a great variety of stories, novels, and plays. Broch's career exemplifies the ancient struggle between philosophy and poetry: philosophy, which tends toward solitude, intransigence, and individuality; and poetry, which aims toward the rediscovery of myth, community, and culture. Hofmannsthal, however, never gave up that poetic ideal, which, as Broch explains, was intimately connected with his post-1918 "idea of Austria." Had Hofmannsthal lived into the 1930s, he would have, like Broch, been faced with a crisis even graver than that of his youth: he would have had to give up

Austria altogether. Broch was able to do that, yet he quite rightly implies that Hofmannsthal would not have been able to.

*Hofmannsthal and His Time* is, as Broch suggested, a portrayal of an entire epoch. It thus obeys Nietzsche's charge that modern biography present a portrait of an individual posited *against* his time rather than *in* his time.[77] As a search for a new understanding of European culture and politics, the study itself becomes an exemplification of the understanding and writing of history as an ethical art.

# Hugo von Hofmannsthal and His Time

# 1

# Art and Its Non-Style
# at the End of the
# Nineteenth Century

The essential character of a period can generally be deciphered from its architectural facade, and in the case of the second half of the nineteenth century, the period of Hofmannsthal's birth, that facade is certainly one of the most wretched in world history. This was the period of eclecticism, of false Baroque, false Renaissance, false Gothic. Wherever in that era Western man determined the style of life, that style tended toward bourgeois constriction and bourgeois pomp,[1] to a solidity that signified suffocation just as much as security. If ever poverty was masked by wealth, it was here.

## 1. Rationality and Decoration

Rationalism[2] often goes hand in hand with an enjoyment of life, for anyone who thinks rationally is likely to believe, in addition, that what is enjoyable in life exists to be enjoyed. On the other hand, rationalism demands a sober, clear, unadorned, and realistic view of the world, and assures the quick discovery that the cruelty and horror of life stand in the way of an untroubled enjoyment of life. In order to attain a full enjoyment of life, either one must transfigure what is horrible into beauty—like the Romans with their gladiator games, like a Nero or a Borgia—or one must keep one's eyes shut in the face of ugliness and cruelty, and distinguish the beautiful so that it becomes an aesthetic "elect" and makes possible undisturbed pleasure. Yet whether it is one or the other, whether the affirmation of cruelty or its negation, despite the rationalistic demand for the unadorned, it is a question of an aesthetic overadornment of the ugly, of its

33

hypertrophy or oversweetening. It is a question of denial concealed by "decoration."

The nineteenth-century bourgeois was just as rationalistic as the Roman; like the Roman he built world empires and war machines. But he was neither a Nero nor a Borgia. For that he considered himself too humane, and to a certain degree he even was. When he cosmeticized and transfigured his world so that it became capable of affording him enjoyment, he did so by concealing all its misery. His passion for decoration was more hypocritical than that of his crueler predecessors, and this brought him the hatred and scorn of Nietzsche, a hatred that would have certainly grown even stronger, had he witnessed the bourgeois's turn to cruelty. No, at that point the bourgeois was not yet cruel, even if he was already preparing himself to become so: for in all aestheticism, in all decoration, even the most harmless, there slumbers cynicism—itself just as much a product of rationalistic thinking—and there slumbers skepticism, which knows or at least suspects that it is merely a sort of "transfiguration game" which is being played.

Where decoration is not naive but the result of rationalism, it is not free creation but artificial, sometimes of good quality, but artificial nonetheless. And, moreover, since it is skeptical, it has no footing of its own, but needs models. Rationalism is earthly, and is on the lookout for earthly prescriptions. The Romans found their earthly norms in Greek art, the Renaissance in antiquity as a whole; and in the Enlightenment the process repeated itself. The rationalistic outlook—directed at extant reality—nearly always leers backward in order to uncover in some former earthly reality the rules it needs for an evaluation of the present; it becomes eclectic.

For, as a consequence of his rationalism, nineteenth-century man was individualistic, romantic, and accordingly also historicizing. The discovery of the individual came about for Christian Europe in the late Renaissance, indeed through the very set of mind [*Geisteshaltung*] that also led to Protestantism: the supraindividual, the Platonic, above all the ecclesiastical as spiritual community was suddenly perceived as something upheld by earthly, visible man, and hence not only something which had to be kept alive by him but something in need of his constant renewal. The individual, with his earthly, individual soul, was placed heretically at the center of the universe in order that he, the measure of all things, might also be the measure of all divine validity. Outside the church, however, this is the attitude of romanticism, the source of its greatness as well as its demise, and the source of its historicism. Since it is here that the earthly-private, the personal, even the intimate are to be raised to a universal significance, and in the end this universal reveals itself once again as the everyday, the romantic view must ratify itself by virtue of the sublimity of those human accomplishments which extend from the past into the present. The superhumanness required by romanticism is projected into the historical so that it may in its turn be retrieved for the present.

In any case, it becomes clear that polarities so dear to historical interpretation, polarities such as rational/irrational, collective/individual, classical/romantic, present-minded/historicizing, etc., represent mere shifts in the center of gravity, which, though they correspond to logically indispensable dialectical motions in the development of the value systems by which human life is determined, have very different periods of variation, so that they can appear in multifarious combinations. The Middle Ages, for example, were theologically at least as rational as modern science—even magic has rational foundations, all the more so a mysticism in the mold of Eckhart—and were nevertheless far removed from any kind of individualism, historicism, or decorativism. Conversely, despite its highly rational basis, romanticism veers with ease into the irrational, as soon as the historicizing elements it contains gain the upper hand. Thus, any attempt at rigid schematicism is wrong. Otherwise in the final analysis one is bound to find that classicism, in view of the romantic schemes of rationality, must be itself irrational. History is saturated with countless polar-dialectical undulations, and the styles of particular periods are nothing other than manifestations of interference produced by the coincidence of such undulations. And it is no different in the case of the conditions of the style or non-style of the nineteenth century, in which rationalism, individualism, historicism, romanticism, eclecticism, skepticism are all imbedded and sustained in a kind of Manchesterism calculated for all eternity, all converging in an inextricable bond, yet each retaining an organic unity. Realism is not a style but, rather, the fulfillment of the claims of rationality. And inasmuch as every age thinks rationally in its own fashion, that is to say considers itself rational, all genuine art is realistic in the end; it represents, in its own specific vocabulary, the picture of reality of its time.

Clearly the non-style of the nineteenth century is also a style—there is not one product, not one piece of furniture of this most style-forsaken epoch that does not reveal at first glance the decade to which it belongs; and, accordingly, this non-style too expresses a specific epoch-reality. The vocabulary it employed, in literature as much as in the visual arts, was a stringently realistic one, namely the vocabulary of a naturalism, bound to earthly surfaces, which renounced everything decorative, wanted nothing to do with hypertrophy, oversweetening, or any kind of romantic sentimentalizing, and, wishing to express things as they appeared to it without adornment, grasped them at the point where they made the impression of being least adorned—in the depiction of society.

The naturalism of earlier centuries was principally associated with painting, a medium inadequate for the new social naturalism, inasmuch as

35

painting could serve it with mere social caricatures, in other words with something that is neither wholly pictorial nor wholly naturalistic. The graphic or pictorial social caricature—like the short story—is tied to individual situations, which permit it at best to intimate the social totality but never to represent it in its entirety. To do the latter requires a broadening of the scope of exemplification, and this is achieved when the social totality is mirrored in the totality of a human life elapsing within it; just as, conversely, a life can only be grasped in its entirety when the corresponding social totality is depicted. This is precisely what is accomplished by the novel and, in the main, only by the novel. The epic (whether that of antiquity or of Dante) was concerned with the totality of the universe, Greek tragedy with the totality of fate's dominion. And if, thanks to Shakespeare, drama won a multidimensionality that encompasses every human aspect (and not least the totality of an individual life), even here, indeed even in *Hamlet* (and not unknown to Shakespeare), the stage opposes itself to everything that proceeds beyond its own most characteristic level of action: only the immediate conflict in which the hero finds himself is significant; his past and even his future (though the entire dramatic tension may be directed to it) do not—in the truest sense of the word—play a part. Epics, like dramas, are essentially anti- or at best a-individualistic. Only with the novel—the Italian novella was still to a great extent preindividualistic—only with Cervantes does the totality (one could almost say lyric totality) of the individual attain a comprehensive portrayal, inwardly and outwardly unfettered, suited to psychology and society. The novel was prepared, as it were, to be the art form adequate to the nineteenth century and, by means of its individualistic naturalism, to flower to its full maturity.

It was, for all its opulence, a thoroughly gloomy flower, one that sprang from urban ground. The world city, which after the collapse of the Roman empire had seemed gone forever, was suddenly resurrected; London and Paris, joined a little later by Berlin and New York, had become world metropolises; and it was natural not only that the expression of the time should evolve inside them, but also that all their qualities should adhere to it: their multifariousness, their scatteredness, their greed, their gloom. No matter how the novel in its ostensible unadornment confronted the city— whether it let itself grow to the gigantic realm of Balzac; whether it fulfilled itself in the sinister world of Dickens; whether, in Zola's hands, it formed itself into dreams of hope for all future romanticism; whether, the opposite of such an expanse, it unraveled itself, through Flaubert's intense eye, into a ghostly backdrop to the stirring of a single soul; or whether, having degenerated into a mere erotic novel of society and its idiocy, it could and

36

still can turn even the unadorned into adornment—the novel remains
relentlessly overshadowed by the gloom of the city.

But why was this sort of gloom never transformed into its opposite? Why
did it persist, and why did it never find relief in a truly satirical novel? Why
did the urban gloom of the nineteenth century preclude the sort of work so
masterfully achieved by Voltaire and Choderlos de Laclos, Laurence
Sterne, Jonathan Swift, to say nothing of the monumental satire of Cervantes and Rabelais? It is more than anything else satire itself and satiric
structure, which can be held responsible. For satire in its innermost being is
after all polemical and (in a broad sense) political, and the great age of
politics, the age of the formation and consolidation of the European states,
in short that most eminently political age of the Baroque, had been stilled
forever with the Congress of Vienna. And if Baroque politics were still
practiced as a form of art—a form of high art, which like all art had
something frivolous about it—and could indulge in the laughter of satire,
the age that followed and the social problems it contained were, quite
simply, deadly serious. One has merely to compare drawings by Hogarth
with drawings by Daumier; one might claim—*cum grano salis*—that the
former are dramatic and political, the latter epic and social; the former are
for the most part grounded in the burlesque of the individual situation, the
latter are always aimed at the social totality and are consequently thoroughly gloomy. Where then, as in the novel, the social totality in its full
reality achieves (or merely purports to achieve) expression, satire can
scarcely have a part. The novel was certainly capable, though rather infre-
quently, of achieving humor, but in general it remained overwhelmed by
the gravity of the epoch—and this as a direct consequence of its realism.

Nevertheless, lively satire still existed in the nineteenth century, if only
as the heritage of the eighteenth century; it survived in the theater.

It conforms, politico-socially and dramatically, to both dialectical conceptual polarities that the theater stands in a structurally natural consanguinity with the Baroque, whereas the nineteenth century by virtue of a
similar relationship brought the novel—which it discovered for itself—to its
maturity.[3] All the same, polarities invariably prove themselves unreliable,
and the result in this case is the opposite of what would have most naturally
followed from them: not the novel, but rather the theater, and beyond that
the opera, at least as far as its external aspects are concerned, became the
representative art form of the epoch. With the theater, the eighteenth
century reached into the nineteenth, just as the principle of Baroque theater
construction remained exemplary, now as before.

Theater is makeup. It could never have made use of the naturalistic unadornment to which the novel aspired (but which not even the novel could attain). Indeed, the daring breakthrough engendered by Stanislavsky's genius at the turn of the century promoted totally new scenic possibilities, but they were not those of the total naturalism he intended. In the nineteenth century, notwithstanding the insignificant dilettantism of the Meininger Hoftheater,[4] there was no breakthrough of that sort; the theater could never have risked it. After all, the theater, as long as it wants to remain a whole, must address the entire public; to a far greater extent than the novel, it has a social and economic function. The "people" [*das "Volk"*] of the nineteenth century most assuredly read no novels—least of all, since they were looking for "something beautiful" in art, novels depicting mass society and misery. And even if this type of novel ever gained the acceptance of the bourgeois and his bad social conscience, especially if it reached him in a tasteful, romantically scintillating guise, he always considered the reading of novels a carefree summer pastime, best left to his female appendage. In short, for all its social airs the novel was banished to the sidelines. The theater, on the other hand, ensnared everyone, the bourgeois along with the "people," the former especially with the incentive of preferential orchestra stalls, while others had to make do with the gallery. And for that very reason the bourgeois, seated beneath the ecstatic gaze of the "people," found in the theater all the decorative beauty that he—not only he, nay, the entire epoch—required, in order to satisfy the demand for a secure, in part ceremonial, in part carefree enjoyment of art and life. Of course, these are superficial symptoms, but symptoms nonetheless, and behind them looms the "stylistic indifference" of naturalism, its incapacity to create its own style, an incapacity which like all others reveals itself in the unerring testing ground of the reality of the theater.

Amid the eclectic conglomeration of styles which made up the non-style of the nineteenth century, the theater, or more precisely, the art of the actor, was the sole domain in which a true stylistic tradition continued to flourish, and because it was a tradition, it was not eclectic. It was Baroque art; during the classical period it had acquired a certain simplicity and breadth, and it was this that was practiced with an almost noble rigor at the Comédie Française and the Vienna Burgtheater.

This high dramatic art was in conflict with its repertory, in almost natural conflict. Its tradition was rooted principally in France, schooled on Racine and Corneille, and if its power of expression was hardly sufficient to master ancient tragedy, it was certainly strong enough to amalgamate quite perfectly Shakespeare on the one hand and, on the other, the works of the great German writers of the Weimar period. To all that, the tradition was adequate, and it found no successors in the late nineteenth century. Grillparzer[5] was a last straggler, whereas Hebbel[6] belonged to an entirely new type of production, one that indeed still considered itself classically conservative and tradition-bound, as it treated principally historical and, hence, political themes, but one that in truth had long since fallen away from that tradition—how could it have been otherwise?—and now occupied itself exclusively with specifically bourgeois concerns. In France this change had been swifter. For although French drama, much to the benefit of its effectiveness on the stage, held on so conservatively to its own peculiar technique, which it only now developed into supreme virtuosity, it was nevertheless so broadly influenced by naturalism (that is, also by the city and its gloom), that it was able to cast off its historical costuming and become the Sardouesque society-piece, which, regardless of its generally aristocratic cast of characters, revealed itself as a pure product of the bourgeois spirit and the bourgeois problematic. Whether its action was based on erotic or—however exceptionally—other motives, this drama no longer mirrored the ethical (and thus in the broadcast sense political) superiority of the hero in victory and defeat, but rather his social success and failure, all the more so as psychological interpretation came increasingly to supplant moral foundation. Thus the sphere of duties of the actor which the classical repertory had staked out was extended into entirely unfamiliar territory, one which had nevertheless to be exhaustively traversed; if the theater wished to remain alive, it had to confront such unfamiliar tasks.

The confrontation came about by way of an intensification [*Übersteigerung*]. Of all the realism and naturalism once offered to the theater in the hues of romanticization, there remained nothing; for, elevated into the superrealistic and supernaturalistic style of an old-fashioned heroic scene, the theater achieved a new and hence more genuine reality. A style of theater, modeled—now as before—after kings, usurped the domain of the bourgeois, transformed the bourgeois problematic into that of a royal drama, transformed bourgeois existence into royal existence, turned bourgeois successes and failures back into victories and defeats, and was able to do so, was compelled to do so, because this method of acting had moral intentions and therefore had to make visible a moral, human background, even where it had to reproduce bourgeois issues and their psychologizing structures. And this was essentially more than the fulfillment of another one of those fantasies forever fostered by the bourgeois who would see himself as a king. To be sure, it was "transfiguration-drama," but insofar as it was genuine drama, the transfiguration—into the human—was also genuine; it was genuineness achieved by means of intensifying the nongenuine and the decorative into the essential, a genuineness that lay, so to speak, on the frontier—one step farther, and the conversion of the decoratively nongenuine would undergo yet another dialectical transformation, namely, into the operatic. No wonder an epoch filled with the insatiable desire for decoration sought and found its highest representation precisely in the opera.

On the stage, the non-style of the period became a style again. In the truest sense, or the most correct double-sense of the word, the theater became the showground of the epoch's poverty, masked by wealth.

## 2. The Turn Away from Decoration

Nevertheless, the breadth of late nineteenth-century culture and civilization, the multiplicity and substantiality of its corresponding artistic expression, is far from exhausted by the formula "poverty masked by wealth."

What in fact took place outside—or really in opposition to—this style of the period, and yet was in every manner and form connected with it, born from it and raised with it, and nonetheless aspired at the same time to dissolve it (any organism is ambivalently faced with such processes)—this was surely no less important, indeed if anything more important, than what was happening within its own more narrow framework. For in, and in spite of, Second-Empire Paris, far from the splendid caryatides of the Haussmann facades, far from all official art, far even from the most accomplished art of the theaters, but no less far from the practiced forms of naturalism and especially from its romanticism, indeed often in conscious opposition to this last, there arose—quite miraculously—a new art: on one hand, the new French poetry inaugurated by Baudelaire, averse to all superficial naturalism and, more especially, to every kind of romanticizing, and, on the other, impressionism, an autonomous outgrowth from the foundations of painterly tradition, void of any literary influence, certainly the legitimate heir to naturalism, yet bearing within it from the start a revolutionary, antinaturalistic kernel.

Every genuine work of art is at once new and bound to tradition: later generations see before anything else its place in tradition and thus grow increasingly blind to revolution, whereas contemporaries (for their part blind to tradition) see in it only the unfamiliar and the new: for the general public an insolence meriting punishment, for the artist a revolutionary act, all the more so since he considers that its success depends on newly discovered insights and resources of artistic technique. The mastery of geometric perspective and its applicability on canvas: this was Dürer's pride, and the impressionistic pride is presumably to be found in the optical, physical knowledge of the fundamentals of color-producing, color-produced shades of light. Yet artistic revolutions—and certainly one as brilliant as impressionism—are autonomous; they themselves can make use of scientific discoveries provided they are themselves suited to revolutionary purposes, but they cannot be caused by them. Artistic revolutions take place when preexisting conventions of symbolic language are thrown overboard, and art sets to work once more to search for primal symbols, with which to build a new direct language aimed at attaining a higher artistic truthfulness; this alone is at stake in art.

Not at one stroke, but step by step, it became clear to the impressionist painters that the impression of reality which a painted picture can transmit depends on two medial layers: the first is the medium of light, which makes objects visible and awakens them into being, forms their shapes with its shadows, colors them with its refractions, envelopes and outlines them one and all with its impenetrable transparency. The second is the medium of the flecks of color applied to the canvas, which (themselves dependent on the light) are by virtue of their arrangement, distributions, nuances, and contrasts, capable of forming symbols, symbols which can indeed only be referred to the other medial layer, that of light, and are never intended to be more than symbolizations of light, but, because of this very integrity, penetrate the light-induced reality of objects. In other words, painting has always to be reduced to the media of light and flecks of color, because any visual commentary about the reality of the world must take place exclusively between and upon these two medial layers, and, by such a reduction of the painting process to its ultimate nakedness, its most naked, primal principles will provide access to that sphere, from which the primal symbols of art and hence new truths arise. This and nothing else was the revolutionary discovery of impressionism, and in this and no other way can impressionism be defined: it was a new attitude toward object reality; it discovered the medium as reality.

Yet is this mode of perception confined to painting? Does not the representation of reality always and everywhere require a medium? Painting is the expression of reality, a specific language in which visual reality is brought forth, but does not the same hold true for every language, for the language of speech as much as those of music and painting? And behind all these communicative potentials of the reality symbol, does there not stand an ideal, Platonic language as the last, and precisely Platonic, vessel for reality? The most recent phenomenological and positivist linguistic investigations lie entirely in this direction; indeed they often expressly analyze the "phenomenon of the medium" as such. And when they become metaphysical, as above all in existentialism, and want to break through the impenetrable medial layer, for the purpose of grasping an "immediate reality," they consistently find behind it—nothingness. Art, on the other hand, is allowed, nay, more than that, is enjoined, to practice metaphysics: without a concern for reality, there is no genuine art! For only the producer

41

of reality, namely art, and only art, can and may raise this concern with the aid of its primal symbols, which in turn become accessible to it only—as impressionism exemplifies—when the metaphysical concern is addressed. Indeed, metaphysical necessity is graduated in accordance with the different artistic media. The language of painting occupies a sort of middle ground between those of music and speech, for in music one apparently finds a convergence of the level of symbol and the level of musical reality—of "meaning" and "meant"—whereas the process that leads to the symbols of words and precisely to the poetic must undoubtedly pass through a whole sequence of other medial layers, and can thus only be understood as a symbol of a symbol of a symbol, etc.; hence the wish to extract primal symbols from the medium of the word appears all but hopeless. And yet even this is not completely hopeless: it is no accident that it was through a contemporary of the impressionist movement, Baudelaire, that language attained individual life and meaning, extending far beyond the mere function of communication to the point where language, in gratitude, as it were, for its newly received devotion, becomes itself a source for the conception of reality, the poetic conception of reality.

Baudelaire's relation to language is certainly not lacking in mystical infusions, since mysticism indeed proclaims itself everywhere in his work; yet fundamentally it is not a mystical relationship but a technical one. By the same token, the impressionist painter is no mystic but a technician of the phenomena of light and color. Yet fanaticism for truth always has something mystical about it; hence an artist who directs all his strength toward an artistic truth, to the "correct" solution of his problem of light and language, presumably has the right to call himself a mystic, a mystic of his own artistic technique, all the more since this very attitude has produced a most specific phenomenon: *l'art pour l'art.*

*L'art pour l'art* has always existed. Every honest artist, and for that matter every honest craftsman, has been and remains under an obligation to it, and there is nothing mystical about it. On the contrary, it is a thoroughly rational attitude, and during the nineteenth century—not unlike its logical and social counterpart "business is business"—it acquired if possible an even higher rationality, all the more so after the shift in artistic orientation away from the central value of religion and the church. And what was an art which, like impressionism, defined its notions of truth exclusively from its own peculiar medial layers, to do with an orientation toward goals that lie outside such a framework? All this combined to make the notion of *l'art pour l'art* typical of the nineteenth century and, moreover, to imprint on it an entirely typical trait, namely, that of "social indifference": neither does this art seek to address social themes, nor does it seek to insinuate itself into the social fabric as a gratifying, instructive, uplifting, or otherwise marketable product. Clearly this does not mean that "success" has become irrelevant to the *artiste pour l'art*; but his relation to the "public" has altered nonetheless. As long as society remained grouped around a central value, art had, so to speak, a natural place within it; artist and public were unified from the first as to the kinds of themes and modes of representation that would prove either admissible or inadmissible. Yet with *l'art pour l'art* that harmonious relationship was transformed into one of antagonism and violation. The artist tries to convert and to violate the bourgeois, and knows in the process that it is an almost hopeless undertaking, that the bourgeois will calmly let him starve, and that one must hence consider oneself lucky, if—like Cézanne—one is able to put aside all momentary ambition and direct everything to future success. For posthumous fame to exceed fame is a phenomenon previously unknown in the history of art.

It is in this manner that *l'art pour l'art* thinks itself and wishes itself to be posited outside every society and, above all, outside every bourgeois society, and yet forgets, in doing so, that no one, not even the artist, can leap over his own shadow: the artist's very opposition to society places him within its framework, precisely as a heretic can only exercise a meaningful function within the church; outside it, that function becomes simply meaningless. *L'art pour l'art* and "business is business" are two branches of the same tree. Whether one has feelings of harmony or of discord toward the society in which one lives, as circumstance and problematic one cannot escape that society, and it is that society which implants the same social indifference in the unsuspecting bourgeois and in the artist alike. But when the bourgeois clings to his business principles with a rationally grounded and unassailable unconditionality, and is blind to anything that might possibly repudiate them, and when the artist with the same unconditionality clings to his own artistic principles, both act in the same way both logically and sociologically, and in both cases the unconditionality of social indifference intensifies to a state of genuine cruelty; in both cases it is the cruelty of bourgeois society, a cruelty which it is true was bound to be surpassed as dictatorial society stripped the last shackles from bourgeois humanity.

And this very cruelty explains the antagonism that reigns between the bourgeois and the artist. Not that the bourgeois was overly affronted by the crass and cruel naturalism of art. No; he may remonstrate with it a little, since misery appears to him as unsuited to enjoyment, especially when not sufficiently romanticized, but in the end he accepts it nonetheless, for it produces no guilt feelings in him, he does not know that he is exploiting misery, and there is no realm of misery for which he feels himself responsible. Not even the representation of the social totality, as in the novels of Zola, can rouse him, to say nothing of the partial representations of which painting is capable. Moreover, impressionism retreated far from social description. Paintings like Manet's *Balcony* or *Theater loges*[7] have nothing to do anymore with the social efforts of a Millet, a Courbet, etc., and the idyllic lyricism of most impressionist landscapes must surely have been thoroughly pleasurable to the romantic bourgeois sensibility. Why then the furor at the Salon of 1865 over Manet's perfectly lovely *Olympia*? Why this unsuitedness for enjoyment? The answer is relatively simple: the social descriptions of naturalism had shown the bourgeois what he was doing and the base deeds he had committed, whereas the *art pour l'art* of impressionism showed him what he was and yet did not want to be. For not in its themes but in its mode of representation, this art—even if it may once again appeal to later generations—proclaims that the unconditional cruelty of the epoch is making itself ready and yet is already present.

The bourgeois practices his cruelty, whether consciously or—more frequently—unconsciously, directly on his fellow man, especially when the latter is of more feeble economic capacity; the artist's cruelty, on the other hand, although no less unconscious, is sublimated in his work. The more the impressionist *art pour l'art* developed, the more clearly this tendency to cruelty was brought to light; the paintings of Cézanne, Gauguin, and Van Gogh, the poems of Baudelaire, are in their acute directness (and certainly not in their harmless themes) nothing but cruelty, unconditionality, inconsiderateness, harshness—all in the purest sublimation. This has not the slightest thing to do with the private tendencies to cruelty of a Baudelaire or a Gauguin, just as, in the converse process, Van Gogh's private (and alas so futile) efforts for a socially helpful life did not relieve the cruelty of his paintings one iota. Even the wish that haunts every artist, the wish to *épater le bourgeois*, although it plays a part, is clearly of no consequence, not merely because social logic dictates that the *épateur du bourgeois* will find himself on the same plane with the *bourgeois épaté*, but, much more, because the bourgeois will accept every *épatement* as long as it seems harmless to him, i.e., as long as it remains rational. Within the bounds of the rational he will permit any hypertrophy of the "ugly"; it thus becomes a "Grand Guignol" for him, in short, something he can perceive as legitimate romanticism. Yet the *Fleurs du mal* are unacceptable to him. For the cruelty brought to consciousness within the poetry (with complete poetic unconsciousness) reveals the utmost horror: the irrational in itself.

*L'art pour l'art* guided art back into a totally irrational sphere, and that was its great accomplishment. Like everything great it contains the moment of necessity, a rationally derivable necessity at that: just because the rational principles of this naturalism-turned-impressionistic attained their utmost radicality in the absolutism of *l'art pour l'art*, it was along this frontier, which one may well call a frontier of infinitude, that the dialectical reversal into the opposite, into the irrational, was bound to occur. For every approach to an absolute contains qualities of infinitude, and all infinitude contains qualities of the irrational. This is the point at which mysterious depths open up: the abyss of the human soul, of human existence, the abyss of the world. And for that very reason every reversal into the irrational threatens to become a reversal into the anarchical as well; anarchy lurks constantly in the depths. It is not only the bourgeois whose security has been threatened who shrinks back in terror here; the artist himself hesitates, and how could it be otherwise? Will his power of sublimation still be equal to the new mission assigned him? Will he not have to conjure an additional sublimation in order to conquer the radically unknown, the anarchical, a sublimation of which neither he, nor indeed art itself, will be in any way capable? To be sure, even great masters like Monet, Renoir, Degas, to say nothing of a Pissarro or a Signac, no longer risked this leap into the unknown but remained in the sphere of the known—i.e., in a mode that was already on the way to establishing itself within the known and even to being able to command a public. Manet had taken the first step; the second, the breakthrough into the totally irrational, was reserved for Cézanne and Van Gogh, and only very seldom in the history of art—probably not since Michelangelo and Rembrandt—has the irrational presented itself with such vehemence as in the works of these two artists. With Cézanne and Van Gogh, impressionism overcame its naturalist heritage.

Where the irrational shows itself with its full vehemence, it does so in the form of primal associations and primal symbols. The world is seen once again for the first time, and with an immediacy otherwise known only to the child and the primitive (and accordingly to the dreamer, if with different coloration); hence the expression of the world becomes that of the child, the primitive, the dreamer; it fulfills itself in the creation of a new language. The achievement of Cézanne and Van Gogh was to create a language, and even if it had its origins in the impressionist vocabulary—indeed it would have been inconceivable without its ground-breaking medial symbolism— what sprang up was nevertheless something totally new: the primal symbolism of an irrational, immediate vision of the world. This was the very same upsurge, the same sudden presence, as the one which, three decades earlier, had made audible Baudelaire's primal sound, his primal vocabulary, the same recklessly cruel unconditionality of the primal as Baudelaire's, the same primal stare of primary existence. If Baudelaire and his successors— including Verlaine, Rimbaud, Tristan Corbière, Péguy, even Mallarmé (though just barely)—still reveal certain impressionist, naturalistic, and romantic touches, it was the primal association reawakened by Baudelaire that was once more placed face to face with language. And the power of primal association—which is precisely what precedes all linguistic creation—continued to function: in the shadow of his work, poetry after Baudelaire created a new language within the French language, a language which, mainly under Mallarmé's guidance, developed to an ever more acute constructiveness, and thus—like all painting after Cézanne—became, in an astonishing manner, more and more suited to represent the essence of being, the essence of man—i.e., to transform the irrational into a new, acutely precise rationality.

This was the artistic revolution at the close of the nineteenth century, and, seen from the outside, it was a quite harmless, quite restricted revolution of a few artists in the out-of-the-way province of *l'art pour l'art*. Nevertheless, this breakthrough of the irrational did not stand alone in the sweep of time—there are no isolated phenomena. The superrational nineteenth century had everywhere begun to "irrationalize," not last in its intoxication with machinery and production. The fact is that at that time a pleasant state of suspension still governed, one in which nothing had yet been decided, and where the possibility still remained that the threat of anarchy festering within the irrational could be tamed. The taming did not succeed, could not succeed. For new symbols, new languages are generated by a new breed of men, and such a breed had announced itself in that new art of the nineteenth century. The revolution of spiritual expression, ostensibly restricted to art alone and hence ostensibly harmless, was an initial symptom of a world-shaking whose end we cannot perceive even today, and the artists of that time, themselves full of artistic self-discipline, were heralds of anarchical dissoluteness, forebears of the new breed of men. The twentieth century was to become that of the darkest anarchy, the darkest atavism, the darkest cruelty.

There is no doubt that *l'art pour l'art* conclusively discarded the decorative mission previously assigned to art. With its tendency toward the undecorative, indeed the antidecorative, *l'art pour l'art* has no desire to fulfill any sort of social function; it wishes to be asocial, is often even antisocial, yet cannot refrain from forcing its products on the public. What kind of social role, then, does it seek to assume?

Where primal associations, primal vocabulary, primal symbols are at stake, where the irrational enters a work, mythos does not seem to be far away, and in fact deep in the unconscious of every art—every great art—there slumbers the desire to be allowed to return to mythos and once again to portray the totality of the universe.[8] It was in mythos that all human history began, in mythos—i.e., in the poetic language of its epics—that those primal associations, that primal vocabulary, that primal symbolism first took form, and each new historical epoch has since rediscovered them for itself, even if in varying forms; in other words, it was in mythos that every new epoch created for itself an adequate language, together with the new creative symbols suited to it. Should not an epoch of the most powerful breakthrough into the irrational—like the present one—be capable of advancing back into mythos? Clearly, poetry and painting, in whose territory the impressionist breakthrough into the irrational fulfilled itself, had never previously been the true domain of mythos, but does that mean it must forever remain that way? Moreover, this kind of breakthrough into the irrational must necessarily expand, must little by little seize every branch of artistic expression, and not remain restricted to a single one—was not the novel, then, as the specific artistic genre of the nineteenth century simply predetermined to be seized by it? In this role, the novel may once again provide the irrational with a partner of the sort it had not had since its encounter with epic in primitive times: is the breath of great epic not already evident in the works of a Balzac, a Dickens, and does not the choice of subject, a century later, in Joyce's *Ulysses* and Mann's *Joseph* indicate the approaching fulfillment of a development which from the beginning had aspired to mythos?

With Zola, the minstrel of rationalism, of the age of the machine, of socialist man, the idea of the modern mythos had already assumed a distinct form—without of course being realized. His naturalism remained undisturbed by the breakthrough into the irrational of contemporary *art pour l'art*. Yet even the case of Flaubert is hardly different, even though his perfectionism of form was at least common to impressionistic and postimpressionistic poetry, from Baudelaire to Mallarmé. It is with Joyce that the picture first changes, for his ambition is focused purely on the mythical. Notwithstanding the mythologizing structure which to a large extent Joyce gave to his novel of a day and a night, and notwithstanding the symbolic wealth which, by dint of his polyhistoric genius, he was able to compile from the total range of human ontogeny and phylogeny and incorporate into his work so as to increase its mythological weight, it was Joyce who truly realized—and this is by far the most essential point—the conjunction with impressionism. Joyce eavesdrops on language and languages, in order that they out of gratitude might supply him with the correct word-symbol and with this the essentials of reality, and such linguistic mysticism (by contrast with which Flaubert's becomes schoolmasterly pedantry) is nothing but a resumption of the medial method invented by the impressionists—and is every bit as rational. For all true mysticism is rational, and linguistic mysticism is mysticism of the medium. And, just as with the impressionists, the breakthrough into the irrational emerges here; it is to be seen and felt everywhere in Joyce's work, sometimes, as in the chapter "Anna Livia Plurabelle," roused to the greatest intensity. Yet the analogy with impressionism goes even further: as little as impressionism, whether in painting or in poetry, actually became mythos, so little was Joyce's success; even here the naturalistic system of coordinates remains undisturbed, and in the end the story remains a representation (often even a romantic one) of Messrs. Bloom and Finnegan, though certainly in an accomplished comprehension of their living totality.

Even such highly developed novelistic art proves itself unable to attain the rank of mythology. Why is this so? Is it simply because of its naturalism, without which living and social totalities cannot be comprehended? No, the causes must lie deeper, and they do. It is not only that every late-developing art which sets about to recapture the irrational must—in order to do so—undertake a break with tradition, which is exceedingly difficult (the impressionist revolution is a prime example of the intricacy of this sort of process of detachment), and it is not only that there can be only partial detachments, simply because nothing can ever totally escape from its own epoch and the effects of its traditions—all this stands in strict opposition to the mythological function as such. Mythos breaks with no tradition, because no tradition precedes it, and it adheres to no tradition, because logically and temporally all tradition begins within it; whatever paths of development tradition might have established, however diverse may have been the branches that grew out of it or continue to grow from it, no matter whether they tend toward the irrational or rational, artistic or scientific attitudes and modes of knowledge— all these paths together are fundamentally indistinguishable as one single unity embedded in the mythical germ-cell. This is an unrepeatable situation, and can least of all be restored atavistically, so to speak, with the help of a breakthrough into the irrational. And this holds true more than ever for such a late form of expression as the novel.

In short, with inadequate means, namely those of naturalism, the novel pursues an unattainable end, namely the mythical. And yet means and end are simply insolubly linked. The novel, incidentally, assumes the same relation to myth as postimpressionist painting does to primitive art. Both naturalistically impeded in their artistic wills, that is, by a naturalism which belongs to all styles and is hence forever incapable of providing them with a style-building symbolism indispensable to all great art, they were both ultimately forced to orient themselves to a primitive art, which adhered to no style but in its mythical unity is the source of the formation of all style. Joyce and mythos, Gauguin and primitive art: one like the other revolves around the realism of early art, its "primal naturalism," with which it endeavors faithfully to delineate the world and human existence as it sees them, and in the process reaches beyond the naturalistic into the essential. For primitive man, unencumbered by any expressive tradition, is capable of grasping what is "essential" to him, capable of expressing it with total

48

purity, unburdened by any outside influences, and it is precisely here that the style-producing strength of his "primal naturalism" lies. Every genuine style signifies the accentuation of a world-essentiality, signifies the transformation of chaos into a sytem of essential elements; yet only the "primal style" of the immediate beginning also possesses the naiveté of an absolutely undiluted realism, that naiveté which is at the same time the most highly and—as with Homer—the most refined artistic intellect.[9] It is artistic intellect and nonetheless suitability to nature, it is the style of nature itself, which reveals itself in the art of the immediate beginning, and the more advanced the evolution, the more seldom do reminiscences of this glorious, truly mystical naiveté emerge. They emerge surely not with Gauguin, yet they do with Henri Rousseau, surely not with Joyce, yet probably with Kafka.

Figures like Kafka and Henri Rousseau are unique not only on account of their genius but more because theirs was a genius that succeeded—in the center, so to speak, of European artistic tradition and hence of contemporary art—in keeping itself almost entirely free of tradition. What is remarkable and enduring about them would have been less striking outside their environment, outside the European mainstream. Certainly, at the time of Henri Rousseau and Kafka there was no longer a no man's land beyond the bounds of tradition, yet in the nineteenth century such a periphery unquestionably existed, for Russia and America were still peripheral countries. All the influence of central and western Europe notwithstanding, these were "youthful" countries, countries of the "beginning," not of course a mythical beginning but one in which tradition could be and indeed was newly endowed. Where American poetry became autochthonous, as with Herman Melville and later with Whitman, there surfaced, even if merely by suggestion, that primal naturalism from which primal associations, primal vocabulary, primal symbols had once arisen. Thus the naturalism of Tolstoy stands closer to that of Melville than to that of Zola, however much it may surpass the social breadth of the American. For monumentality—and this is here the *tertium comparationis*—entails not so much social breadth as social depth, and the latter is a function of the choice of symbol. The characteristic of monumental art is not a wealth of symbols, it is rather the single essential symbol, the symbol which in a single image, in a single twist of fate, grasps and subsumes a totality along with all its limbs; the rape of Helen is an event whose symbolic power stamps the total fate of the Greeks and Trojans into a single, common inalterability, and Melville's vision of the hunt for the white whale, the vision of lonely seas and lonely worlds, the vision of infinite inalterability, reveals more than a single seafarer's fate, and the war portrayed by Tolstoy is the one which from time immemorial has been relentlessly foisted on mankind in terrible helplessness. Where narrative is guided by a symbol of inalterability, structures develop which in their innermost composition can be accurately measured against the greatest epics of world literature, indeed, against the greatest myths.

Nevertheless, no mythos evolved. Be it Tolstoy, Dostoevsky, or Chekhov (who demonstrated, contrary to Western narrative art, that a genuinely satirical epic is possible): all of them drew the ultimate conclusions from the realism of the novel and, indeed, forged ahead to its frontier of infinitude, i.e., to the frontier of "primal naturalism," the boundary at which the naturalistic prepares to turn into the essential; nevertheless, the novel remained the novel. And even if these masterworks have long surmounted the nature of the bourgeoisie from whose non-style and narrowness they emerged, and even if their concern is no longer the bourgeois, although he is portrayed, no longer his problems, although they are dealt with, but, simply, man and mankind's earthly-divine existence, and even if in this manner—especially with Dostoevsky—a grandiose metaphysics unfolds whose irrationality has only little in common with the Joycean breakthrough into the irrational, for all that, the distance from the mythical is no smaller than with Joyce. In short, even here the bounds of the novel cannot be overstepped; here also the "inadequacy of the means and the inaccessibility of the end" are brought to light. And even here, precisely here, the novel remains in that curious hybrid state in which it is a work of art that is never able to rise to the rank of perfect art, the rank of style-creating "perfect poetry" which is the property of lyric poetry, drama, and not last, precisely of the great epics. Contrary to these, the novel is not a producer but a consumer of style, not a subject but an object of style, and the symbolism it creates falls into utter triviality, becomes an accessory. In other words, the task which was assigned to the novel directs itself principally, now as always, to its duty to represent the totality of life, and with far less intensity toward its duty as an artistic creation. Balzac is more important for the novel than Stendhal, Zola more important than Flaubert, the formless Thomas Wolfe more important than the artist Thornton Wilder: the novel does not stand, as does true poetry, under the measure of art but under the measure of "writerliness," and even the monumentality of the Russian epic is now as before implanted within the region—so utterly characteristic of the nineteenth century—of apoetical and at times almost antipoetical *belles lettres*.

Does this mean that the new artistic tradition of the nineteenth-century Russian epic was not sufficiently radical? Or does it mean, rather, that the criminal, bloodthirsty Nazi intellectuality was right when it maintained that only after a gloriously atavistic self-annihilation of the world would a new mythos first be able to rise from it—the Nazi mythos of the twentieth century?

50

A concern of this sort will once again suggest the attempt to anchor mythos in the irrational, in this case even as an apology for atavistic murder. Once again, then: mythos cannot be identified with the irrational, yet neither can it be identified with the rational; it is rather both these combined, and is consequently greater and more pregnant with meaning than the mere sum of its united parts. Man's development, however, consists of the progressing autonomy of individual rational attitudes, and thus removes itself further and further from the mythical unity of once upon a time. Even the poetry of Dante, born in a far less divided epoch than the present one, can no longer be described as mythical. Yet the Italian Renaissance of 1300 was surely no less radical than that of nineteenth-century Russia.

It is not on the mythological maturity of the world that this depends— that is the Nazi aesthetic—but on the turning away from the decorative mission of artistic endeavor and on the emphasis upon its ethical duty. Here, however, one further commonality is revealed between the poetry of Dante, which prevailed over the decorative *Minnesang*, and the great Russian epic; both rediscovered the ethical within the inalterable, just as the Attic tragedy of fate had done, driven by the necessity of humanizing the intensely terrifying fatalism of the Homeric mythos. The cognitive goal of poetry, its goal of truth, is no longer simply the beautiful in its compassionlessness, no longer solely the reality of fate; above and beyond that, it is the reality of the soul and of the struggle against fate which it must wage if it wishes to remain human. In this manner the novel, and precisely the Russian novel (as opposed to the Western, e.g., Joycean novel) broke through the boundaries of *l'art pour l'art*, and up into the open: it flung open the door to "the ethical work of art," it at last became political, indeed it even achieved satirical possibilities (Chekhov), and, although "merely" a novel, although mere *belles lettres*, although—as a result of its naturalism— not really style-creating, it rose to a valid aesthetic representation of the epoch, which the West had achieved only in the theater—and that indeed only as an ersatz, because Western narrative art, despite its adequacy to the times, was not able to raise itself above the romantic, above the psychological, above the decorative nature of its bourgeois origin.

## 3. The Value Vacuum of German Art

From the West and from the East came the factors that determined European literary and pictorial expression; Germany, which between 1750 and 1850 had earned a decisive right of codetermination, had practically nothing more to contribute.

Interpreted mythistorically (which is clearly not admissible), it is almost as if the German spirit had known that with Goethe and Hölderlin it had exhausted itself for a long time to come, and that artistically, or more precisely poetically—curiously enough, painting had been long lost—it was condemned to silence. Grillparzer, surely a playwright of extraordinary stature, a historical intellect of the first rank and a totally worthy heir to Schiller and Kleist, did remain prominent into the new era, but his place soon became vacant, all the more so when Hebbel, far too much an epigone to fill the breach, claimed his inheritance. It was different, however, with poetry, where it was still practiced as true literature—in remote areas, in the provinces, in crotchety little bourgeois towns. Here one must single out Gottfried Keller and Conrad Ferdinand Meyer, and also, though at a certain distance from them, Theodor Storm and the Austrian Ferdinand von Saar.[10]

The European significance of recent German literature was now totally lost. There was a sole exception: Nietzsche. The lonely summit he claimed for himself and which has since been reduced to platitude was truly his own; there he stood, he alone, separated from all the lesser spirits. Yet he did not want to be included in the ranks of literature, least of all German literature. And for this very reason he was as German as one can be German. Because, despite his powerful artistic temperament, he remained aloof from art and poetry, and—apart from a few poems which, significant as they are, remained completely secret—felt himself to be an exclusively rational thinker, he merged perfectly into the new posture of the German spirit. The mystical causes that had rendered poetry forbidden ground to the Germans had their effect on Nietzsche too.

The causes may have been mystical; for the reasons there are explanations. The fact that the people stripped the poet and thinker of his poetic domain, and that this happened exclusively to the domains not of the thinker but of the scholar and the musician, can be traced at least in part to the radicalism of which the German spirit is often—unfortunately all too often—capable. By virtue of this radicalism, the German spirit developed one of the principal features of the time, its rationality, to the extreme, to extreme abstractness. And in such abstractness, only the sciences and music remain as justifiable means of expression. In fact, the revolutionizing quality of the epoch was in the first place scientific—even the impressionist revolution in painting points in this direction—and there is hardly a field of science to which Germany in the second half of the nineteenth century did not make the most significant contributions; in the field of music not only had the strongest impulses once come from Germany, but now too the most significant revolution was introduced by Wagner.

But why then did Germany's so-called "take-off" period [*Gründerzeit*], the years 1870–90, create the impression of a total intellectual void?

52

In literature and painting, in fact, nothing at all was produced, and scientific revolutions, which for the most part take place in the seclusion of laboratories, libraries, and studies, are seldom so turbulent as to be observed by more than the narrowest circle of colleagues. Who, for example, was aware at the time of the revolution in scientific axiomatics being prepared in the work of Gottlob Frege and Georg Cantor—not to mention the fact that work of this kind penetrates a wider circle of knowledge. The situation is clearly different in music; here there was no stagnation as there was in literature and in painting but, rather, a genuine revolution, one that proceeded not in isolation and hiding but in all openness, turbulently, noisily, and arrogantly, and aroused just as turbulent and noisy an opposition, so that it could actually have brought about the disappearance of the "value vacuum," as the condition of these decades may rightly be called. Why did the vacuum nonetheless have to persist? Why was it only after the epoch had passed that Wagner—and for that matter his immortal antagonist Nietzsche—were granted standing and lasting currency? The allusion to Cézanne, who allegedly sold only one painting in his lifetime, is no answer; a much more reliable answer lies in the radicalism of the German spirit, expressed also in its revolutions (and which in the political sphere makes monstrosities of them). Above all, the explanation is to be found in the revolutionary work of art itself, that is, in the very mechanism of revolution.

Revolutions are tuned to the "new." And both science and art, as forms of knowledge, would be nonexistent were they not unerringly aimed at the new. But revolutions demand the renewal of the "whole," and for this reason there are relatively few scientific revolutions in the true sense; scientific novelty is most often the product of "progress," i.e., the patient, logical, step-by-step probing into the riddle of the world totality, which must be wrung ounce by ounce from "supplemental" knowledge. Art, however—and its individuality and its justification lie in this opposition—is impatient: it contains neither something "supplemental," nor any true "progress"; rather, it must strive with each and even the slightest work—if it is to become a genuine work of art—for an immediate grasp of the world totality. For this reason its development proceeds exclusively in revolutionary thrusts.

Yet when a work of art truly grasps the world totality, it embraces along with it *eo ipso* the period of its own formation. Science is hardly capable of anything similar. A Cézanne still life, for example, at least for anyone who is not totally dense, makes one breathe the entire atmosphere of the turn of the century (and it does not even have to be a Cézanne); whereas the theory of relativity, which in 1905—as one of the few scientific exceptions—was a revolutionary event, requires truly complicated theoretical-interpretive feats of analysis if it is to be taken as a statement about the entire structure of the spirit of the time. Science does not burden itself with understanding the period of its formation, yet the moment it crosses the boundary between theory and praxis, it has a direct bearing on life, in that by dint of its own needs it awakens new needs and so becomes a crucial factor in the growth of a new epoch, in the creation of the "historically new." The artist, however, the genuine artist, does not concern himself with the needs of the epoch, yet he feels and knows what it is and wherein its novelty lies, knows this thanks to an intuitive insight that one might simply call the "feel for the epoch." Though he lives in the midst of a confusing multiplicity of a myriad anonymous and petty events which fill out and constitute the epoch, he is able nonetheless to grasp it as a whole; he grasps it, so to speak, from "the inside out," and as it is the new epoch which thus enters his work as a totality, the epoch becomes the "new" in his art. The average man (and with him the average scholar—also, indeed, the artistically motivated nonartist) is seldom faced with the same situation; he remains submerged in the anonymity of the events which surround him, and for him the epoch first loses this anonymity when it has expired, when he can view it from "outside" as a historical unity and whole. When a new period has established itself, the preceding ones reveal themselves as historical wholes.

This, however, is also the mechanism of so-called artistic "success." A work of art that reproduces the entire content of an epoch (and not only its style) and consequently presents something uncannily "new" to its contemporaries, will most often achieve a status of familiarity only after the period has passed; that is, it will be first understood and acknowledged when the period of its origin has become a historical whole. This occurs most often with the emergence of the succeeding generation, which actually shapes the beginnings of posterity, so important to the artist. In other words, the major work of art usually only achieves a lively currency at the "edge" of its epoch, whereas the minor work, that is, the one that neither grasps nor wishes to grasp the totality of the epoch but satisfies itself by serving the epoch's needs, i.e., in being a part of the structure of the epoch and its style, is usually extinguished at the close of the epoch. The phenomena of obsolete art and belatedly acknowledged art are reciprocal.

In the middle of an epoch, two main groups of art works share between them public acclaim: first the products of transient, "minor" art (which is often simply non-art), and second the kind of major art that stems from the previous or an earlier period and has already succeeded in crossing the threshold of understanding. These curious bedfellows are the backbone of the opposition to a period's contemporary major art, an opposition that

54

grows necessarily sharper the sharper the revolutionary claim of the new art.

When a political, social, or economic vacuum has set in, its corresponding political, social, or economic revolution is not far away, and the more complete the vacuum, the more the various "partial" revolutions—as they simultaneously sharpen their tendencies—will converge in their struggle to become a single, all-encompassing revolution. The same holds true for artistic revolutions, and the major work of art that carries them is what clearly reveals the total mechanism, through its position and especially through the counterrevolutionary opposition it evokes. For if an epoch totality is centered in a value vacuum, the major work of art in which it finds its expression must also express that vacuum. The work of art becomes the mirror of the vacuum, and in doing so vindicates its revolutionism, yet at the same time immediately arouses counterrevolutionary opposition—must arouse it, because a mirror that shows the vacuum is an uncanny thing, and even the man who manages to live in the vacuum cannot endure the sight of it. This is what occurred in the second half of the nineteenth century, with particular acuteness and radicality in Germany: the Wagnerian artwork was big, remains big, and is the mirror of the vacuum.

Just as the style of the time—above all where it was determined by romantic naturalism—was a non-style, so was Wagner an unmusical music genius and, moreover, an unpoetical poetic genius. He was precisely the genius of the vacuum, and where the genius is interrupted—because no genius can be constantly a genius—it reveals a non-style in the worst possible abomination, in the form of empty bombast, as in the Faust Overture, or of empty sentimentality, as in the Wesendonck Songs. But Wagner also possessed the naiveté—in part carefree, in part refined—of a genius. He knew that works of art could be made from any material, provided an architectonic appropriate to the material was employed, and, theater genius that he was, he knew that the theater and opera of his time already contained the elements that could be used—intensified into the superromantic, superrational, and even, when necessary, into the untheatrical and the antitheatrical (e.g. *Tristan*)—in the construction of the necessary vacuum architecture. It was a question of constructing the so-called *Gesamtkunstwerk*.

This was the proving ground for Wagner's special feeling—indeed his positively unerring instinct—for the epoch. He knew that the age he was born into would choose the operatic as the form for its representative total expression; he saw how the new bourgeois cities were seeking a community center that would replace the cathedral and how they strove to raise the Place de l'Opéra to that honored status—and all this red-plush, gilded, and gaslit ceremoniousness corresponded to his own blueprint for the tasks of modern art. But he knew also that opera in its present form had not met the demands of such ceremoniousness; for that a Meyerbeer was not sufficient, however esteemed he may have been by the public and by Wagner himself; for that, not even a Verdi was sufficient, to say nothing of the otherwise routine repertoire, which consisted exclusively of superannuated romanticism and would have been altogether intolerable without the insertion of ballets. Aware of all this, Wagner knew very well that his plan for an operatic *Gesamtkunstwerk* would satisfy a genuine need of the time. On the other hand, it was far less clear to him that a plan that is supposed to serve the immediate needs of its epoch, and thereby reap immediate success, will possess all the characteristics of "minor" art and will be condemned from the start to remain in the style of its time, which here means in its non-style, in the false truthfulness that imprinted its indelible stamp on the Wagnerian life and work. Whatever happened, it was rational and romantic, naturalistic and ceremonial, sentimental and gloomy, catholicizing and mythologizing, and above all (despite *Die Meistersinger*, and perhaps there more than ever) perfectly humorless, as humorless as only a vacuum can be. Nevertheless it was major art, had become major art, and was able to unite all the disparate elements of the non-style into a single style, the specifically Wagnerian style—one could almost say brew them together, because behind the scenes stood the radicality of genius which, with utter, radical shamelessness, exposed the nakedness of the vacuum.

Wagner was rejected and assailed by his contemporaries, and the reason, as usual, was blindness to a major work of art; as usual, the assailers thought that it was non-art (in this case non-music) that they were dismissing. Of course Nietzsche, who launched the most significant, indeed the only significant attack, saw deeper, for he was Nietzsche, and he saw through Wagner because he saw through the epoch, saw through it with hatred and scorn because he saw into its vacuum. And whereas in his own work, which he looked on throughout as an ethical and ultimately metapolitical work of art and hence a conclusive representation of the epoch, he raised the epoch to utmost clarity so that some day by virtue of such clarity the vacuum might be overcome, he saw justifiably in the emergent Wagnerian work, with its similar claims of representation, the exact opposite of his own. None of the contemptible and odious inclinations of the epoch are combated in it; none of its hollowness, its specifically German hollowness, is brought into the open; no, nothing of that was allowed to be touched, for it was needed as the basis for theater, as the requisite of a theatricality with which the inarticulately hollow, mystical, patriotic, and decoration-craving appetite of the philistine German public could be tickled and gratified. For Nietzsche, then, Wagner offered no synopsis or comprehension of the epoch but was, rather, one of its attending components, a minor artist who had strayed into the gigantic, a mere opera composer who dared to break with the main operatic tradition because he felt himself incapable of furthering it, and against whom the minor Bizet had to be posited as a major counterexample. Yet did this not shift the discussion to another track? Was Nietzsche not unintentionally attending to the affairs of the anti-Wagnerian music philistines? He was indeed, just as half a century later—surely against his will even in death—he was forced to serve as a spiritual pretext for the affairs of the philistine beast.

In other words, when discussion is limited to the sphere of music, we no longer have the seer-philosopher Nietzsche confronting the fundamentally unprophetic Wagner, but a fundamentally nonmusical genius confronting a music genius, even though an unmusical one. And Wagner is thus attacked where the musically philistine public were wont to attack him, and where he, vis-à-vis this public, was just bound to be in the right. The public (and one dares not say perhaps even Nietzsche as well) had preferred Liszt to Wagner, but Liszt knew how far his genius son-in-law had surpassed him. The public—and this with a mite more justice—had preferred Verdi to the antimusician Wagner, but under Wagnerian influence Verdi found the style of his old age and created *Falstaff*, his most splendid work. The public treated Bruckner and, a little later, Hugo Wolf, the two most genuine and profound musical geniuses of the epoch, just as badly as it had treated Wagner. In symphonic as well as song literature, it preferred the strictly conservative, tradition-bound Brahms (probably to his detriment), but he was more and more eclipsed by the work of Bruckner and Wolf, and their styles are both unthinkable without Wagner.[11] Even if we were to dismiss the revolutionary in Wagner as too rational, it was precisely through this rationality that he acted as the necessary catalyst for the musical revolution that he initiated. For Nietzsche, despite all his clairvoyance, this was absolutely inconceivable.

Yet why, we may ask, did a genius like Bruckner, who was well able to stand on his own two feet, need a catalyst for his development? The somewhat childish personal reverence he extended to the master of Bayreuth is surely not a sufficient explanation; for all the reverence, a Bruckner needed no kind of support from Wagner or from anyone else. He did, however, need the world, the world totality, the epoch totality, to whose expression he as an artist was called and bound and which, despite his search for it, he was probably unable to grasp once and for all, although, artist that he was, he had surmised not only it but its vacuum as well. Locked into his solid Catholic beliefs, in which there is no value vacuum, Bruckner was first made aware of the world, the epoch, the vacuum through the Wagnerian work of art; in the art of the vacuum he found the worldly stance that could serve as the point of departure, from which for the first time he could gather the world up to the higher state of his own work, overcoming the vacuum and surpassing Wagner. Of course, it could be objected that Bruckner was unique, but did not something similar occur in the case of Hugo Wolf? If his was a unique case, it was a paradigmatic one, paradigmatic for the uniqueness of a world caught in a value vacuum, paradigmatic for the uniqueness of Richard Wagner, in whom this vacuum was uniquely embodied.

The value vacuum of the world presented an extraordinary situation. In Germany it had adopted forms more visible than anywhere else, since intellectual production was reduced almost completely to the fields of science and music, yet that does not imply it was not visible elsewhere. The cruelty, for example, that emerged with increasing intensity in impressionist and postimpressionist painting can be taken as a symptom of vacuum. For even if every value vacuum is primarily a break in the flow of tradition, an empty spot in that "patchwork process" by which epoch styles are generated, each in the womb of the preceding style—though they develop in mutual dependence and influence through the revolutionary rejection of this "mother style"—this is still, so to speak, only the technical view, the "historico-mechanical" view of the problem; in truth, a particularly ethical phenomenon stands behind it. In the nineteenth century, the dwindling of the old European systems of beliefs had begun, and with the collapse of this central value, the splintering of the comprehensive religious value system gave rise to autonomous individual systems (of which *l'art pour l'art* was one). In other words, the universality of the governing ethical attitudes began to disintegrate, and the desires they had until now ethically subdued began to be unleashed. Here, however, the circle closes: every value vacuum is an incitement to revolution, but for the fulfillment of revolutions the unleashing of desires is indispensable.

Nietzsche was aware of the mechanism of the value vacuum and of this superimposition of epochs (the union of which appears to be a historical law), and he was aware of the sinister consequences slumbering within them, all the more so as he could see Germany, burdened with evil, before his own eyes. Wagner knew nothing of this; for him, every potential vacuum was always filled by the *Gesamtkunstwerk*; and the Twilight of the Gods, in reality a glorification of German being and German fate, was a theatrical apotheosis whose carryover into life could be at most an unfulfillable wish. But those who followed, the philistine beasts, were no longer able to differentiate between the ethical *no* of the prophet and the *yes* of the theater aesthete, so that Nietzsche and Wagner, in a strange communion, bore the spiritual responsibility—presumably distasteful to the former and

58

pleasing to the latter—for the shameful events which after not too long a time were to rock Germany and the whole of world civilization.

### 4. Vienna's Gay Apocalypse of 1880

In Vienna, too, the value vacuum ruled from 1870 to 1890, but whereas in Germany these years constituted the "take-off" period, here they constituted the "roast chicken era" [*Backhendlzeit*] and were therefore taken as lightly as befits a vacuum.

Were there such a thing as a complete value vacuum, man would be reduced to the level of the melancholiac, for whom life is not worthwhile. But there is no complete value vacuum, and although the stagnation of artistic value production is no isolated phenomenon but portends a non-style encompassing all areas of life, that non-style will not commonly be considered by its contemporaries as a detriment to life. There remain sufficient realms of activity into which life values can be projected, and substitute values are usually by far the most gratifying. Daily life always continues. Germany in the "take-off" period had a full and overflowing daily life and not only created within it geniune scientific values but was also so busy with the construction of its ominous economic and national dimensions, that it could easily disregard both value vacuum and non-style. Germany was the country of rational work-intoxication. Yet did the Austrians, the Viennese, work less? Was this really nothing but the roast chicken era, a period of pure hedonism and sheer decoration of life? And, if so, why?

Of course the Austrians worked too, perhaps in somewhat less possessed a way than the Berliners, yet certainly no less than the southern Germans. Daily life presented the same demands everywhere. Austrian science accomplished no less than German science: Ernst Mach worked in Vienna, and even if his physical-philosophical life's work went unnoticed there, the same would have happened to him in Germany. Vienna was the source of the most important technological innovations (for instance the propeller); but above all Vienna was the seat of a medical school which in a period of development of more than a hundred years—since its foundation under Joseph II—under the direction of men like Van Swieten, Hyrtl, Rokitansky, and finally Billroth, had raised itself to be the foremost in the world.[12] In the light of such achievement one could certainly—just as in Germany—disregard the value vacuum.

Yet the desire was not only to disregard it but also to gloss over it. One played at great art, not as crudely as later under Wilhelm II, to say nothing of the Hitler period, yet still not quite unconsciously, hence not without untruthfulness. Munich designated itself "Athens-on-the-Isar" because within its walls a kind of "neo–Van Dyckism" and "neo–Velazquezism" was practiced (admittedly not by the strong and willful Leibl) and there was even some poetry on the side. Now for all the acknowledgement of the painterly qualities of a Lenbach and even his successor Habermann, or of the literary qualities of his poetic fellow citizen Heyse,[13] "Athens-on-the-Isar" was a farce, in part the effort of Bavarian particularism against Berlin, but in part the farce of an unintended self-directed irony fully approved by the Munich *Fliegende Blätter,* the humorless comig rag of the German burgher of the time. Not for nothing was the word *kitsch* coined in Munich at that time. And yet, involuntary as this self-directed irony may have been, Bavarian national sarcasm did not leave it in the unconscious but turned it back into the conscious and thereby back into the genuine, and for that very reason "Athens-on-the-Isar" won that humorous veneer which provided the city's peculiar charm, its art, its entire atmosphere.

Although Vienna felt itself just as much an art city, indeed an art city par excellence, its atmosphere was entirely different. It was really far less a city of art than a city of decoration par excellence. In accordance with its decoration, Vienna was cheerful, often idiotically cheerful, but with little sense of indigenous humor or even sarcasm and self-directed irony. As for literary production, aside from the catching feuilletons practically nothing existed. The passing of Stifter and Grillparzer, who had provided Austria's only important contribution to German and hence to world literature, and who were now without successors, touched almost no one. Poetry was an affair of gold-edged books on the parlor table, and for that a Rudolph Baumbach or at best a Friedrich von Halm were the most appropriate.[14] The visual arts, on the other hand, were necessary for the decoration of life, and they were valued according to their usefulness; Viennese decorative art rightly named its non-style after its most representative painter, the beauty-virtuoso Hans Makart. He was the greatest decorator of the epoch, and the epoch became—at least in Vienna—the Makart period. If in Munich the game was "neo–Van Dyck," Makart conjured in his paintings a kind of Rubens opera, to the astonished delight of his contemporaries. In the 1873 Imperial Parade, which he designed, he actually appeared disguised as Rubens, riding a white saddle horse. And all those who, out of artistic honesty, could not or would not conform to the Makart style—for instance the brilliant, often nearly impressionistic experimenter Pettenkofen, or the Viennese *veduto* painter Rudolf von Alt who, though thoroughly original, was still frankly reminiscent of Canaletto, or the important painters of Viennese landscape Jacob Schindler and Tina Blau, as well as many others—all were inevitably overshadowed by this kind of high decorative style.[15] But Vienna stood on its "decoration rights," and—this is the essential point—was to a substantial degree entitled to do so, not only because decorativeness was a fundamental characteristic of the epoch, but far more because it had exerted its purest and finest effect in the musical and theatrical tradition of Austria. Dutiful concern for this tradition removed from Viennese decorativeness the farcical spirit with which the Germans—especially in Munich—were trying to gloss over the value vacuum, and if, despite that concern, this decorativeness was far from being granted true legitimacy, the legitimacy it did achieve was more defensible than it could have been anywhere else in Europe.

If anywhere, decorativeness was legitimate in Vienna; only it was more or less that kind of legitimation which befits the establishment and maintenance of a museum. In fulfillment of its duty to tradition, Vienna confused culture with "museumness" [*Museumshaftigkeit*] and became a museum to itself (unfortunately not in its architecture, where it was guilty of the most outrageous devastations). Because Haydn and Mozart, Beethoven and Schubert had miraculously converged on this spot, had been badly treated and had nevertheless composed, Vienna set itself up as a musical institution. Germany never set itself up as a poetic institution, in spite of Weimar, and not even "Athens-on-the-Isar" did anything of the sort with its painting. The "museumish" [*das Museale*] was reserved for Vienna, indeed as a sign of its ruin, the sign of Austrian ruin. For in despondency decay leads to vegetating, but in wealth it leads to the museum. Museumishness [*Musealität*] is the vegetating of wealth, a cheerful vegetating, and Austria was at the time still a wealthy country.

The Viennese have always felt uneasy with the Germans, especially the northern Germans, and the wish to differentiate themselves from the Germans, even at the price of this museumishness, would probably have always gained their consent. The fact that this museumish posture also distinguished Vienna from Paris, however, would have met with less approval. For Vienna has always been proud of its similarities to Paris.

Clearly the two cities have much in common, mainly in atmosphere. Paris of course was never the explicitly musical city that Vienna was, but it surpassed Vienna, if possible, in its love for the theater. The lightness of the theatrical and the love for the theater, the lightness of the ever present desire for pleasure and entertainment, in short the love of spectacle was innate in the people of both cities, and in each had become the breeding ground for a dominating theater culture through which that love, in turn, was continually reawakened and kept on the move. The Comédie Française and the Vienna Burgtheater were parallel institutions, and their high style had its effect beyond the theater, reaching out as a model into every stratum of the population (not only to the bourgeoisie), setting the pace for language and conduct, and influencing more than ever what remained of the genuine and vital popular theater of both cities, even popular musical comedy, which for its part was still in a state of dependence—part imitative, part satirical-polemical—on grand opera. In no other place was the entire texture of life so tightly interwoven with that of the theater as it was in Paris and Vienna.

Such common interests point to resemblances in national character. But national character is correlated to historical conditions and experiences; each determines the other. During the seventeenth and eighteenth centuries, Paris and Vienna were the power centers of the European continent, and the rivalry between the houses of Bourbon and Habsburg was the axis around which world politics rotated. France and Austria had won exceptional positions within the European balance of power; they had to defend themselves against each other, and thus both required the most highly developed organization in order to accomplish the world-political tasks this situation presented them with. They in fact became the two most modern continental states of the Baroque. This new state organization was centralized—in France even more than in Austria—yet it was unable in the name of this centralization to deny or even to destroy what might be called its natural administrative foundations, which were anchored in feudal and ecclesiastical institutions. Nor could it become tyrannical, since it needed the people and especially the bourgeoisie as a counterweight to the power of the feudal and ecclesiastical lords. The solution to this extremely difficult problem lay in the indigenously Baroque, downright oriental hypertrophy of the courtly. Through the splendor of the court, the minor nobles and collateral lines could be alienated from the great noble families, and through the court it became more and more possible to secularize spiritual and cultural spheres which until that point had been directed exclusively by the clergy—for example, through the foundation of scholarly academies as principally courtly institutions. And if, with all this, the people were seldom assigned anything more than the role of an astonished spectator—a role they had genuinely accepted—they felt themselves becoming more and more of a political factor, and certainly the one as much as the other and even both together were from then on thoroughly calculated to influence decisively the national character. As a participant in the new consciousness of power and splendor, the people of the rival cities Paris and Vienna had become bearers of a common lifestyle. Rivalry and affinity have always been siblings.

The secularization of spiritual life was initiated by Protestantism; thus its imitation in the court also had a religious-political goal, namely, the reconsolidation of Catholicism within the new framework of the state. Art was not the last thing to be affected. Insofar as the bourgeois private intimacy, into which the Protestant secularization process had necessarily to flow, was replaced by the spectator-oriented "amusement of the sovereign" (with the salon providing maximum intimacy), secularization was caught in a domain which for technical reasons alone had to remain practically unattainable for the bourgeois and his artistic pursuits. Grand concerts, grand opera, and above all the theater, all of them removed from the sphere of the private, were antithetical to chamber music and still-life painting, and for that very reason they formed one of those bridges that could bring the people into immediate contact. The tradition from which the Bourbon and Habsburg residences emerged as theater cities began in the two court theaters and always drew new sustenance from them. And there were no Protestant theater cities.

In any case the monarchic-courtly element became more and more superfluous, in other words an empty convention. For every self-solidifying tradition becomes autonomous in the end. The tradition of the Comédie Française has smoothly survived every royal deposition. It would probably have been no different with the Burgtheater; but there was no Austrian revolution—the cleverly timed administrative reforms of Joseph II did more than a little to avoid one, and so courtly convention remained intact for Viennese intellectual life and especially for the theater. Academic life, too, long remained under the protection of an imperial prince; the opera long kept its gala performances, at which the attendance of the emperor transmitted to the spectator a morsel of participation in the luster of divine right. And for a long time the private theaters, officially unvisited by the court and therefore excluded from its luster, maintained—even the smallest of them—a royal box (like the equally unused "royal waiting rooms" in the major railway stations) clearly visible, its plush-red, rather cheap ostentation constantly in the public's eyes, so that pleasure in theater continued to be ordered around the scheme of monarchical value hierarchy. For a truly seeing eye, this continuously unused, continuously dark box clearly had the effect of a museum piece and, indeed, because of this very museumishness, of a symbol of empty convention of monarchical Baroque gesture.

Austria in the nineteenth century had become museumish, not only intellectually but also politically (no organism, at the very least a community where one part conditions the other, contains isolated zones). The path of revolution, which may well have been in the mind of the reformer Joseph II, treads on the razor's edge, the precipice into revolution on its left, that into reaction on its right, and he who would follow it needs an instinct for balance of the type that may have developed only in insularly assured England. Austria, threatened from without and nationally torn from within, possessed nothing of this instinct, could not possess it, and where it did not fall into reaction, it had to become stagnant and museumish. While

Paris surmounted its Baroque structure through revolutionary thrusts and so made possible the development of the world city already germinating within it, Vienna remained a Baroque city, far from that passionate gloom and latent revolutionism that is indigenous to every world city, that smoldered beneath the cheerfulness of nineteenth-century France and even today is not extinguished yet could well be extinguished when Paris loses its status as a world city. For an uprising to transcend itself and turn into a revolution—as was the case in France in 1789—it must achieve a worldwide effect; it must—as became ever clearer in the nineteenth century—strive toward world revolution, and this demands a world center as a stage, at least a potential world city and not just some kind of national metropolis. And Austria, as a country that had partly lost, partly squandered its world-political mission, was utterly unfit to contain such a city. After 1848, the city—its working-class quarter not excepted—moved ever more deeply into the unrevolutionary, the hedonistic, the skeptic-courteous, courteous-skeptic. Vienna became an "un–world city," and, without thereby becoming a small town, it sought small town tranquillity, small-town narrow-mindedness, small-town pleasures, the charm of "once upon a time." It was still a metropolis, but a Baroque metropolis, and one for which there were no more Baroque politics.

At this point, their resemblance in atmosphere notwithstanding, the primary commonality between Paris and Vienna is annulled. A city in an acute value vacuum, a city turned museumish, no longer has anything essential in common with one that finds itself in a stormy value upheaval. And a people turned provincial has a different character from a cosmopolitan people and therefore must also produce a different kind of art. This is immediately visible in popular art. If one compares the three types of operetta embodied in Offenbach, Sullivan, and Johann Strauss, the third—contrary to the first two—lacks any satirical tendency. The ironic note that had distinguished the Viennese popular stage in its classical epoch in the first half of the nineteenth century (the romantic irony of Raimund and the biting irony of Nestroy)[16] had completely disappeared, and nothing remained of it but the totally idiotic counterfeit of comic opera and its sometimes appealing, sometimes insipid romanticism. What was spreading here was the flat cynicism of sheer, i.e., exclusively decorative, amusement, and the adequate carrier of its immorality was the waltz-genius of Strauss. To be sure, comic opera lives also in the satire of Offenbach and the social caricature of Sullivan, and surely these contain almost as genuine an amusement and cynicism, but it is that exceedingly cosmopolitan cynicism whose aggressiveness stems from political aspiration and finds its moral support in such aspiration—an aggressiveness that is for that very reason indispensable to the realization of satire. All this was lost to the Viennese after 1848, so that the operetta form created by Strauss became a specific vacuum–product; yet as a vacuum–decoration it proved itself all too durable, and its later worldwide success can be taken as a *mene-tekel*[17] for the submergence of the whole world into the relentlessly widening value vacuum.

Vienna, center of the European value vacuum—surely a somewhat absurd honor and distinction, yet not so absurd when one takes into account the sociopolitical texture of the city, the social texture of Austria itself, unique in Europe.

## 5. The Political Vacuum[18]

Of the seven European major powers, France in 1871 had definitely become a republic. The remaining six, still monarchies to be sure, were nevertheless in no way structurally alike. Two of them, Russia and Spain, had held onto an apparently unchanged Baroque political form; that is, they adhered now as before to the monarchical (in Russia also theoretical) centralization of the state established in the seventeenth century, which had cast off the medieval feudal system, had de-autonomized it with the counterweight of the non-noble estates, and had continued nevertheless to use it as an instrument of administration, hence endowing it with its final nature, which has lasted until the most recent times. They were able to do this because their bourgeoisie—still numerically insignificant—was in no position to impose a further shift in equilibrium, and they had to do it, because with the bourgeoisie as weak as it was—a weakness Lenin was the first to perceive as common to both countries—economic and social revolution lurked beneath the numbness of the superannuated state. Conversely, the long solidified bourgeois economic order of the new Italian and German monarchies—*parvenu* and rabble monarchies in aristocratic eyes—needed no such help. Italy could have followed France down the republican path without further ado, and the German empire, this hyperdecorative resuscitation of the now thoroughly Protestant-centered and no longer Roman "Holy Empire," was in the end a Bismarckian trick for the union of German National Liberalism with the Prussian feudalistic *Junkertum*, the trick of a pseudofederalism that camouflaged nothing but Prussian hegemony—the perpetuation of its mastery over Habsburg as over all the constituent German states, which had been conceded shadowlike autonomous existences within the bounds of the empire. The circumstances were completely different, however, in England and Austria: the representative mission of the Victorian as well as of the Francisco-Josephinian monarchy was dictated neither by decorative—let alone hyperdecorative—nor by tricksterish, least of all by economic necessities, but by political necessity.

Behind this nonetheless curious English-Austrian resemblance, analogous causes were at work in both countries, clearly presaging opposite results. (England had been on the rise for two hundred years, Austria in decline.) Notwithstanding the symbolic meaning of the crown—in England as a sign of the everlasting continuity of British power and its growth, in Austria as the expression of the old German, mystically based, imperial glory that had once been experienced and to which one held fast in spirit despite its loss—notwithstanding such emotional impulses, by no means unimportant politically, the crown erected in both places a thoroughly rational, practical, indeed indispensable state-building institution; in the case of Austria it lent a secure, legally tenable unity to the complicated and scattered conglomerate of autonomies and semi-autonomies that formed the Habsburg empire, in the case of England it provided the same for the even more complicated, ever expanding world empire of colonies, dominions, mandates, etc. In both cases, the unifying strength of the crown was a political necessity. Borne by such necessity, the English as much as the Austrian-Baroque monarchy was able to conform to the demands of the times in a more or less constant evolution, without drastic breaks in tradition. (Even the Cromwell interregnum hardly counts as a break in tradition, much less, therefore, a brief reign like the Viennese March revolution of 1848.) In contrast to the still Baroque-feudal monarchies of Russia and Spain, yet also in contrast to the artistic, decorative structure of the German and Italian thrones, only in England and Austria was constitutional monarchy (with great-power status) realized in a "natural" manner.

The "natural," evolutionary constitutionalization of a state fufills itself as a gradual, step-by-step transfer of crown privileges—above all the authority to set laws—to the sovereignty of the people. Defeat in foreign policy, lost wars, and other emergencies are what generally force the crown to settle for such popularly appeasing concessions. The constitutionalization of Austria in the nineteenth century is an example of this. And the much older English constitutionalization was initiated by the very same causes. But then the picture changes. The more England found the path suited to it—the colonial-imperialist one (and thereby differentiated itself structurally from the continental powers), the more its democratization became the concern of the entire people, and the more it was advanced through foreign success rather than defeat, through welfare rather than distress. Even if the upswing was broken by a political or an economic crisis, the position of the crown became all the more solid, for it was this very upswing that increased its necessity; aware of this, the crown was forced on its own behalf to yield to the wishes of the people. Thus, from the original (fluctuating) three-cornered equilibrium of royal, noble, and bourgeois power, the immediate influence of the throne slowly lost its place, and the weight of the bourgeoisie, which united increasingly with the nobility, was bit by bit replaced by that of the proletariat. Yet, whatever it may have been like, this totally unique power game, comparable to none on the continent, brought on an eminently political result—the conservative-progressive consensus on which English democracy rests, and through which it became exemplary.

Concrete politics, whether good or bad, are made by concrete men, through dictates in a true absolute divine monarchy, through compromise in true democracy. Yet an absolutism compelled into compromise (and wanting still to remain absolute) begins to tack into the wind, and he who wishes to dictate in a democracy (without robbing it of the democratic) tacks into the same ambiguous course, even if he is able to justify himself—as is usually predetermined—with the ability to steady himself on abstract, unshakable dogmas. No abstractly oriented politics, from Plato to Wilson, has developed into politically enduring action, and as much as tacking may belong to political technique, never, not even with Franklin D. Roosevelt, has it led to a founding political idea. Richelieu and Mazarin, with a disregard for all abstract and for that matter all Catholic principles, practiced concrete absolutist politics, and England never deviated from the concrete but attached herself to it all the more tenaciously as she became more democratic. Austrian or, more precisely, Habsburg politics were from the very beginning attracted, in a strange combination, to tacking and to the abstract, and because of that they were later compelled to remain so by virtue of the relations they had created.

Surely every action attended to by concrete men is concrete; yet that does not prevent it from mirroring the concrete-abstract discordance of its motivations. And the Habsburgs were not ones to allow such discordance to be absent. They were endowed to an overwhelming extent with political instinct, yet one which ultimately focused on the antipolitical. Beneath their extraordinary talent for the Machiavellian, as well as for every kind of political intrigue and maneuver, lurked often a lack of determination and the abstract-playful propensity to a tacking for its own sake, but one that remains fixed to one spot, and for this—senile and skeletonized—Charles V's ghostlike clock-making mania offers the clearest evidence. But where the Habsburgs, however rarely, were truly human and, like Maximilian ("the last knight"), found true contact with the people, this connection became—as the popular legendary anecdotes about Emperor Max show—a paternalistic, home-oriented family connection that corresponded to their unpolitical ideal. The issue was the fear of politicization, the deeply rooted antipathy to the masses politicized through questions of faith (other causes were at that time hardly involved), and this fear was so fundamentally corroborated by the bitter experience of the Thirty Years' War that Jesuitism, already enlisted against the masses in a similar way, came to be granted not only the direction of the Counterreformation but also a decisive influence on the nature of statecraft. Through Jesuitic teaching, Habsburg abstractism wins its theoretical footing, through Jesuitic rules, its tacking becomes methodical and nearly indomitable, through Jesuitic determination, its discordance is raised to the systematic.

These were the weapons with which Habsburg encountered the emerging democratization of the period between 1789 and 1848. Joseph II's famous reforms, sprung from under the shadow of the French Revolution and the threat of its contagion, were an act of Jesuitic schooling and Machiavellian tacking, although Joseph himself—rationalistic and hence dogmatic, politically unconcrete and hence purposive, humanitarian and hence undemocratic, feeble and hence vitreously inflexible, in short a man of utmost coolness and utmost disunion—considered himself a convinced defender of human rights, unaware that in his state-centralized efforts (admittedly not racist) toward Germanization, he simultaneously withheld those rights from the non-German Austrians. Momentary compromises of an absolute ruler, his reforms could be eliminated without further ado at the outbreak of the Napoleonic wars, in which the reforms no longer acted as preventive measures, but rather as fifth-column instruments of French ideas. This happened promptly, brutally, and without success through his successors Leopold II and Franz I; without success, because in the post-Napoleonic period, the peril of Austria and Habsburg was more evident than ever (never yet have the ideas that carried a usurper and that were carried by him been destroyed together with his overthrow). The French danger was replaced by the German one, on one hand in the form of the revitalized Prussian desires for hegemony, on the other in the form of every foolish irredentist democratic movement that longed for a parliamentary Greater Germany; and alongside the latter, no less irredentistically, the centrifugal forces existing in the so called "nationalities" suddenly revealed themselves—in part of course also as a consequence of the Josephinian campaign of Germanization, not yet it is true among the Czechs and southern Slavs, but clearly among the Poles (who refused to get over the fact of their lost kingdom) as well as in Venetia and Lombardy. And every one of these dangers had necessarily to abet the strengthening of the intra-Austrian democratic tendencies. No wonder, then, that under the paternalistic reign of Franz I, who—similarly cool but essentially more straightforward than Joseph II and, in compensation, equipped with a certain underhanded wit—sought, partly through exhortation, partly through malice, to bring his subjects to reason, the "secret ones," as the Austrian state police[19] of the time were popularly designated, became omnipotent, the censors continuously gained in harshness, and the notorious Spielberg Prisons became even fuller of "political" prisoners. For what went on here in the form of aggressive Metternichian radical conservatism (in domestic as well as foreign politics) was more than mere reaction. Not one of those concerned—not even Gentz or even Adam Müller,[20] although they saw most clearly through this conservatism—saw that the Counterreformation, in an immense final effort, had become completely political and, according to its mission, was making a final attempt to rescue the integrity of the Austrian state through radical depoliticization.

Eighteen forty-eight made it clear that this effort had become futile. When Ferdinand I, the most harmless of tyrants who always softened in the face of revolution, abdicated and with the historic words "All right, Frankie, be good" ("Schon recht, Franzl, bleib brav"), handed over the imperial command to his eighteen-year-old nephew Franz Joseph I, he handed over at the same time an empire that no longer was an empire, in other words a state already rejected by the overwhelming majority of its population. For all the proletarian participation, this was clearly a predominantly bourgeois revolution, loyal to the emperor and hence one in which the typically bourgeois freedoms of constitutionalism were demanded; it was also an Austrian revolution and hence affirmed Austria and desired its continuance. For even if the intellectuals and students, the spiritual leaders of this revolution, were in many ways opposed to their predominantly Catholic fathers, they were still, like them, rooted in their home institutions, partly through class interest and partly through romantic sentiment, and they knew, at least they suspected, that without the unifying crown of the Habsburgs the state structure would crumble. Their dream was Austrian freedom, a freedom with which they hoped to gather the separately struggling nationalities back to a new Austrian unity, and they did not consider the fact that in the majority of the provincial cities even their own linguistic and class contemporaries were already infected by irredentism and pan-Germanism, and, indeed, that the revolutionary sympathies of these contemporaries, not to mention those of the nationalities, were not striving for state consolidation, but for the accelerated destruction of the state. In its illusions about Austria, the Viennese revolution was just as abstract as the regime it battled, yet in the unleashing of the centrifugal forces of the nationalities—the very fear Metternich had held for forty years—it was concrete; it was the most concrete of dangers.

Fundamentally, this was already the dissolution of the Austrian state, even if for the time being it revealed itself only as a paradoxical situation. Even if the young, inexperienced emperor had had the finest democratizing intentions, the partiality of the Viennese revolution would have prevented him from finding a point of departure for them. For to democracy—as is the case in England—there belongs a total population prepared to be responsible to the state, whereas here the majority of the population was at most prepared to live within the state as a responsibility-free, yet respected, in any case grumbling guest, and to wait for the opportunity to destroy it. Aside from the Viennese *Bürgertum*, revolutionary-liberal as well as Catholic, devotion to Austria was extant only among the resident peasantry of the (German Alpine) "hereditary lands" [*Erblanden*]; for them, loyalty to the emperor was a purely mystical tradition maintained in the depths of their being, surpassing everything political (the similarly disposed Croatia stood under Hungarian dominion); and, even if one takes into account the splinter groups of great-agrarian and feudal type whose adherence to the state, regardless of nationality, depended above all on the guarantee of their special position—even then, hardly an eighth of the population, hence a vanishing, tiny segment could be regarded as a life-carrying substance of the state. Eighteen forty-eight made it unequivocally clear that, without the crown, the Austrian structure was absolutely void of substance; that concentrated within the crown was the state's entire principle of intertia—the most important requisite for its existence; in short, that the crown alone represented the substance of the state. A kind of totality function was incumbent on the crown, a kind of involuntary "L'état c'est moi," and if this expression had actually been as proud in the mouth of Franz Joseph as it had been in the mouth of Louis XIV, it would have been a cry of despair.

In other words, whereas the politically unifying function of the crown is compatible with constitutionalism and democracy, as the English example shows, its totality function—no less necessary for Austria—craved absolutism in an almost terrifying way. The relapse into the old regime, inaugurated with the Schwarzenberg ministry, was upbraided for its counterrevolutionary vindictiveness; actually it was a solution to a difficult predicament and owed its astonishing decade-long lifespan to the equally astonishing foreign political successes of the anti-Prussian course of the time. Yet after the triumphant defeat of 1859 (defeat in war after victory in battles had become Austria's lot), after the cession of Lombardy and Venetia to the newly unified Italy, a major change in course could no longer be avoided. Schmerling, who as a liberal had led the Austrian union in the 1848 Frankfurt parliament, was called to the government in place of Schwarzenberg, and in 1861 the emperor established the first pan-Austrian parliament. The Austrian constitution was born, much later of course than the English one and determined by a completely different state structure; yet, like the English constitution, it was the final, necessary phase in the steady development of a monarchical tradition unbroken since the Middle Ages and the Baroque.

Austria had entered the closing phase of its existence as a state, and it could well be that Franz Joseph, who in the meantime had grown to manhood, had such premonitions as he drove along the debris of Vienna's now demolished city walls, over the still undeveloped glacis—where the

Ringstrasse would later arise—to the provisional wooden houses of the new Parliament in front of the Schottentor, to open its first session. It was a parliamentary assembly by means of which government was still possible; a subtly crafted class suffrage guaranteed unconditional majority to the loyal Austrian party led by German liberals, and thus pressed the "nationalities," despite their popular majority, into a helpless minority and confined their centrifugal forces, at least in terms of legislating capacity. By this time, it is true, voices had already been raised—not least from the ranks of the nationalities—demanding the initiation of a "just," federative parliamentary system, but how could that have been brought about? The mere attempt to establish it had fired disputes to the boiling point among the kaleidoscopic overlapping settlements of the nationality groups, and it had justifiably to be accepted that their counterachievement of "repatriotization" (the very expectation of the revolutionary idealists of 1848) would become more than insecure. It seemed absolutely impossible to create a federative "justice," and in its place there emerged almost necessarily the peculiarly Habsburgian system of political preferences, a system which— clearly at the price of discrimination against Austria by Hungary's special position—understood actually how to make weakness into strength through a Machiavellian exploitation of the nationality dispute. In other words, it turned the centrifugal mechanism into a kind of equilibrium, or at least imposed on it a temporary suspension of the problem. It was a process of constant "tacking" and of more or less official reforming, of constant negotiating both inside and outside Parliament (mostly the latter). But it led the way to 1873, and indeed, in a whirl of revolutionary tendencies and temperaments, which at every external loss of power threatened to flare up to double the danger, it led Austria to a final heyday which—even if it was only a false heyday—reached into the twentieth century and became the swan song of Vienna.

But this was a heyday of an abstract structure. The more vocal the nationalities became, by dint of the ever growing concessions which they had forced—the preference system had a purely retarding effect—the more Austria disappeared. The German minority, until now loyal to the state, robbed of its preferred position and hence embittered, degenerated altogether to a pan-German irredenta of sheer pre-Hitlerian character. Its place was filled by the Christian Socialist party of Lueger, later mayor of Vienna. Under a Catholic banner, yet with a demogogic employment of pre-Hitlerian methods, he had once again, if through a different stratification, gathered the imperially loyal elements, first of all the Viennese petite bourgeoisie and then, with the aid of the clergy, the Alpine peasantry, and from this tradition-bound, indeed democratic basis—the same occurred in Hungary from a Croatian basis—he intended not only to reinstate the situation of 1850 together with its reactionary course but also to convert the nationalities to that course and thus resolve their problematic through a kind of intra-Austrian Catholic International. The latter was a goal modeled on that of the rapidly growing Workers' Party, which likewise presumed it would be able to engender an intra-Austrian International bridging all nationality quarrels, just as long as it were granted equal, direct, and universal suffrage. The nationalities did support the demand, but when suffrage was achieved, they did not adopt the tendencies of the two Internationals to preserve the state. The centrifugal forces remained untamed, indeed were becoming constantly more untamable, and began to wear away the structure of the state with increasing speed so that the parliamentary machinery, which surrendered the stage to this—allegedly toward the goal of an Austrian legislation—became a specter of its own goal. What subsisted of the Austrian state was the specterlike skeleton of a theory in which no one any longer believed.

The state was one thing, and the political machinery existing inside it quite another; between the two lay a kind of impenetrable insulating layer, at which apparently both of these became abstract. Just as Machiavellianism is in itself mere political technique and as such not politics, so parliamentary rules of procedure, for all the ardor of the battles waged within their boundaries, are far from being democracy, because democracy goes hand in hand with democratic consensus and democratic compromise, and these in turn go hand in hand with the state together with the common weal for whose sake compromises are sealed. Here, however, in a rejected state, in the state vacuum, non-democracy reigned, and the only thing it still shared with more genuine democracy was the overcoming of absolutism. Step by step, in an almost never explicit, tacking, retreat operation, Franz Joseph had given up the last bits of absolutism that remained to him. Yet not only does every strategy that merely masters retreat, that is in itself, so to speak, a retreat strategy, inevitably become abstract in the end; in this case it had to become all the more abstract as it drifted more and more, in the final third of the century, into the state vacuum and hence to the spot where all concreteness is extinguished. And so it happened. The Machiavellian perfidy of the early Habsburgs (even if Austrian abstractness was already pronounced under Joseph II) was a lively concreteness in contrast to the correct bureaucratism by which Franz Joseph I ran his government operations, never overstepping the constitutional boundaries which he had once accepted. Precisely because the substance of the state was ever more acutely reduced to the crown, and because the subsisting remains of the state became ever more identical to the crown, the remarkably vacuumlike character of the state had likewise to be taken over by the crown. The discordance of a constitutional state in which "L'état c'est moi" is still to have value—albeit only as substance, yet for this reason no less absurdly—also impinges on the "moi." Thus the crown became as abstract an institution as the state it embodied, and the insular layer which severed the state from the events happening within it surrounded the crown now more than ever.

The older Franz Joseph I grew, the more he immersed himself in the vacuum of his vocation and the more identical he felt with the state, whose fatal destiny was tied to his own, and whose insulated abstractness he was thus forced to carry. Habsburgian in his sense of coolly unapproachable, hierarchical dignity—his most conspicuous characteristic—he drew from this situation a single corresponding consequence, namely, absolute seclusion. He had never been paternalistic—for that he had acceded to the throne too young; yet now men no longer valued him, and his existence became hermetic. They had all betrayed Austria in compelling him toward such calamitous political advancement; even his own son—no doubt a crucial trauma—had allied himself with them, and thus the apaternal raised itself into the antipaternal, disclaiming humanity altogether. Whether commoners, nobles, or princes of the royal house, all of them were empire spoilers searching for reform, an undistinguishable mass, a world of variability before which he, monarch and guardian of imperial subsistence, was compelled to retreat into the immutable. Every reform, every technical invention no matter how insignificant, every modernization of life—whether an automobile, a bathroom, or a wardrobe—that was not allowed in the imperial palaces, became for him a symbol and a symptom of those forces that had brought Austria to the edge of the precipice. He opposed new buildings in the city (for example on the Mariahilferstrasse, through which he rode day after day from Schönbrunn to the "castle"), and his former consent to the demolition of the Vienna city walls and thus the destruction of the old city plan must have haunted him all his life as a sin of youth fraught with the gravest consequences. Surely such an extreme penchant for the immutable can be looked upon as senile, as the private court ceremony of an imperial senile old man, perhaps even as the devious private magic of a helpless creature; all the same, dignity prevailed. It was the immutability of an invisible and undefined inprisonment in which he had found himself drawn into a seclusion infinitely more bitter than that of the Vatican because it proceeded in a vacuum and its stubbornness was that of a solitude that reached out far beyond the individual. Immense was the shell of solitude in which he lived his uncannily bureaucratic, abstractly punctual official life, no matter whether in the Vienna "castle" or in the simple Biedermeier villa at Ischl where annual hunting vacations took him, always in abstract exactness, always in solitude, always in dignity. Wilhelm I was called the first soldier of his empire, Edward VII was the first gentleman of Europe, Franz Joseph I was the abstract monarch par excellence.

And this was exactly the effect he had on his subjects, on the archdukes no less than on the nobles and the burghers and even the working class—this was the effect. He, a man of very meager proportions, a Habsburg who revealed in small measure the inherited qualities of that breed, thus a man with little sense for political and social happenings, yet without immediate access to his fellow man, above all because he lacked any kind of humor and most of all the Habsburg wittiness, in short a truly visionless, narrow, and small-dimensioned man, he was able all the same to become the essence of majesty, in a different way from Louis XIV, it is true, yet with no narrower significance. And this did not occur because a sheer Greek-tragic excess of personal misfortune weighed upon him, neither did it occur from the awe-inspiring effect of such misfortune—this kind of awe-inspired compassion simply disappears from view when the masses are not a public and therefore know no compassion—but it occurred because, perhaps even as a result of all his deficiencies, he had become capable of taking upon himself the thrilling dignity of absolute solitude. For thrill is constantly and instantly extant in the world, and it lurks in every human heart. And so he was seen. He was the opposite of a people's emperor and nevertheless "the" emperor in the eyes of the people.

## 6. Sociology of the Gay Apocalypse[21]

In accordance with its still predominantly monarchically determined political structure, the European social picture of the nineteenth century—the French republic not excepted—was of a predominantly feudal color. Clearly it was only a tint, a surface, but aristocratic society was still "the" society and for that very reason international. Its life forms were generally the same everywhere; all over Europe there were castles and social exclusivity, hunts and races, and everywhere the nobility was entitled to participate in the court hierarchy that every monarchical head of state was obliged to maintain. Beyond the court, the hierarchy extended to government appointments, to the leading diplomatic and military posts as well as those in internal administrative service, so that out of spite the facade of the state aristocracy—even in France—remained seemingly untouched by all democratic hostility. It had the resistance energy of an autonomous tradition, all the more so when this tradition, having a kind of "natural" affinity with the monarchical tradition, shared an even closer affinity with the state tradition. Historically and economically, feudalism emerged as a result of the possession of the prevailing part of all national power by the nobility (who became nobility in just this way). And since even Baroque monarchy, although it broke feudal autonomy, changed nothing in this respect, it became the charge of the state and a branch of its tradition to protect the possessions of the noble class and guarantee its poor relations, in particular "younger sons," positions appropriate to their rank. The nobility (especially when it grew poor as a consequence of the rise of the bourgeoisie) grew loyal to the state, and for all its antipathy toward the usurping monarchical institution, it used the monarchy in its pact with the state, indeed as an agency, which it then reimbursed with the required court attendance. (The despised "parvenu" monarchies of Germany and Italy also profited from this.) But the pact was always with the state, never with the crown; hence the disappearance of the French crown could be accepted: monarchical tradition is in fact younger than feudal tradition, and the case of France made it clear that it is also shorter-lived.

In any case, the steady, sociologically "natural" relationship between monarchical institution and feudal upper class that unquestionably exists can be understood as follows: where the upper class is despised as the bearer of economic and political oppression—as in Russia and Spain, but equally, for example, in Hungary—the crown is also imperiled; where, however, on account of a lack of tradition the monarchy is insufficiently developed, as in Germany and Italy, the nobility loses the ground from under its feet. And in France, where the throne has been definitely brought down, the upper class—although it still functions as such—has necessarily been reduced to a shadow. Yet to whatever extent the monarchy enjoys political affirmation—in England by the entire population, in Austria by the populations of Vienna and the "hereditary lands," the nobility belonging to it is also affirmed. The Victorian and Francisco-Josephinian nobilities were "popular," more popular by far than the bourgeoisie of the same period, which was becoming ever more suspect; and where an upper class gains popularity, its manner of living sets the trend for all the other classes. They all adopted—with mainly quantitative variations—a common "lifestyle," in England that of the "gentleman," in Austria that of the "cavalier" (both debonair, but in the Protestant-Catholic polarity); and since a common lifestyle represents the "most natural," the most naturally engendered sociological affinity, the crown was to a certain extent included in that sphere.

One could almost speak of a style-democracy. For example, the fact that races organized by jockey clubs—aristocratically exclusive all through Europe—were generally accessible certainly did not make them into democratic institutions. At Longchamps they were a fashion show; in Grünewald, Karlshorst, and Hamburg they were predominantly plebeian betting grounds; yet the fact that at Epsom Downs and at the Vienna

75

Freudenau they took on the character of folk festivals, in which every class up to the court participated equally, gave them, like any other folk festival, a democratic hue. And a similar thing held good for the English and Austrian noble classes themselves. Since they were not under attack, they had no reason to be arrogant, in contrast to their other class contemporaries, the *Junkers* for example. As to the Austrian nobility, which far more than the English had always been tied to the land—this popular affinity was even revealed in the language. The Austrian aristocratic language is indeed "high German" and, moreover, frequently Frenchified, yet it is rooted in dialect and is itself very nearly normalized as pure dialect. Hofmannsthal (his purpose of dramatic characterization notwithstanding) may be said to have been "linguistically entitled" to let Baron Ochs auf Lerchenau of *Der Rosenkavalier* speak in pure popular dialect; and since linguistic normalization is a social mirror, it also became clear that, in closeness to the people, the aristocracy considerably outflanked the burghers, whose touches of dialect continued to fluctuate. Clearly the gentleman and the cavalier were class-conscious nonetheless; clearly they understood each other best in terms of their proficiency at horsemanship and hunting, where they were both unsurpassable, yet the unaffectedness of their democratic attitude played an equal role in this kind of understanding.

Still, for all the affinity between the English and Austrian aristocracies, many things must be taken as opposite omens—as was the case in the comparison of the two monarchies. The English rise and the Austrian decline, the total politics of the English democracy and the non-politics of the Austrian vacuum—this contrast had to have an effect on the status and habits of both noble classes. In England, the pact between state and nobility had become brittle, for the democratic consensus had upset the relationship. Public appointments were no longer made under the influence of the court and its officials, but were used rather (side by side with plutocracy) as a reservoir for the replenishing of the court nobility. Conformity to the new relationships and a corresponding productivity was thus the sole means by which the old nobility could hope to maintain its status as ruling upper class, and their success in doing so was due to the strength of character with which they demonstrated their zeal for the state, and to a maximum of political schooling. Not so in Austria; here the state had to maintain the pact and elicit support from the feudal class as an accessory to the court, all the more so as the feudal class alone was indifferent to nationalities and its members were thus the primary candidates for public positions, to which—in view of the jealous nationalities—the German *Bürgertum*, even if it had remained partially loyal to the state, could be admitted only in limited quantities. Thus without any special effort, governmental prerogative fell to the aristocracy, and when its Hungarian branch continued to fill a slew of important offices, above all in foreign service (profiting from the "Compromise" of 1867), and to exploit these toward securing the Hungarian class-state, with great adroitness, the Austrian in turn needed for his task a minimum of schooling and strength of character, simply because no one demanded anything more. Of course the main difference between the noble classes of England and Austria lay one level deeper: the English believed in their state; the Austrians had no point of reference to justify such faith.

For the Austrian nobility, with its existence bound to that of the state and thereby to that of the crown, could merely participate in the crown's political rearguard actions; and, like the crown, it knew where the path was leading even if it did not generally acknowledge it. No strength of character, no political schooling could have done anything to change that; yet was it necessary for the entire noble class to follow the example of Franz Joseph I and persist in heroic solitude? The nobility chose the lesser, more humanly natural path. Like the Parisian aristocratic society of the Rococo (the resemblance between the false Baroque of the nineteenth century and the genuine Baroque of the eighteenth cannot be denied here), the Austrian nobility was driven by a sense of decline to the most ephemeral pursuit of pleasure. Thus, where the English-Austrian resemblance breaks off, the French-Austrian resemblance begins. And even if the range of comparison was in both cases relatively meager, the Viennese were proud of and happy in the one as well as the other: they loved the solid, anglicizing elegance of their aristocracy; they loved the lighthearted atmosphere of their city, reminiscent of Paris, which the aristocracy kept in motion. And even while sensing the approaching downfall (the portrait of the lonely emperor was his contribution to that), for those who through inherited rank and property were in any case accustomed to the light sense of lightheartedness, the flight into the unpolitical was only right. Whether it was a question of Lueger, of a workers' movement, even if they themselves happened to be involved, they understood the cavalier who would not take it seriously, indeed they were even somewhat ashamed of their own behavior, and the political clamor of others, above all of the "nationalities," struck them as a fundamentally comic and senseless grotesque.

The attitude of the political being has much in common with that of the ethical being. Both would improve the world or at least the state, and in this capacity both want to persuade, educate, and if necessary coerce their fellow man to fixed values which they have determined. The scheme remains the same, no matter if composed of ethical, anethical, or even criminally antiethical politics (like those of Hitler); politics and ethics are structurally the same in their activities. Their affinity reveals itself not least in their ultimately consistently hostile relations to the aesthetic. The strict ethicist, the pure ethicist—Savonarola, Calvin—sees in the aesthetic nothing but the work of the devil, nothing but seduction toward a pursuit of pleasure, the dissuasion of man from his ethical duties, to the extent that it all must be cleared from the field of view in a holy iconoclasm. And if the politician does not go so far in theory, he does so in practice nonetheless. This is true as soon as politics, in the final analysis, achieves mastery, and—whether in domestic or foreign warfare—tramples down any aesthetic human creation. Conversely, where political thought is entirely lacking, either because it has not yet developed or because it has been stunted, the aesthetic category moves more and more into the foreground, and, notwithstanding the exceptional cases in which it evolves into truly artistic production, it generates more and more the tendency toward the ornamentation and decoration of life, culminating in a form of ethical indifference—the counterpart of iconoclasm—that expresses itself as naked hedonism, naked pleasure seeking. There is no doubt that Vienna, having become politically incapable, contributed to such a condition.

The lifestyle of the aristocratic upper class was already in this state; Vienna's swan song of the final third of the century had advanced it, and now it advanced its imitation as well. What the Jesuit Counterreformation and the Jesuitically schooled Habsburg politics, culminating with Metternich prior to 1848, had unsuccessfully striven for for centuries—namely, the attainment whenever possible of a depoliticized, homogenous, harmless pan-Austrian population mass, devoted to a simple pursuit of pleasure and its peaceful aesthetic values—was suddenly realized, belatedly and uselessly, in Vienna and its surroundings. From archduke to folk singer, but also from the *Grossbürgertum* down through the proletariat, the hedonistic attitude prevailed. It was the basis of that particular "style-democracy" that united the nobility with the people, guaranteed their mutual understanding—while still maintaining social distinctions—and made it into that very specifically Austrian *gemütlich* familiarity. Of course this cavalier-conditioned "style-democracy" was markedly different from that of the English gentleman, behind which the genuine political democracy of his country was at work. Austrian social structure had absolutely nothing to do with political democracy. As the product of Austrian vacuousness, in which no one could take anyone seriously because, aside from the national substance of the crown, there was nothing to be taken seriously, the social structure too lost substance and became a sort of gelatin democracy [*Gallert-Demokratie*], in which, when it came right down to it, counts took on the allure of coachmen and coachmen the allure of counts.[22] It was a state of social suspension (for Austria the most adequate right from the beginning) and it was able to be so because the reigning heyday held everything in suspension.

If anywhere, a stateless society was realized here, not merely because, aristocratic and aristocratizing as it was, it constantly peered beyond national boundaries into the international, but, much more so, because these boundaries enclosed an abstraction rather than a state. Yet this abstraction was still a state or, at least, a piece of functional state machinery, and for better or for worse the machinery was attended to by the society which belonged to it, no matter how stateless that society may have been; otherwise it would not have continued to function. In other words, with its existence contingent on the continued existence of Austria, this society, together with its upper class, despite its partly aestheticizing, partly fatalistic hedonism, was in no way ready for suicide and was thus obliged, willingly or not, to submit to a minimum of political thought and political ethics. Yet where were the necessary guiding values? There are aesthetically advanced cultures—and Vienna assuredly did not belong to these—in which a sound political-ethical value system (for example, that of the medieval church or of French Baroque absolutism) achieves such a degree of self-evidence that it grants the aesthetic program which is incorporated in it every liberty to unfold itself. There are also aestheticizing decadent cultures, the stages of degeneration of most great empires since antiquity, which for lack of any indigenous ethical center are forced to allow their most vital foundations to be dictated by an "external" or in some other way "higher" ethical authority. Austria, undoubtedly belonging to this second category, was forced to seek its value orientation where its only substance existed, i.e., in that unifying function of the monarchy which (quite uniquely) fell to the Austrian crown and locked within itself the crown's political as well as its ethical authority (the latter supported by the solitude and the Catholicity of the emperor). It was a social authority, and as such—not as a political authority, which had strayed into a void—it was impressive; indeed, its ethics became sacrosanct and utterly mystical, since rational-skeptical frivolity felt itself obliged to accept them.

And it was all the more mystical when a mere glance at the emperor, and an empty glance at that, represented ethical profit. For the ethical substratum that was mediated there was thoroughly eclectic, and thus truly meaningless. The epoch was eclectic in its ethics as in its aesthetics. The fact that purely ethically oriented communities (contrary to the purely aesthetic orientation), for example those of the Puritans, Calvinists, or Jews, were during their ethical prime aesthetically unproductive and, insofar as they did not altogether reject aesthetic values, accepted them eclectically from external authorities, does not imply that aesthetic eclecticism must have an ethical background. And if Franz Joseph I (mainly as a result of his want of humanity) opposed blindly and obtusely the aesthetic phenomenon and in so doing resembled the genuinely ethical personality, he was nonetheless, despite his ethos of solitude, nothing of the sort. It was no concern of his if the ethical values for which he lived were eclectic, for he accepted them dogmatically, and the aesthetic eclecticism all around him concerned him even less, for he did not notice it at all. And still it turned out that a glance at this mediocrity could give to the Austrian the ballast of social authority—presumably incomprehensible to an Englishman, were he to compare it to his sentiments at the sight of the queen. Yet the eclectic values, not only ethical but also aesthetic values, did undergo an extraordinary invigoration through the mere existence of the imperial old man. In the technical realm of civilization, his inclination to changelessness could not hold life up, but in the far less compelling ethical-aesthetic sphere his conservatism set the trend, because a community that finds itself in decline, and in such a beautiful decline at that, will much sooner follow mystical inclinations than revolutionary ones.

This sort of ethical-aesthetic tie to the crown achieved its clearest expression among the Viennese burghers, to the extent that they were not overpoliticized by pan-German and Christian Socialist elements. The Viennese tradesmen, the Viennese industrialists, the Viennese "purveyors to the court," the Viennese faculty members, the Viennese judges, and the Viennese attorneys—all were related to the well-known figure of the Austrian "privy councillor" [*Hofrat*], and, just as politics was forbidden to the Austrian officer, who often sprang from these ranks, they forbade themselves politics. Their political conviction was simply "loyalty to Austria." Because they thought and acted in a manner truly ethical to the state (if not politically), the head of the state, despite its abstractness, was for them an ever surviving, living point of orientation onto which they projected their entire sense of value and from which they extracted all their values. They were a happy mixture of tranquil industriousness and nimbly hedonistic pleasure-seeking, not totally ethical, not totally aesthetic, inwardly steady enough, yet in their judgments in need of corroboration. Neither totally individualistic nor totally collectivist in essence, they were first and foremost a public, the public of the court theater, the court museums, and the concerts and art exhibitions under the court's patronage. Their understanding of art was highly developed, yet unable to deviate an inch from the aforementioned eclectic artistic tradition, and was thus focused exclusively on the virtuoso—on the actor, not the play; on the musician, not the music. All the same, they possessed in the imperial Burgtheater an art in which the eclectic was elevated to originality, the purely aesthetic to the purely ethical. And they were well aware of that, these burghers.

There is no doubt that, apart from the burghers, who were loyal to the emperor and to Austria and representative of a very minor cross section of Austrian society as a whole, things had not changed much. Only that here, where the nobility alone set the trend, respect for the courtly was lacking. For feudalism, which for three hundred years had been pouting at the crown and was still flaunting its former, superior, and more venerable dominion, regarded the monarch at best as primus inter pares and had respect only for itself. Disrespectfulness, however, was no less a fundamental attitude, for that matter an exceedingly un-German fundamental attitude, of the Viennese populace; it belonged solidly to the heritage of the Romance and Slavic influences which were constituent parts of "Austrianness," perhaps the final remains—now of course depoliticized—of a once indisputably extant revolutionism. In this disrespectfulness the populace and the nobility found themselves in the happiest community; indeed they instantly formed the putty for their classless society, the putty-gelatin of their gelatin democracy. And in this sense Franz Joseph I was right after all to lump them all together and keep them without exception at a distance. They all shared the utmost hostility toward him. Yet this grumbling hostility was the single somehow politically colored resistance remaining in this disrespectfulness. Thus the resistance had no effect, not even in the aesthetic. The conditions had become too depoliticized, too lacking in substance, to allow even the slightest movement toward revolution, even toward satire. The farthest any such movement went was the travestying and frivolizing of the courtly values and their ethical-aesthetic content, now appropriated by the burghers; it went as far as the world of the waltz. And precisely because the values which granted some kind of solidity to this society had their origin beyond the insulating layer of the emperor, in the abstraction of the crown, precisely because they aroused at once high and low esteem, horror and confidence, they were not taken seriously, and, through such intensified lack of seriousness, Viennese frivolity maintained that peculiar note which set it apart from any other major city: the note of nonaggression, the note of its utterly mixed-up lightheartedness, amiability, and *Gemütlichkeit*. No doubt there was a measure of wisdom in all this—*Gemütlichkeit* and wisdom blossom in close proximity, the wisdom of a soul that senses demise and accepts it. Nevertheless, it was operetta wisdom, and under the shadow of the approaching demise it became spirited and developed into Vienna's gay apocalypse.

The ultimate meaning of poverty masked by wealth became clearer in Vienna, in Vienna's spirited swan song, than in any other place or time. A minimum of ethical values was to be masked by a maximum of aesthetic values, which themselves no longer existed. They could no longer exist, because an aesthetic value that does not spring from an ethical foundation is its own opposite—kitsch. And as the metropolis of kitsch, Vienna also became the metropolis of the value vacuum of the epoch.

# 2

# Formation and Assertion of
# a Personality
# Inside the Vacuum

The present dictates forms. The creative lies in breaking out of this charmed circle and attaining new forms.

There is more freedom within the narrowest bounds, within the most specific task, than in that boundless non-place which modern consciousness imagines to be the playground of freedom.

The philosopher—in the ancient sense and in the eighteenth-century sense—has good standing both in a grandiose epoch and in a wretched epoch: he will stand out from both. But an epoch that nullifies itself nullifies the philosopher too.

Insofar as by "reality" one predicates something in some sense comprehensive, one is already near to dream, or rather to poetry.[1]

These four maxims from the extraordinarily significant *Book of Friends* contain almost the entire life plan of Hugo von Hofmannsthal, the life plan of a creative being who has discerned the value vacuum surrounding him and has posited against it his own personality. And it was—so much can be affirmed—a very early life plan. For Hofmannsthal, raised in a Vienna ruled by the vacuum and in a specifically Viennese milieu, was bound before anything else to be a man of knowledge; the genius-naiveté of the artist first developed in him as a supplementary function of such knowledge.

82

## 1. History of an Assimilation

At the end of the eighteenth century a constantly increasing number of Jewish merchants from Bohemian and Moravian ghetto communities moved to Vienna. This migration was set into motion by the Josephinian Patent of Toleration and could not be checked, let alone suspended, at its subsequent revocation. Without much deliberation or regret, these immigrants left behind their tightly defined village and provincial lives, and they did so with an even lighter heart in the thought that this time too they would take along with them their tightly defined yet rich and introverted individual culture, which they had carried with them during centuries of wandering from land to land. They did not consider that this time it would have to be different: tolerance is intolerant and demands assimilation.

The motives that had set the Jews on their way were almost exclusively economic. The magnetism of a major city and certainly one in a capitalist efflorescence is predominantly economic, and the wealth of the few privileged Jews who had settled in Vienna in the eighteenth century had surely undergone fantastic embellishment in provincial gossip. Even then the mythical name of one superrich figure, Salomon Rothschild of Frankfurt, may have cropped up here and there. If you were a shopkeeper in the provinces, in the capital you could, and had to, become a wholesale merchant. Moreover, many of these Jewish merchants had amassed specialized knowledge through trade with peasant populations; they had learned not only how to meet the needs of the peasant but also how to buy horses, livestock, grain, handwoven articles, etc., advantageously, and they knew that the Viennese market held abundant profit in store, especially since the current period of war had made the army into a major customer. Such were the economic dreams of the immigrants. For many they were not fulfilled, but for Isaak Löw Hofmann, who arrived in Vienna from Prague in 1788 at the age of twenty-five, they were.

In the relatively short period of thirty years, Isaak Hofmann succeeded in building an extraordinarily large fortune, not of Rothschild dimensions—that was reserved for bankers—but certainly one that brought him within reach of that uppermost of classes. Perhaps with the aid of military contacts he had generated a wide expansion of the textile trade, his apparent point of departure, mainly through the introduction of silk imports from the Italian provinces, whose silk cultures and industries fell more and more into his range of activity. No doubt he rendered significant service to the Austrian political economy and to the Austrian state; otherwise the solidly anti-Semitic Franz I would hardly have let himself be persuaded to confer upon him a title of nobility.[2] In 1827 Hofmann secured the title "Edler von Hofmannsthal" and chose as the insignia for his appropriately double-fielded coat of arms the mulberry leaf of the silk spinner and the Mosaic tablets—the first symbolizing his industrial virtue, the latter his religious-philanthropic. For, thankful as he was for his new Austrianhood, which had borne him so high, it became a duty for him to care for those who had taken the same path as his own without having been equally favored by fate. There were already more than fifty thousand of them, and they needed funds for prayer services, for religious schools, and finally for the cultural and administrative center established for the purposes of poor relief. In short, the Israelite Religious Community [*Israelitische Kultusgemeinde*] of Vienna was coming into existence, and next to the Rothschilds, who had meanwhile established their Vienna banking house and had been promoted into the Austrian barony, Isaak Hofmann played a conspicuous part in its foundation. He became the first director of the community, and under his leadership it moved into a new headquarters built by the famous Viennese Biedermeier architect Kornhäusl on the winding Seitenstättengasse. The area behind it was occupied by the stately temple (only Catholic churches were allowed to give directly onto the street in Austria at that time), one of the finest and stylistically purest edifices of the period. The granting of his noble title and the inauguration of the temple were surely the high points of Isaak Hofmann's success-filled career.

It is less sure, however, that he counted among these high points the 1839 engagement in Milan of his son August to Petronella von Rho, the daughter of a Catholic patrician. For the son, the marriage was not only a bond of love, which it decidedly was—customary as marriage between aristocratic men and Jewish women had already become, the opposite was all the more unusual—but also a solution to the assimilation problem, which confronted him in a way completely different from the way it confronted his father. To the generation of Isaak Hofmann, an assimilation that did not hold fast to Judaism was absolutely unthinkable. The fact that the Rothschilds, Wertheimsteins, Sinas, Eskeles, Arnheims, with whom now the Hofmannsthals were also to associate, were socially, or at least halfway socially, accepted by the old aristocracy was based not so much on economic motives as on their Judaism, that is, on their membership in an exotic lineage which in them had dispatched its princes to the capital with the claim to equal status with the nobility. This is how they felt themselves, and this was the ambition of these banker barons, an ambition dedicated to the creation of a Jewish-feudalistic noble class, insane as such, even more insane in its fulfillment, nevertheless one of the few social realities grounded purely in romanticism and in this case supported above all by the penchant for the international, for the foreign, for the exceptional, to which the Viennese nobility of the time fell prey. No wonder the end of romanticism signified the end of this too, all the more because the migration of Jews to Vienna and their constantly increasing naturalization—the very foundation of the "Religious Community" indicated the decisive turning point—had turned the Jews from an exotic into an economically as well as a socially undesirable foreign body. To be sure, the Rothschilds had guarded their special position, but that they owed exclusively to their uniquely international family and business structure. For the others, all their wealth notwithstanding, the dream of a subfeudal pseudoassimilation was fundamentally exhausted. Although it was a dream of his father, August von Hofmann refused to spin it any further, unrealistic as it was. He had renounced it when he brought home from Milan a Catholic bride of the minor nobility, and he probably encountered no less severe opposition in his father's house than he had there; he had after all begun a new, more modest, more solid, yet no less radical dream of assimilation. By a complete transition into the non-Jewish camp he wished to earn for himself and his children a lasting social position in the circle of the minor nobility.

By itself, whether in Austria or elsewhere, the minor nobility—the "bagatelle nobility" as it was called in the eighteenth century—was always and everywhere a diffuse and not clearly defined class. It consisted of landowning hereditary nobility, of moneyed nobility as well as the nobility of officers and bureaucrats, and of these only the last two, as long as they remained in military and public service, formed a solid, unified caste. Of the others, whereas the landowners did enjoy a certain social connection with the feudal aristocracy—an incentive for the moneyed aristocracy to obtain land—the remaining number and by far the majority were limited either to withdrawing into social isolation or to seeking their place among the burghers. Coexistence with the burghers was also brought about by appropriate "adaptation," professional if possible. For contrary to feudal society, which liked to ridicule and disobey every imperial act and, above all, made its own decisions as to who should belong to it and who should not, the Viennese burghers respected the granting of noble titles as a genuine elevation of rank, and were flattered when it was accompanied by genuine burgher conduct with its corresponding burgher breadwinning. All this was true of August von Hofmann and his family. His prosperity and the expansion of his business no longer had anything "seigneurial" about them; they became more and more a burgher-class business operation, no different from other industrial and wholesale undertakings and like these caught in the economic stagnation of Austria's mid-century crisis years. The secession of Lombardy in 1859 had proved ruinous for many Viennese firms, especially for those in the silk trade, and it speaks for the solid prudence of the forty-four-year-old August von Hofmann that he was able to keep the family fortune intact, apparently by way of a gradual liquidation of his interests. Nevertheless, his son Hugo, born in 1841, did not join the firm but prepared himself for the legal profession, the exercise of which was later to allow him to assume the directorship of the Wiener Grossbank. The family fortune was largely lost in the stock market crash of 1873—a difficult loss for August von Hofmann's old age, which lasted until 1888—and from then on Hugo von Hofmann had to depend financially on his own earning power. The induction into the *Bürgertum* was thus complete.

And so was the turn to complete assimilation. Dr. Hugo Hofmann von Hofmannsthal, himself now only a half-Jew and raised a Catholic, spouse of a pure-Catholic wife of half-Austrian, half-Swabian peasant extraction (the daughter of the provincial district attorney Laurenz Fohleutner), was reminded of his Jewish descent neither from without nor from within (with the possible exception of those occasions when his path through the city took him past the Seitenstättengasse). He lived the normal, tranquilly industrious, mildly hedonistic life of the Viennese patrician, whose political ideals exhausted themselves with loyalty to the emperor and to Austria. More important to him than his public offices in the Court, etc., were assuredly the performances at the Burgtheater—he would never have given up the patricial family box; more important for him were the concerts in the new caryatid-crammed hall of the Musikverein and in the intimate Biedermeier Bösendorfer Hall, the scenes of the triumphs of Liszt, Clara Schumann, Bülow, Rubinstein, Brahms, Joachim. Summers took him to the Austrian Alps, mostly to Fuschl, winters to his Vienna "mansion" (as every Viennese house with a minimum of four rooms at street level was called), Salesianergasse 12. This was one of those quiet Viennese side streets in which smaller and larger middle-class residences alternated with noble palaces; opposite the Hofmannsthal windows was the little Baroque palace of the Vetseras (whose eighteen-year-old daughter Mary was to meet her death with the crown prince Rudolf in 1889); and where the Salesianergasse joined the main street, the "Rennweg," at the famous Metternich palace, the Schwarzenberg and Belvedere palaces were visible behind the Salesianer Convent. In these very uncommon Viennese surroundings, Hugo von Hofmannsthal junior, a Viennese and an Austrian through and through, was born on February 1, 1874. Had he grown into the precisely ordained path that lay open to him, had he for example taken up an academic career, he would have become an Austrian privy councillor, assimilated into the long line of privy councillors before him and beside him, and indistinguishable from them.

But it turned out differently.

## 2. *Wunderkind*, Wondrous Child, Child Gazing on Wonder[3]

It turned out differently, and what turned out, un-bourgeois as it was, probably complied with the most secret hopes that District Attorney Hugo von Hofmann had harbored for his son's career. It turned out this way perhaps because the legacy of the four grandparents, Swabian and Austrian, Italian and Jewish, presented a particularly fortunate (or, from the standpoint of normalcy, a particularly unfortunate) combination.

The decade of the 1880s was for Hugo von Hofmannsthal the period of those decisive youthful impressions which determine for almost every man the fundamental themes and the specific schematic of the challenges of his future life. Whereas the childhood and youthful impressions of the average individual, however, are limited to the influence of the family milieu, for a *Wunderkind* of Hofmannsthal's caliber they are not only more intense but also more extensive. Genius, not always but often, is in some measure predeveloped, as if this were necessary for it later to transcend childhood. The expansion of the nursery to the social milieu, which proceeds with the average child in strictly successive stages, one step at a time, is achieved with the child genius in a few leaps. That speed is a constant source of danger, evident in the child "spoiled by neglect," who in the same manner, though of course from other causes, shifts over all too quickly, or bypasses altogether, the path from family milieu to social milieu, and is thereby unable to form in himself either a norm-supplying superego or the social sublimations so necessary for "normal development." Whether because of specific or diffuse gifts, there are more *Wunderkinder* than is generally believed, but the one not equipped from within with the strongest defenses—like those which develop from the particular vulnerability of true geniuses—requires from his outside encounters exceptionally protective psychic circumstances for the achievement of "normal development." Otherwise he will slip into the condition of the "wasted genius"—so akin to the one "spoiled by neglect." Indeed, one might almost contend that educational methods attempting to create a premature social milieu are sometimes guilty, just because they correctly perceive in such a milieu the possibility for the earliest free expression of a young man's latent gifts, even qualities of genius, of generating an immoderate percentage of narcissistic cases and even cases "spoiled by neglect." The young Hofmannsthal, however, stood in his early development under the loving educational influence of his father (probably a much stronger influence than that of his mother), and that was decisive for his life.

The educational influence of Dr. von Hofmann can be compared with the influence Leopold Mozart exerted on his son; the parallel will also show the difference between the two eras. Mozart learned from his father the profession practiced by his father; yet it could hardly have occurred for more than an instant to Dr. Hofmannsthal to prepare his son for the legal profession or, for that matter, for a banking career. He concentrated his guidance far more on imparting *Bildung* and a keen eye [*Schaufähigkeit*], that is to say, on the development of those abilities through which the leisure hours of the burgher class were being transformed to "noble enjoyment," to the enjoyment of art in winter, nature in summer—or, more precisely, in the "resort months" [*Sommerfrischenzeit*]. Clearly the burghers of the epoch, with their solid industriousness, were in no way a "leisure class" as the feudal nobility unequivocally was; nevertheless they behaved as if they imagined they were, since they shifted all their life values, all the wealth worth striving for in life, to what would today be described as leisure activity but what then went under the rubric "Art and Nature." Whereas Leopold Mozart wished to bring up his son to be an able musical craftsman and held all other worldly conduct as self-evident and needy of no individual prescription, it was the opposite with Hofmannsthal. His father abstained from any direct interference in the son's choice of vocation, yet he would certainly have considered it an insult if his son had not followed in his world view. Both Leopold Mozart and Hugo von Hofmann acted "morally," each in his way; both found reward for their efforts in the genius of the objects of their education; yet it was the difference between the ethical and the aesthetic that proclaimed itself in the goals of their education, the difference between the Mozartean, active and production-directed "ethical morality" on one hand, the bourgeois "aesthetic morality," as it can best be called, on the other; for the latter in essence remains directed toward passive "appreciation," even when it revolves around an appreciation as noble as that of Hofmannsthal.

It can clearly be protested that *Bildung* has always been "aesthetically-morally" oriented, and not for the first time in the bourgeois era. The monastery Latin school, which by Mozart's time already had a history of many centuries behind it, was oriented to the classical texts and their mastery; this was preparatory training only for theologians and philologists, no one else. The same holds true for the offshoot of the monastic schools, the *Gymnasium* in Austria and Germany, the *lycée* in France, and so forth. Indeed, the teaching in these institutions occasionally managed permanently to excise any aesthetic appreciation whatsoever—for how many are the classics forever spoiled—but occasionally it managed to have positive effects, to deepen exceptional aesthetic ability, and to be of use to a young man in choosing or not choosing an academic vocation. To prevent so far as is possible the negative effects of school, to strengthen in advance its positive effects: this was the thoroughly legitimate, so to speak "natural" pedagogical intention of Dr. von Hofmann in his wish to guide the educational path of his son to its optimal result. And to that goal he felt all the more committed when, just before the boy's birth, the family fortune was devoured by the crash of 1873. No one could be held responsible for a *force majeure*, not even August von Hofmann (at that point a robust man in his late fifties), who had administered the fortune; nonetheless, feelings of guilt emerged, first with regard to the ancestry whose inheritance was squandered, second with regard to the son, who someday would have enjoyed its benefits. For the saying "What you have received as your fathers' heir, earn it to possess it!"[4] had not only become a general bourgeois financial axiom but, in this case, had also gained (if only unconsciously) a meaning for assimilation, that of the assimilation legacy which had to be upheld through the possession of money. Drastic losses of this sort could only be made up for by a select program of education, the likes of which young Hugo von Hofmannsthal was prepared for in 1884 when, at the age of ten, he entered the Wiener Akademisches Gymnasium.

A whole row of the most important Austrian minds, headed by Grillparzer, owed their education to the Akademisches Gymnasium. Following its separation in 1864 from the university, whose preparatory school it had been, it had maintained a university level rivaled only by the two Viennese monastic schools of the Piarists and the Scottish priests, who made equally exacting demands on their students. The Gymnasium was very close to the Salesianergasse; so it was only natural that it be chosen for the young Hofmannsthal. And it was just as natural, that even before entering school, he should become the Gymnasium's preferred student, their prospective *Klassenprimus*, certainly no primus inter pares.

On the contrary: Hofmannsthal the schoolboy must have soon ascertained how far his talent and education lifted him above the average level of his peers, and the feeling of being outstanding is closely related to arrogance. After all, he was still a child, and his gifts were almost all too many. Not only was he mentally far superior, he was also better looking than most of the others; the image of the "beautiful youth" (in those stereotyped words) which pervades his entire poetical work testifies to the persistence of this childhood discovery. Moreover, he was distinguished by the noble title *von* in front of his name, which dubbed him as something even more "noble." In any of the feudal teaching institutions, for example in the Theresianum or the Kalksburger boarding school run by the Jesuits for the nobility, the little *von* would have been more than meaningless, but here in this bourgeois school, which, without detriment to its scholarly level, could not escape the restricted milieu of its teachers and students and thus presented a model of burgher society in miniature, the aristocratic particle had a nimbus about it that instilled respect. From all this emerged an exceptionality which was justified at least in part but became hypertrophied by young Hofmannsthal's childlike sensibility and thus burdened his still too weak shoulders with an all too heavy, all too proud, indeed almost mystical experience. The exceptionality gave way to seclusion. According to the accounts of the time, Hofmannsthal the schoolboy kept to himself, courteously to be sure and never offensively, yet consistent with the *Wun-*

*derkind* whose unchildlike nature no longer wishes, indeed is no longer able, to have anything in common with the childishness of his peers. The awakening of a vehemently narcissistic feeling for life was only to be expected, and if through scholastic success that sense had not achieved a concretization by which it was possible for the boy to adopt as his own the discipline of school and thereby maintain a certain contact with reality, he would have been in danger of losing all stability.

The youth's psychic mainstay was his family home, and the relationship to his father. Yet in no way did this support keep narcissism in check. It is well known that there exists a collective narcissism—the principal instrument of all politics—which expresses itself as group consciousness, as "national consciousness," as "class consciousness," etc., and curiously enough it is nourished far more on passive than on active achievement. Ruling groups, conquering peoples, stabilized upper classes, in short, all who have become "style-setting" exude an "aesthetic" pride, a pride in the specific, corporal "beauty" of the group, in the specific nature of its everyday incarnation as well as in its ways of seeking enjoyment—in both artistic and culinary contexts—whereas the active achievements that predate and pertain to that pride, such as national conquests or class victories, are inserted into the narcissistic group memory through mythological transformation, though they usually dwindle away in the form of commemorative celebrations and monuments. In the case of "subjected" peoples, however, it is somewhat more complicated. They assimilate the style of the national, economic, or however-defined upper class in order to take part in the latter's narcissism, which is meanwhile compounded by the pride of successful assimilation; hence their one-time humiliating situation can never be forgotten. All assimilated minorities reveal this curious "two-tiered" narcissism, fundamentally a mechanism of overcompensation, yet one that does not eliminate the original sense of inferiority but endeavors to conserve it as a springboard for the joy of compensation. Not only does this type of narcissism in assimilated (or for that matter rejected) minorities surpass that of the upper class; it is, moreover, a thoroughly knowing self-irony, which the ruling class totally lacks. In this manner the strange "inner anti-Semitism" of assimilated Jewry is a phenomenon of "two-tiered narcissism." Even after an assimilation achieved through the course of several generations, a "nobly isolated" externality is held onto (if only in the twilight of unconsciousness); and the milieu of assimilation, long familiar as a homeland, is seen through a psychic distance that turns it into something foreign. The assimilated individual thus perceives himself as a chosen one of high degree, a chosen one among the chosen people. And precisely because all these judgments, although principally social judgments, move in aesthetic-aestheticizing categories, nineteenth-century Viennese culture supplied them with the most propitious breeding ground, the most propitious for the narcissism-hungry soul. Hofmannsthal's home was likewise rooted in this ground.

In this context one might almost speak of a definite hereditary narcissism. The *Wunderkind* Mozart was clearly not narcissistic; the *Wunderkind* Hofmannsthal clearly was; and if the former was to a large extent free of psychic problems, the latter was completely overwhelmed by such problems, including those of an only child burdened by a concentration of love and education that can only induce narcissism. Neither home nor school could change any of this. The Gymnasium teachers of the time were at best scientific specialists, but not psychologically trained pedagogues, and among those who taught the young Hugo von Hofmannsthal there seems to have been none who through natural pedagogical inclination might have attained superior insight. For had this been the case, a conspicuously gifted child like Hofmannsthal would certainly have achieved a personal and quite likely a lucrative teacher-student rapport, and such an experience would almost certainly have left its trace in Hofmannsthal's works; nothing of the kind is even suggested. Of course just as little is suggested in his work as to the father-son relationship, which was for Hofmannsthal without a doubt a concrete experience. Clearly Hofmannsthal's "discretion" [*Dezenz*], which he mentions again and again, was prominent, and he had a bashful aversion to divulging personal experience. Nevertheless he did compose, if always, so he thought, under a mask: "The beautiful, even in art, is not thinkable without shame."[5] Yet the mask was torn away with the composition of his most mature work, *The Tower* [*Der Turm*],[6] and suddenly the father-son relationship as well as that between teacher and student showed their true form: both terrible. What had happened? Had the former silence, the former shame, been that of guilt, the guilt of an insufficient response to a father's love? Was the narcissistic form that pervades the entire work at once an avowal of guilt and an apology? No; long before that the entire work with its narcissistic central form, first fully revealed in *Death and the Fool* [*Der Tor und der Tod*],[7] is a single indictment, a knowing indictment, of the aestheticizing burgher existence in which he was born and raised and which, for all his wisdom, he hardly ever escaped. After the long, silent latency, the sudden eruption in *The Tower* shows how long the resentment had been accumulating. It is clear that already as a child he was led to suffering and confusion by the gap in his education—hedonistic or, at the very least, hedonoid aestheticism alongside morality. This narcissistic, exaggerated set of problems would have been insoluble had the guardian angel of genius not arisen and found the solution. The solution was that of dreams, of the fairy tales embedded in dreams.

Every child lives in dreamlike imaginings; every child is a fairy-tale figure to himself. But whereas other children's experiences of reality cause them to feel like Tom Thumb or Cinderella so that they may likewise become princes and princesses in their fantasies, young Hofmannsthal was already in reality—in any case his reality—a thorough fairy-tale prince, singled out by beauty and spirit and triumph, singled out by his own seclusion, singled out by the emperor himself as a "nobleman," to the point where he felt a closer identification with the emperor, that ornately costumed figure gazing down at him from the portrait on the classroom wall, than he did with his teachers and peers. And in this way, unchecked, admitting no proof—if indeed without counterproof—and unnoticed, the dream and dream solitude was incorporated into everyday reality. Like the Jewish Biedermeier barons who imagined themselves—and hence actually were—exotic princes, he traveled as an exotic prince without companions—a specific Hofmannsthal theme—through a real world in which he "dreamed away" his ever deeper and wider solitude, and which in just that way became a fantasylike consolation for his solitude. As the fairy tale that was imaginary for others became real for him, it separated his imagination from that of the others. The city was a dream, and the emperor a dream within the dream; it was a dream when daily, at high noon, the red-costumed, gold-shimmering "Arcieren" bodyguards[8] with their halberds took up their position in the palace to protect the emperor; a dream when, an hour later, as the first stroke rang out from the hammer of the palace clock, the drum major of the palace music corps and the detachment for the changing of the guard entered the inner palace in parade uniform, while the emperor once in a while appeared at the window of the audience chamber; and it was a dream when, a little later, he rode out toward Schönbrunn, his huntsman-in-ordinary with a white feather-plume blowing in the wind next to his coachman, and everyone took off his hat as if in church, while in the midst of that sudden silence the watch resumed the beating of the drum. The vision of the emperor would never quit Hofmannsthal's imagination. It remained a dream within a dream, fairy tale within a fairy tale, the embodiment of both. For it is most likely from that vision that the child seized the essence of the poetic.

Everything around him was at once native intimacy and yet removed, removed to a distance where it became as foreign as a fairy tale, and precisely because of this double vision, the *Wunderkind*, the wondrous child, developed into a child gazing on wonder. For the ignorant see no wonders, and the dream within a dream, which here united reality, not least the true reality of the vision of the emperor, into a dreamlike affinity with all the fairy-tale domains of East and West, was at the same time the dreamer's knowledge of the dream. Hence the guardian angel of genius could intervene and guide the *Wunderkind*, whose precocious pre-maturity is open to all knowledge, to the dream within the dream, so that he may win the knowledge of the dream character of observed existence, and hence become a poet, once the revealing essence of poetry is revealed. There can be no doubt: just as Mozart would still have composed without his father's guidance, so would Hugo von Hofmannsthal have become a poet, with the same immediacy, without the early, almost too early, knowledge of poetry conveyed by his father. From this point of view, the aesthetic education had been superfluous—a probable cause for his resentment of it, yet in some respect it had a beneficial effect. Most likely his father, with a guiding love for his son, for poetry, and no less for Austria, introduced him at an early age to Raimund and to Grillparzer, and most likely Raimund's fairy plays and Grillparzer's *Dream as Life*, often performed at the Burgtheater, were his first experiences in the theater. As such—as a receptive child's first encounter with the magic of the stage—they were bound to be lasting; yet these plays were lasting even more because they confirmed his own unliterary, wonder-gazing individual experience, namely, the reciprocal saturation of the reality of life and the reality of dream and their mutual elevation to a higher, rapturous, fairy-tale reality. Even at that point, the danger of rapture had also made a lasting impression. Dream and life forever blend into one another; such blending is forever an impenetrable enticement, forever requiring one to hold on to the dream in order to hold on to life, and forever holding out the threat that life will transform itself to dream.

And because this was a knowledge gained in childhood, it became a lifelong problem, a lasting temptation to literature. From Calderón's *Life is a Dream*, the model for Grillparzer's *Dream as Life*, *The Tower* emerged.

### 3. Dream as Life: The Call to Poetry

The fundamental mentality of this childhood existence was that of absolute isolation. Yet in his father the boy saw the example of a man who, without isolation, led a daily life in the community and from time to time simply retired into a dreamworld, into the dreamworld of poetry and art. The ethical question was posed—urgently posed. And yet it was not to be solved through his father's example. The isolation as well as the dreamworld, both permanent conditions, were too strong either to be readily broken through or to be interrupted, but all the same not strong enough to allow the ethical problem to be put aside completely. Once the ethical has presented itself together with its demands, it can no longer be silenced.[9]

The nearest available solution would have been that of religion. Little is known about the religious attitudes of young Hofmannsthal. It is of no consequence that his school report card boasted an "excellent" (the highest mark in the Austrian *Gymnasium*) in religion, for not only did the superior student Hofmannsthal easily achieve the highest marks in almost all subjects—only the formal sciences, i.e. mathematics, physics, etc., gave him difficulties—it was also easy to satisfy most religion teachers, the "catechists," by simply appearing on time for mass and confession. And since the traditions of the Austrian peasantry, including confession and mass, ran in the blood of Anna von Hofmann, she of course held them up to her son. Hence he was certainly confronted with the problem of religion, whether or not it was connected to the strong influence of his father (all the more so if it was not). Notwithstanding ecclesiastical ritual, whose symbol-laden pomp must have left a deep impression on the child's supersensitive receptivity, the teaching of religion itself did not pass him by without leaving an impression, insofar as the history of the saints which was presented to him touched on the ethical problem of seclusion. For the saint lives in a mystical seclusion, and he has solved the ethical question of the secluded child, having cast away everything "evil" from seclusion—its conceit, self-sufficiency, dreamlike-aesthetic narcissism, hence permitting, indeed requiring, that it be maintained. Children—especially those predestined to saintliness—play with fantasies of saintliness, and these often extend over an entire life. Their earnestness is greater when such fantasies lead to the priesthood; narrower, as with Hofmannsthal, when they merely occasion the entry into a lay monastic order, so that some day one's body will be buried in the garb of the order.[10] Yet this was by no means the mere expression of fantasy: Hofmannsthal knew the true meaning of saintliness, and it was the most earnest form he could give to his own rejection of it. "Ceremony is the spiritual work of the body,"[11] is what it meant for him, and this was the last ceremony to which he entrusted his own.

But saintliness is at once monastic seclusion and surrender to totality, in this life as well as the next. That surrender entails service, yet allows a higher freedom in the spectacle and meditation that come from seclusion. Saintliness is a difficult grace, and the young Hofmannsthal recognized it as such when he renounced it and turned to the artistic. For nothing is more like a saint's existence than that of a genuine artist; he too lives in seclusion and in a dreamworld, and he too overcomes seclusion. He too surrenders to totality, at least in this life; hence service and freedom converge for him too. The artist too has a share in a burdensome grace, one that does not shatter his narcissism but simply brings it under control. And this is precisely the difference—for all the ethical similarity of structure a world of difference in the truest sense of the expression. Saintliness rises beyond the ethical, whereas the artistic at best rises from the aesthetic into the ethical; and thus, even when such self-transcendence [*Über-sich-Hinauswachsen*] leads to the purest art form, even when the artist lives like a true saint, he can be called at best pseudosaintly. In an assault on the burdensome grace which he also carried, Stefan George refused to admit any difference between the two whatsoever. Hofmannsthal accepted the difference, perhaps because he, the supposed aesthete battling against his aesthetic education and its after-pains, had so early seen himself confronted with the ethical question (the early breakthrough of the *Wunderkind* into the social milieu). Knowing that the burdensome grace demanded compliance, knowing that if he did over-come the aesthetic and renounce the saintly, this grace would transform the dreamlike seclusion which held him permanently captive not into the seclusion of the saint but into the cold and sober dream of art, he gave himself up, for the sake of his return into community, to the ethical quest. This was the impulse behind his poetry.

He remained alone with his knowledge. The times, precisely because they did not yet notice it, had already fallen into a Babylonian mental chaos—the very title *The Tower* implies Babel—in which it was no longer possible for anyone to come to an understanding with anyone else. Who was still concerned with the difference between sacredness and art? Who still attached a meaning to the word "sacred?" This semantic disorder reaches back into the eighteenth century, where copious discussion was already given to "sacred beauty," to the "sacred flame of art," and romantics such as Schiller (Hölderin was still too little known) gave these metaphors to the common vocabulary. This once well-defined word had become so unde-fined that the extent of its applicability had passed into the immeasurable, extending—then as now—from the "sacred aims" proclaimed in every profession, to the grotesque and blasphemous proclamation of the sacred-ness of art as the proper religion of modern man. Yet the artist himself was granted not "sacredness" but "freedom," another word that had lost its definition. In the eyes of the bourgeois, freedom means the twenty-four leisure hours a day that the artist could apply to the production of sacred beauty in order that the spirits of the seriously employed could be lifted during the scant leisure time after office hours. With his freedom the artist lifted himself out of the bourgeoisie and became enviable and suspect in their eyes. His freedom was (and is) the most important element of his existence, except that he still doesn't know whether he is a saint or a salesman. Here as always and everywhere, behind the terminological chaos there is a spiritual and social chaos, above all the disappearance of religious-ness as a meaning-giving central value, its displacement through commerce and the magic of the commercial balance sheet, its degradation into an instrument of political, aesthetic, or whatever ends. The "horrible experi-ence of the nineteenth century," as Hofmannsthal calls it, robbed the soul of the treasure of language, and reduced it to the "worldless ego."[12]

The seclusion of the schoolboy, which he would never totally lose, became an ethical exceptionality, the ethical exceptionality of the poet, and this position left him once again without companions, if this time under a

95

different omen. When at age seventeen he was introduced into the leading Viennese literary circle presided over in the Café Griensteidl by Hermann Bahr, he encountered an aestheticism from which he distinguished himself with the ethic of his newly found poet's vocation, in precisely the same way that he had once distinguished himself in his aestheticizing dreamworld from the activities of his school and his peers. With the exception of Beer-Hofmann, who perhaps resembled him most, and Schnitzler, who resembled him least, they all spoke a foreign language—that of mere literature, hence, especially in Vienna, a language divorced from ethicality. For where there is no genuine connection with death and where death's absolute prevalence in this world is not continuously recognized, there is no true ethos, and Vienna, capital of a dying monarchy, had every connection with dying but not the slightest with death. The renowned Viennese sentimentality was the knowledge of farewells, a sense of leave-taking, the fruit of a perpetual condition of dying whose end one did not foresee and did not wish to foresee; death defined itself in everything from which one had to take leave: "Es wird ein Wein sein und mir wer'n nimmer sein" (There will be wine, and we'll be no more),[13] as a truly poetic Viennese popular song puts it, at once lighthearted and melancholy. Hofmannsthal, however, took death seriously because he took life seriously, because his concern was ethical earnestness. Most likely he had already been preoccupied with death as a child, punishing his arrogant isolation with the fear of a lonely death and of loneliness in death. At the same time he legitimized that isolation, since to face the magnitude of death allows one to see the doings of others as nothingness, in which participation is unnecessary. And it was most likely this early concern with death which had rendered its form so intimate to him, so that it remained from the start constantly associated with his entire poetic activity. From *The Death of Titian* and *Death and the Fool*, products of his eighteenth and nineteenth years, to his mature *Everyman*,[14] the shape of death, in its religious incarnation, plays the central meaning-giving role. But the concern is ethical purification in death and through death.

The concern is ethicality, not sacredness. This is the fundamental difference between Hofmannsthal and Rilke, whose poetry sought the sacred, indeed nothing other than the sacred, in the Catholic sense a venture of the highest presumption, since its aim was self-redemption, carried out in addition with the immoderately and perhaps even blasphemously overextended means of poetry. By this means and this means alone, poetry was able to advance to the radicality of poetry for its own sake. For Hofmannsthal this was unattainable. Likely as it may be that the young Hofmannsthal had come to poetry by way of fantasies of sacredness, he would never have granted it such a temerity of sacredness. Rilke, who had been informed by an unfortunate youthful rebellion and hence a self-imposed, lonely heresy, removed himself more and more from Catholicism, whose abundant legends had initially been an aesthetic accessory for him. Rebellion and heresy were totally foreign to Hofmannsthal. Not only would Catholic doctrine have prevented him from allowing the secular—in this case poetry—access to the true problem of faith; not only—the extent of his own faith notwithstanding—did his Catholic humility cause him to repudiate poetic pseudoholiness (even though he had once been seduced by it) and never allow it to serve as the springboard from which to aspire to the experience of holiness; he had also become far too knowing and perceptive, far too skeptical and cautious and, in a way, too Viennese, seriously to consider poetry tied to his own spiritual salvation, as Rilke had done. Nevertheless, Rilke's earnest expectation of holiness before the phenomenon of art was far less solemn than the skeptical yet extravagant valuation it received from Hofmannsthal. For the former considered art a cognitive instrument for the gaining of faith, the latter as a simple ritual of knowledge, an aesthetic ritual, with whose earthliness one had to be satisfied if one were not to be guilty of what was ultimately a blasphemous exposure of the soul and its most intimate holiness: "In the end, everything written is indiscreet."[15] Hence, unlike Rilke, whose task was the poetic knowledge of faith, Hofmannsthal was unable to direct the process of grace to the sublation of death; he uses that process, rather, as an earthly-ethical ritual peak. He knew that faith was a matter of grace, and poetry, within the sphere of tasks he had assigned to it, could still express that, inasmuch as it no longer dared venture near grace as such. For Hofmannsthal, poetry was the ritual of ethicality.

To the two original chief motives of his poetry, dream and life, a third is added: that of death as an element of ethicality; and on the triad of life, dream, and death rests the symphonic structure of Hofmannsthal's complete opus. Yet what is the ritual structure that will unite these three prime elements with one another? One of the little poems, whose title "Life, Dream, and Death" suggests an epigrammatic condensation of the whole (although almost every genuine lyric poem is such an abbreviation), goes:

| | |
|---|---|
| Life, Dream, and Death . . . | *Leben, Traum, und Tod . . .* |
| How the torch is blazing! | *Wie die Fackel loht!* |
| How the bronze quadrigae | *Wie die Erzquadrigen* |
| Over bridges fly, | *Über Brücken fliegen,* |
| How it soughs down below | *Wie es drunten saust,* |
| Thundering on the trees | *An die Bäume braust,* |
| Hanging on steep banks, | *Die an steilen Ufern hängen,* |
| Black tree-tops stretching | *Schwarze Riesenwipfel aufwärts* |
| upwards . . . | *drängen* |

| | |
|---|---|
| Life, Dream, and Death, | *Leben, Traum und Tod,* |
| The boat goes softly . . . | *Leise treibt das Boot . . .* |
| Green riverbanks | *Grüne Uferbänke* |
| Moist in evening's glow | *Feucht im Abendrot* |
| A pond for silent horses | *Stiller Pferde Tränke* |
| Horses without master . . . | *Herrenloser Pferde* |
| The boat goes softly | *Leise treibt das Boot* |
| | |
| Goes past the park, | *Treibt am Park vorbei,* |
| Red blossoms, May. | *Rote Blumen, Mai,* |
| Who is in the leaves? | *In der Laube wer?* |
| Say, who is sleeping in the grass? | *Sag wer schläft im Gras?* |
| Yellow hair, lips of red? | *Gelb Haar, Lippen rot?* |
| Life, Dream and Death. | *Leben, Traum, und Tod.* |

Neither in form nor in substance is this a significant poem, and it invites criticism of many kinds. Under the glaze of the first two stanzas, reminiscent now of Böcklin, now of Marées,[16] Austrian summer holiday landscapes are easily recognizable, Finstermünzklamm and the Mondsee, perhaps. The third stanza stems directly from the display window of the Neumann art dealership on the Michaelerplatz in Vienna (opposite the Café Griensteidl), and the line "Say, who is sleeping in the grass?/Yellow hair, lips of red?" has faithfully adopted all the coyness of its merchandise. And, however unsure one is at first whether the word is quádrigae or quadrígae (all the less sure for the fact that in the brief moment the poem describes there could have been at most one quadriga—without a rhyme—on the little short bridge), one is just as unsure why the entire triptych is focused on the refrain "Life, Dream, and Death." Many of Hofmannsthal's poems invite such malevolent analysis, but that analysis is almost always shocked into self-destruction. Like this triptych, they nearly all exemplify dream landscapes on a dream stage; they are dream ritual and dream declamation. And not only may the dream take its subject from anywhere and everywhere, including the window display of the Neumann art dealership, it simply infects everyone who would share the dream. Those with an analogous dream vision capable of grasping the dream happenings together with the dream stage on which they occur are seized by the dream ritual, "incorporated" into the dream ritual, and they become aware in their dream terror of a single pulse, so that in the thundering quadrigae on the bridge and in the still horses at the pond and in the yellow-haired, red-lipped wax doll in the grass, borderless life and borderless death run into one another. The poem speaks to a dream public, nonetheless to one found in reality: the actual theater public in its peculiar dream situation. For this audience Hofmannsthal dreams his poems, and he dreams them in the form of imaginary theater scenes for an imaginary great actor who has entered, "arms akimbo," into imaginary theater scenery in order to conjure up Life, Dream, and Death. Dream ritual becomes stage ritual.

In the end, ritual is always a scenic demonstration, and this holds for Hofmannsthal's ethical ritual as well. His early turn to art and poetry reveals itself from the very start as a thoroughly unambiguous turn to the theater, and so radical a turn as to transpose even lyrical poetry onto an imaginary stage. In other words, the poet does not develop the lyrical situation from its own kernel, which is also his own, but rather confronts both it and himself—as an observer like his public: "We do not possess our self; it drifts toward us from without."[17] The dramatic is always "determined from without"; this, however, does not imply that it has to take the form of "scenic lyric," or that it will form lyricism's one presupposition. For example: [Stefan] George's lyric poetry, born of the monstrous tension between a will to total assertion of being [*Seins-Aussage*] and just as strong a will to total ego suppression, [*Ich-Verschweigung*] and for that very reason "determined from without," is "scenic," yet not in the same way as Hofmannsthal's, whose "discretion," working as a similar if milder agent of tension, tends to the theatrical. As a counterexample, the Shakespearean sonnets, although created by the most powerful dramatic spirit of two millennia and created in a historical epoch, found by way of their "determination from without" their principal poetic expression in the dramatic, yet bear an unmistakably "inner-determined" character; are lyric inner-assertion. And to a certain extent this contrast suggests the contrast between Germanic and Latin thought. Shakespeare's inaccessibility notwithstanding, it is not to his dramatic genius that Hofmannsthal's corresponds, but to Calderón's. Just as in George the presence of the Rhineland does not deny the Latin influence, the Austrian in Hofmannsthal felt a deep affinity with the Latin. The Latin rigor of form, together with its "determination from without," became a model for his creation, and its strength, combined with that of the Latin theater, transposed his lyrics into a scenic dream-world, perhaps not through theatrical "dramatization" or "monologization," but rather through a true "about-face." The primal lyric content of poetry is not impugned but is placed under an "external view," and the poet, instead of simply conjuring up an image of "evening," sees himself acting on the lyrical scene, so that in the end we hear—a renowned Hofmannsthalian result—"And yet he who says 'evening' says much."[18] It is a "restratification of vision" which at once reveals the poet in celebration of the lyric ritual and the kernel of the ritual itself, the crystal-sharp stratification of vision of that cold dream with which poetry responds to its burdensome grace. Such was the new necessity that Hofmannsthal's "scenic lyrics" brought to German and hence world literature.

Yet behind lyric ritual and its imaginary scenes stands the true theater, theater ritual. In the pure Latin tradition, Hofmannsthal felt the theater imprisonment of his being and creations as something thoroughly Austrian, tied to the Austrian love for spectacle and decoration, tied to the Vienna that resonated with it, tied to the childlike and the unpolitical in which he took part as a poet, only, of course, in order to raise it to the ethical. Yet he rarely, if ever, acknowledged that this too involved a truly Austrian compromise. No matter how much he abhorred the aestheticism of his youth, and however offensive slogans like "the sacredness of art" or "the priesthood of art" were to him, indeed no matter how hard he strove to overcome all this through the nature of his own artistic practice (not least in the fact that he took the pseudosacred nimbus of art and banished it back to earthly, ethical ritual), he was never able to free himself totally from the celebration of beauty that had marked his youth. The word "beautiful" remained among the most frequent in his vocabulary, and for just this reason the theater was the earthly dream par excellence—the preordained, absolutely logical locus. For the public goes to the theater in order to recognize onstage its own essentiality and see it transformed into beauty, and the artist must accede to this wish, for the theater is unyielding in its demands. This was the compromise with the stage that Hofmannsthal seized upon all too enthusiastically. The world becomes a beautiful theater—"How beautiful is this battle"[19]—that the artist must present to the very same world, he, its ideal observer and hence its ideal illustrator, so that sitting in his orchestra seat within the crowd (a crowd modeled on a bourgeois youth milieu and encompassing a whole range of humanity) he too can wander into the seclusion and solitude of the stage. This double position of internality and externality that the poet fills imaginatively in his "scenic poetry" is transferred into stage reality and must hence, like everything on the stage, adopt a solid form. This is the reason why the "Prologue" and the "Poet" are indispensable figures in the Hofmannsthal cast of characters, one as pre-curtain commentator on poetic affairs, the other charged with fulfilling the compromise between beauty and ethicality as scenic ritual in the eyes of the spectator (Pirandello made this double function of the poet into a theatrical trick).

Yet he who celebrates rituals is a priest, even when they are earthly rituals, and whoever is a priest still embodies, for all his earthliness, a not inconsiderable remnant of the long obsolete holiness fantasies that were played out during childhood. George professed such a priestly office without giving it a second thought, all the more so as it aided his ego suppression, and for the sake of lyrical unity of person and work (not ego and work) he shifted it to a celebration of the self. Rilke, on the other hand, who by means of continuous sublimation left all that celebrated the aesthetic far behind him, lived merely within the work and chose in it the path to a prophetic quest for salvation. Hofmannsthal, however, who by way of "determination from without" stood closer to George than to Rilke—the theater can put a priest on the stage but not a saint—was, because they were mere lyricists, surpassed by both in lack of compromise: by the former's strength of form, by the latter's strength of dream. And although he knew this, and although he knew that compromises are admissible at best in the practical-political realm but never in the spiritual (the difference between the English and the Austrian compromises), and although he knew that he was driven to his own compromise not by his beloved theater but rather by the tabooed quest for beauty that was behind it—the one insolubly combined with and inescapable from the other—he nonetheless had grounds for defense. Is the dream strength of the theater not in a sense a similarly invincible inner necessity? And is the stage with its make-up, with its cloaks and masks, not more "discreet" for its creator than pure lyric? And is its result not that peculiar beauty, born almost shamefully, against the will of the artist ("The beautiful, in art as well, is unthinkable without shame") and nevertheless made visible onstage in near shameless frankness as a natural outgrowth simply seeking acceptance? The dreamworld of the theater is strong indeed, strong enough to render the compromise with it legitimate and downright "radical," radical enough for it to be imposed upon lyricism. Nevertheless, under no circumstances would this have become so absolutely binding for Hofmannsthal had it not on one hand evolved from the unconsciousness of definite childhood impressions, and had it not, on the other, contained certain acceptable qualities which enriched the full consciousness of the artist. Both were the case: young Hofmannsthal's earliest impressions of the Burgtheater resonated ceaselessly and unmistakably in the waking dream of poetry—a legitimating dream within a dream. They did so in drama, lyric, and prose; and they had to do so because, in observing that noblest of scenes in which the play of Life, Dream, and Death was elevated to the strange rapture of a high style, he had learned that even compromise can transcend one's own self, provided it is the compromise of a great tradition. Since his compromise was taken from the Burgtheater, he was able to perceive it as enrichment. For rituals must belong to a long tradition; otherwide they are meaningless.

There is no doubt that for father Hofmannsthal and his son the visits to the Burgtheater—before that to the "Prater" and its Kasperle-Theater—formed the high points of the aesthetic-aestheticizing game of education in which and with which, naturally predisposed to one another, they built and made lasting their relationship. Yet this paternal influence in no way diminishes the discriminating capacity the boy added on his own. That so young a person would prove unable to extricate himself from the decora-

101

tion- and "beautification"-filled epoch was only to be expected; that he nevertheless succeeded in discovering perhaps the single truly fruitful element in it, namely the high performing art practiced in the Burgtheater (that of the Comédie Française was as yet unknown to him), and hence the element in which the decorative artistic practice of the time had transcended itself and had grown into the genuine, the "re-genuine," reflected an extraordinary instinct in a boy; it was an achievement that was bound to have further effect. Not only did the entire soundness of Hofmannsthal's judgment first proclaim itself in this boyish instinct, not only did his entire life's work perpetuate the "high style" of the Burgtheater; but, from the very first moment, the Burgtheater gave the work a decisive ethical significance. For everything the Burgtheater added up to, the elevation of the naturalistic and the psychological into the realm of ethical motive, the unveiling of a higher reality which, though the reality of the stage, does not deny its Platonic heritage, this orderly transformation of the dreamlike into the cold dream of art and, through art, into a new warmth—in short, this attitude of "self-transcendence"—became for Hofmannsthal the basic principle of all ethicality and the basic attitude of his life.

For all the prematurity of the young Hofmannsthal, that half-consciousness which is both the bitter hardship and the delightful ease of youth was also his. The discovery of the "self-transcendence" revealed in the "high style" of the Burgtheater had clearly unfolded in half-consciousness, and had hardly arrived at a formulation; yet it already provided a valid answer to his early question: how is it possible for a human being not born into holiness, nevertheless mystically secluded—and in the end everyone is secluded—to gain a community, to win contemporaries and a social world? The answer he gave himself was valid because he who transcends himself in life and work has chosen what may be the only path leading to community.

## 4. The Second Assimilation

Did the "self-transcendence" formula really resolve the social problem of the artist, which the young Hofmannsthal confronted so early? Does not the artist's problem of community inevitably revert to the problem of his public? And, accordingly, did not that part of the Hofmannsthalian essence correctly conceive of humanity as a single, comprehensive theater public? And for that matter, is not contempt for the public the task of true artistry, a contempt that grows the more the artist transcends himself? What community remains for him then when his community with his audience is denied him?

It is a peculiar state of affairs: the artist of the bourgeois age takes bourgeois aestheticism seriously; in other words he becomes, in the sense of his society, exclusively a producer of beauty, a man of *l'art pour l'art. L'art pour la société* clearly remains in the back of his mind, but even when that corresponds to the public's taste, he remains nonetheless socially isolated from the public's bourgeois existence, and even the high esteem accorded him—especially if he is a playwright—remains hostile. For precisely as a middle class (and because of its specific and other economic contingencies), the bourgeoisie is most inflexible toward every foreign body, and whatever does not totally assimilate to it; for example, the self-made noble as well as the parvenu, or whatever can never achieve total assimilation, like the artist or the Jew, will inevitably be denied access. Even privy councillor Grillparzer encountered isolation and practically perished from his share of high esteem grown hostile; in the case of Ferdinand Raimund it actually ended in suicide. Not even with the beloved artists of the Burgtheater was it otherwise. Although they often led a strictly bourgeois official existence without detriment to their high art, and although the emperor granted noble title to one or another of his "k.k."[20] court actors, to say nothing of the aristocratic marriages of court actresses, no exceptions were made. The rigidity was all the more conspicuous when it entered the realm of the blurred class structure of Viennese gelatin democracy, a gelatinous, soft rigidity whose weapon was an amiably insidious obstinacy—a tenacious weapon nonetheless. The burghers, who (with reason) considered themselves the sole upholders of state and society, wanted to stand out against the other groups, including the members of the artistic world, as an exclusively observing public, and they immediately rose in defense against any disturbance that threatened their isolation.

Thus, despite himself, young Hugo von Hofmannsthal was excluded from the *Bürgertum* when he chose poetry as his vocation. The assimilation into the *Bürgertum* initiated by his grandfather and completed by his father was thus annulled; the ties to his origins remained, but the society of his origins had become a mere public. And could it have been replaced by another? In other words, was one to be satisfied with the bohemia of the Café Griensteidl? Goethe, the constant model for all nineteenth-century German poeticism and from the beginning the object of young Hofmannsthal's emulation, had resolved the question of social position in his own virtuoso manner: he reserved himself complete freedom, and, readily as he had broken with the *Bürgertum* he was always just as ready to do the same with the society of the court and nobility, in which he took care to move with ceremonious ease but only until he felt the need to flabbergast that society or exchange it for awhile with the Roman bohemia. He never forgot that the title "prince of poetry" signified the absolutely unbridgeable gulf between the bourgeois and the princely, but that title became the legitimation of his princely freedom. Goethe the man was a burgher, his public were burghers, in the same way that the Burgtheater was an institution maintained by burgher artists—their noble titles did not appear on the playbill— playing to a predominantly burgher public; and yet in both cases art had transcended itself into an exalted noble sphere whose social significance undeniably carried a fascinating illusion for the socially homeless: the illusion of a hierarchical value-order that could offer him a new home.

In Goethe's time, in the time of the romantics, feudal society—that of the urban courts, not the landowners—was by and large philo-artistically disposed, in a manner thoroughly parallel to its philo-Semitic disposition. In its essential cosmopolitan character as in its taste for the exotic, but also in its deep-seated sense of approaching demise which since the French Revolution could no longer be scared off, it was, in contrast to the burgher class, capable of making exceptions for the exotic. So much the easier for the artist, then, when he didn't appear as the vanguard of the Jews, an entire caste with subfeudal and otherwise feudaloid claims, but remained a unique phenomenon whose economic and social patronage belonged without question to a centuries-old tradition of the court and nobility. With the feudaloid Jewish assimilation of the postromantic period, this came to an end; the artist, however—and here Liszt is an example among countless others— could now as before assimilate his cosmopolitanism even further into that of the high aristocracy. The artistic salon of the nobility persisted, and if no longer populated by true Goethes or even genuine Liszts, it nevertheless became in the West that of a Prosper Mérimée, a Whistler, an Oscar Wilde. In Vienna, however, where the salons had once been renowned for the names of Beethoven's patrons Rasumofsky and Waldstein, the dissolution of the nobility into mere cavalierliness was not without effect, and the renowned salon of Princess Metternich-Sandor[21] was frequented largely by newspapermen. Nevertheless, wherever there is an upper class—and if the nobility officiated as the upper class anywhere, it was in Vienna—it will be acknowledged as the bearer of culture; not only did it always possess members—even in Vienna—who took such a task seriously, such as Count Wilczek and Count Lanckoronsky (to whom Hofmannsthal dedicated the "Speech in the House of an Art Collector"), but the artists themselves who fit into such traditional realms are not automatically to be called snobbish. To level such a reproach against Rilke, for example, simply because he was offered the hospitality of the Princess of Thurn and Taxis, to whom he subsequently dedicated the Duino Elegies, would be quite unjust and, moreover, almost a slur on his poetry.

Hofmannsthal's affirmation of nobility was conspicuous. The fact that it dominated his everyday existence could have been ascribed (the Goethean example notwithstanding) to chance encounters and chance friendships, but the fact that it carries through to his poetic work—Count Kari in *The Difficult One*[22] is obviously a portrait of an ideal—indicates the depth of its roots, and one will not go wrong in looking for it in any of the mystic or near-mystic representations on which the bulk of Hofmannsthal's creative work is nourished. Of course, the representation of exotic, secretly noble fairy-tale princes, which he probably felt himself to be as a boy and which became capable of determining his later life, cannot really be called mystical; everything susceptible of representation draws from a real past—no one is totally free from ancestor worship. The break with the burgher-class existence established by his father and grandfather was in no sense the simple surrender of something one could freely control as one's natural possession; no, it was far more, it was a betrayal, a betrayal of their achievement of assimilation, another violation of the ethic "Earn it to possess it"—and it was thus a sin. It was truly a sin, and like every sin would have been inexcusable—yet was it really nothing but a sin? Was it not at the same time a necessary retaliation? For in destroying the Jewish-feudal purposes of their ancestors and taking the turn toward the Christian-burgher camp, both father and grandfather had burdened themselves with guilt. And so this new defection, in which the bourgeois was abandoned in favor of the artistic, made its amends only through the revival of the entire assimilation process, together with its feudal goal, which had gone wrong with the grandfather's Catholic marriage. The psyche's calculations of justice are of unparalleled intricacy. In the end, not as a Jew—although he was the first Hofmannsthal in three generations to enter into a Jewish marriage—but as an artist and with the artist's claim to nobility, Hugo von Hofmannsthal renewed the mission of assimilation. The spirit of his great-grandfather, embodied in the mystically potent image of the tablets of the law in the family crest, received a brilliant post facto apology, if not exactly the kind of brilliance he might have dreamed of for his great-grandchildren.

The artist's claim to nobility, founded on the strength of self-transcendence—this was the mission of assimilation, and Hofmannsthal would have been the last to think it might be fulfilled through social relations with the aristocracy. For there is no accomplishment with which one can buy one's way into a class; one must be born even into the proletariat for class membership to guarantee a social place within the total population. And, inversely, whoever chooses the artist's freedom is excluded from the class into which he was born and becomes subject to the kind of ancient proscription that is reserved for the "free man," which is what the Germans call an executioner. For class signifies bonds, and to be bound proscribes freedom. To be a guest is the most the artist can demand, a guest of a favorable nobility, yet hardly ever of the bourgeoisie and certainly never of the common people as such, who are on the one hand too hardworking, on the other (especially in Austria) too pleasure-loving to pay attention to or make a to-do about serious art or poetry. As a whole, the common people simply don't take the poet, the eternal guest, into their consciousness; they don't assimilate him. Yet whoever is not assimilated by the entire population must give up any claim to nobility, indeed can fulfill no claim to nobility, even if he is nobility's most welcome guest.

Yet is it really that way? Is the claim to nobility—like that of the great-grandfather—really nothing but a chimera? Is the poet really damned to the role of the eternal guest, someone constantly seeking admittance and without a home? No, he does have a home; his home is independent from the guest role which may or may not be assigned him from one or another social level, and his existence is more lasting than that of his host. No matter which social rank reality assigns the poet, indeed no matter even whether social ranks exist which would ever permit such an association, his life fulfills itself not within their tightly drawn bounds but within the bounds of popular symbol and language, in other words in that spiritual social corpus from which popular symbols and languages are continuously born. And it is precisely here that the duty and the accomplishment of the poet emerge. With the elevation of symbol to language, of language to symbol, he looks after the affairs of the people and implants himself among the actual people even if he is not received into their consciousness. The constant yet invisible presence of the poet in the house of the nation (his secret "princely palace"), whose life treasures are his own because he is their lord and protector, this lofty position of the poet forms the principal theme of Hofmannsthal's voluminous essay "The Poet and Our Time."[23] Yet no matter how high he places the poet, he makes him no more than protector and master. The treasures themselves, their spiritual reality as well as their linguistic structure, originate with the people. For Hofmannsthal, the ancient, earthbound, language-creating peasantry and the poet are eternally related, and since (with a hearty preference for the Austrian) he considered the peasantry thoroughly noble and, to some extent, the democratic fundament of all nobility, it was also the authority by which the patent of nobility—the artist's democratic patent of nobility—was and continues to be drawn up.

The people, as Hofmannsthal saw them, formed a collective fairy-tale image. It is almost as if he fabricated from this image a legitimizing foil for the (likewise fairy-tale-like) image of the "poet," in order to permit the exaggerated tribute due the latter, because of its correlation with the former. But even if that is correct, the fairy-tale image was a reality for

Hofmannsthal. And that fits with the image, totally foreign to reality, that was for him the Habsburg monarchy:

| | |
|---|---|
| Motley peoples in field tents | *Völker bunt im Feldgezelt,* |
| Will the blaze solder them? | *Wird die Glut sie löten?* |
| Austria, varied realm, | *Östreich, Erdreich vieler Art,* |
| Will you defy distress? | *Trotzest du den Nöten?* |

This is the motto with which he prefaced his Austrian War Song (1914), for, until the dissolution of the monarchy, its total population, the "Austrian people," seemed to him cut from the pattern of the Alpine peasantry (who provided his summertime childhood experience), so that for them too the "holiness" of the imperial person had to be one with the holiness of the fatherland. In any case, the state had no substance other than the crown, yet he disavowed both the crown and the hostility of the "nationalities" toward Austria, and of the gray, indefinable, proletarian masses he knew only that they were in need of education; of their mentality he knew nothing. The apolitical nature of his Austrian-burgher heritage reached its extreme in him: where he is concerned with political structures—even in *The Tower*— his aesthetic-mystical vision becomes apparent, as does the wish for a hierarchical order of the type that had been concretized by the old estate system, a wish that could, of course, be considered provisional and not seriously intended. In the end, everything is to be removed from the emperor-people polarity to a sacred natural right of freedom and a sacred natural duty of order, each ethically conditioned by the other, so that the spiritual unity of the nation will emerge from an ethical harmony of obedient rule and free obedience. It is a fantasy of ethics—too apolitical for an ethical utopia, served by the ethic-ritual of Hofmannsthal's poetics through symbols disguised as dreams, allegories disguised as dreams, in an Oriental wealth of disguise, a dream work of the most sensitive construction and most sense-filled significance, yet more beautiful for the childlike nature which it has regained and its inclination toward fairy tale, which allows childlike, primal images to shine forth from one's dreams. The multiply disguised, forever reappearing "emperor" remains in residence in the Schönbrunn palace, wafted around by a fairy-tale world that could no longer be chased from the imagination of any Austrian childhood, and the "people," loyal and servile to this legendary imperial image, can nowhere deny their relationship to the free peasant stock of the Austrian Salzkammergut region.

For the reality of the Austrian monarchy remained now as always saturated with mystical features, and its stately subsistence depended on them to no small extent: a reality that had to support itself on a dream, in order to be real. It was, so to speak, Austria's most human quality, and it was the poet Hofmannsthal's most Austrian quality. He kept his mission of assimilation focused on this dream Austria, a task which after three generations now fell to him, and it was one dream reality speaking to another. Only in the sphere of such an affinity did his purpose, and his claim, have meaning: as a poet belonging to no concrete social class but for this reason at home with the universal spirit of Austria, indeed even feeling himself to be its secret leader and hence its servant, he could, like that spirit—and even to a greater extent—be subject exclusively to the emperor in whose crown it was embodied, subordinate directly to the crown, equal to the highest baronage, and, in a concrete sense, of equal birth. And although this poetic mission of assimilation was thoroughly symbolic, not least in its feudaloid goals, it resembles to a great extent the one which—if with a somewhat firmer hand—Isaak Löw Hofmann had initiated in the Austria of Emperor Franz I.

## 5. Life as Symbol: The Call to Style

For Hofmannsthal, Austria was an entity of the highest reality, indeed even of the highest ethical reality, certainly not in the sense of the Hegelian idea of the state but, rather, in an even more mystical sense: the foundation of reality lay in the symbolization through the emperor. As both reality and its symbol, Austria was invested with such symbolic strength, almost like a popular poem called to reality, that it constantly conjured reality from within itself, without anyone being able to name the poet—Austria poeticizing by itself, unique and created by providence and history for this purpose. Reality is for Hofmannsthal the symbolic come to life.

Yet the symbol emerges from the convergence of life and dream, and at the level of the symbol all poetic knowledge of world reality is kindled; the problem of reality is constantly rekindled and is the constant enticement to poetry. If man did not possess the dream induced by reality, he would confront the phenomena of reality "speechless" like an animal: but because he does possess it and, with it, the symbolic range of language, language itself becomes a second reality. In language, external reality is timelessly stored (indeed, preserved in "form"); yet linguistic reality is once again incorporated into dream, this time by the language-induced, poeticizing dream, is once again symbolized, again to be stored (in "content") at the next level, so that a word truly derived from language achieves a poetic value beyond time— "and he who says 'evening' says much." The fact that such timelessness is initiated by dream, because the dream present is one with the past and future, is all too easily forgotten in the face of the practical use of the "formal" symbol storage of language. Only on the plane of poetry, where there is an interplay between external and linguistic reality and an equivalent symbolic indifference, does the magic origin of the abolition of time once again come to the surface, in other words at the point when the combination of both symbol groups leads to one "contentual" interference point and effects a doubling of symbolic strength. The prophet has power over reality and over language, insofar as his dream, his mighty dream, is engaged by reality as much as by language, and for all the difference between prophet and poet, the same engagement—for better or for worse—grants the poet prophetic insight, whether into the past or into the future. Yet everything prophetic aims toward the ethical, showing that the ethical too is a reality with a timeless claim of symbolization; indeed, wherever a primal reality of any kind is created and elevated by human means, it is ethics, born of the prophet's power of mythos, that is the reality of the human psyche. Poetry, for that very reason so much more insignificant than prophecy, creates no reality, no ethics; nevertheless, if it is to subsist in an eternal interplay of reality and ethics, receiving motivation from both, it must satisfy prophecy's claim to symbolization. When poetry does not stick to the task, the human degenerates, the ethical degenerates, the symbol degenerates, language degenerates—reality degenerates. Even where the rite of ethical symbolization has become a perfected, exalted institution—as in the Empire and the Church—even there poetry has its role in keeping it attached to life, for the task of poetry is the constant recreation of the world. And that is the mystery of the primal task that has been assigned to it, on whose account it exists, the mystery of the ethical ritual that it is, the mystery of renewed creation, fulfilling itself as the formation and concretization of the symbol, as the symbolic order, as the "image" of "symbol essentiality."

It is precisely the unveiling of the essential symbol, its organization, its form and its formation—as the double meaning of the Goethean *Bildung* demands—that is at stake for Hofmannsthal. Expressed in his *Book of Friends*: "What separates the one who has entered the temple of *Bildung* from the one who tarries in the outer court is that, to the former, the wealth of the ethically possible will always represent itself in forms, not in concepts." The issue is the knowledge of reality, the trans-formation of reality into knowledge—*Bildung* is the broadening of knowledge. And all this determined his resolve to artistic expression. It was clearly a resolve at which young Hofmannsthal had arrived very early on. For he grew up at the time of the battle between naturalism and antinaturalism, and he was drawn to neither side; he had no inner affinity for either. The long list of his writings includes not one that came to grips with the great naturalistic literature of France and Russia (unless we take the short obituary essay "On the Artistry of Tolstoy"[25] that way), and one finds only sporadic allusions to

109

the antinaturalism of French poetry, which, from Baudelaire on, strove for an immediate expression of the dreamlike irrational. "The modern psychological poets render profound what should be passed over, and take superficially what should be taken profoundly," Hofmannsthal remarked about naturalism; and yet, as far as irrationalism was concerned, "The deep must be hidden. Where? On the surface."[26] When he glances over at France, he sees Victor Hugo (another model for the poet's relation to the "people"), and even an essay as principled as "The Development of Poetic Form in Hugo"[27] (one of his most profound reflections on literature) pursues that development only as far as Victor Hugo and completely ignores his successors. Abjuring, like Goethe, everything chaotic, Hofmannsthal, unpolemical as he was, retired from the new literature in silence; he found it lacking in the Goethean principle of order. And here too his decision was made on his own. His sharp and even sharply impressionistic capacity for observation, attuned as it was to reality, was receptive to every possibility of naturalistic representation; yet he knew that none of the total realities such representation may strive for, whether of surface events or dreams, was capable of reproduction. Reality is always infinite; a work of art, on the other hand (as conceived by Hofmannsthal but not by Rilke), is always constrained by the finite and thus requires for its creation, even in the case of such unconditional naturalism, a constant act of selection, which imposes order and which, in the end, by dint of the fact that *Bildung* is based on essentiality, is an ethical act. Hence artistic rigorousness must devote all its attention to the act of selection, which can and must be made visible—the dream within the dream and the "prologue" once again come to mind—so that the essential symbol may also become visible.

Visibility is a function of the physical eye and is achieved in physical space—the "mind's eye" is merely a metaphor; hence the question, where is the symbol truly visible? Where is its "spirit" actually manifest in space? Certainly in the visual arts, certainly in architecture, certainly in the theater—certainly as style. For architectural forms are precisely those which represent the "spirit" of an epoch or a country, and make visible the style of that epoch and that country. Even if style has its origin in the innermost reaches of creation and thought, even if it comes to light in every expression of life, thought, and work and hence makes endless demands on the humans subordinate to it, these demands will become most stringent with every effort to render the symbolic truly visible by means of and within a style. And to that end, the turn to the order-imposing act of selection, the essence of the Hofmannsthalian resolve, is necessary. Where there is style, a principle of order and selection governs all forms of human existence and action, and every change of style can be traced back to a change in the manner of selection and ordering. And however much more acute the principle of selection, the more masterly and masterful will be the style, the more symbolically powerful will be the plane of reality it creates, and the more essential the symbols on that plane will be; in short, the more it will enable men to transcend themselves. The ethicality of the principle of selection makes the style ethical and thereby gains visibility itself. Great architectural style is a static expression of ethicality; its dynamic expression is that of the theater. Both are visible to the eye, both are the logical place for the symbol and ritual of ethicality. This was the most profound cause of Hofmannsthal's bond with the theater: not only is the stage predetermined visibly to transform life into dream and dream into life, and not only does that visible transformation finally lift both life and dream out of its status as the raw material of their separateness; it lifts them to the level of art, to the level of symbol, to the level of ethicality, to the level of absolute visible style. In order to reach the level of potential self-transcendence provided by high style, Hofmannsthal needed the theater. And conversely: so far as he would succeed in making visible onstage the process of the moral-mystical evolution of a personality to nobility, in making visible the process of growth as an ethical-artistic ritual (he succeeded with his late work *The Tower* but no earlier), he could hope that this would afford him entry into the sphere of high style and form.

Hofmannsthal knew exactly what style meant. The resolve to the symbolic is not yet symbol, and the resolve to style is far from being style. Even form alone is not style; it can be more extensive or more constricted than style. A basic form, that of linguistic expression for example, contains within it every stylistic change, and a style may remain the same and yet change immensely in its forms. Moreover, every creative individual has his own personal style. Indeed, in an epoch of non-style, of style vacuum, of freedom of style, personal style is all there is, and for anyone aware of it, it is a disquieting and almost paralyzing freedom. Young Hofmannsthal had become aware of it at the moment when, more attuned and perceptive than most adults, he received his first artistic impressions in the Burgtheater, where he not only discovered the one style of the epoch that was still valid, but also became aware of the vacuum that ruled in its vicinity. Already then, with this great void of eclecticism before him, it dawned on him what he would later write down: "The most evil style evolves from the wish to imitate, yet at the same time to make known that one feels superior to the object of one's imitation."[28] Yet his own will to an individual, personal style probably reached further back than he himself knew. It must have soon become clear to him that a style that does not emerge freely from the unconscious does not willingly let itself be invented, and that every attempt at such invention necessarily leads to mannerism (a genuine danger of his Austrophilia). He faced that dilemma insofar as he took the style of the

Burgtheater as "form" and strove to bring this basic form, which could not be imitated but could be stylistically modified, to the limits of its essentiality. The Burgtheater had taught him above all to overcome the sentimental as well as the naturalistic—"In former epochs the sentimental affectation prevailed; in the present one it is the realistic."[29] And in intensifying the accompanying basic form to its utmost and most extended possibility of expression, stretching it over the entire domain of poetry, he found the solution, the path that led him in the end to *The Tower*.

To some, no doubt, this may appear as a mere technical stylistic method, but even if it were no more than that, it would still be a function of the self-transcendence which was above all else formative for Hofmannsthal, even if only in technical matters, since—as "The Poet and Our Time" reveals—he held that to be the poet's highest mission: "We must raise ourselves to a higher level within our selves, where it is no longer possible to do one thing or another, where it is no longer possible to know one thing or another, but where for that reason one and the other are visible, connectible, possible, indeed tangible, which remain hidden to all others." It was an ethical demand, not an aesthetic one, and for that reason alone he was able to exaggerate to the point of perfection the style of the Burgtheater, which was sustained by the same ethicality. Now every stylistic tradition, no matter how great and how perfected, contains a restricting element, and that of the Burgtheater (to say nothing of the petty elegance, which permanently, easily, and somewhat comically, overshadowed its ethicality) was surely no exception. No doubt this entailed for Hofmannsthal's œuvre a forfeit of his original freedom of movement and expansiveness; yet it was a loss only in appearance: from unrestricted freedom of movement came inner excitement, from unrestricted expansiveness came the inner space of moderation. For it is the principle of order contained within style—especially high style—and the higher plane of reality it creates that makes "visible, connectible, possible, indeed tangible" what is otherwise hidden and unknowable. And it is in this manner that the content shared between the words and lines of poetry or between musical tones, the content shared between one dab of color of a painting and another, and not least even the content shared between one architectural form and another, become discernible: in sum, the content shared between the contents, this visible invisibility caused by dynamic tension, by the order and organization of the symbol, at once static and dynamic, so that from within this kind of disciplined symbol-architectonic, all true art—not only that of the stage— asserts the essential. Without this discipline, without this self-imposed Goethean commitment to order, without these strict ties to style and tradition, Hofmannsthal's colossal wealth of images, associations, thoughts and insights, his ultimately impressionistic abundance, would probably

112

never have achieved a collective representation. And it can therefore be asserted that, for him, style carried a thoroughly mystical, even Pythagorean significance, the architectonic-moral significance referred to in his comment: "What in poetic representation is called the plastic, the actual formative process, has its roots in justice."[30]

The Pythagorean cosmogony—knowledge and ethicality and art embracing a common architectonic—is conditioned by the musical as much as by the mathematical. Whoever lives in the symbolic realm of language learns with every sentence he conceives and through which he wants to express a definite substantive (not formally abstract) truth, that the linguistic apperception and representation of that truth is not a question of mere logical determination, but that the perhaps higher, perhaps more profound logic of art must be invoked, through whose architectonic the necessary validity and power of conviction of the utterance will be produced. "Insofar as by 'reality' one predicates something in some sense comprehensive, one is already near to dream, or rather to poetry." The realms of knowledge and poetry, and indeed of dream, converge relentlessly. Novalis knew of the Pythagorean relation of poetic logic to mathematical thought; Hofmannsthal, an unmathematical spirit, heard in that relation the architectonic of music, the penetration of the musical into the linguistic, the ubiquitous resonance of the musical world of expression in the word, reaching beyond the word, yet contained within it and conferring on it the cognitive content of "visible invisibility." "What art, if not music, can express this? to capture a piece of heaven and usurp it?" reads one of Hofmannsthal's letters to Richard Strauss.[31] Music is uninterpretable through words, and yet, in a common architectonic, it informs the word of its meaning; it is an uninterpretable convergence, but one with a pregnancy of meaning derived from unity and indicating its mystery. For, "a thing is an uninterpretable interpretability."[32]

Hence language—discursive language—alone becomes inadequate and "uninterpretable." Surely the "crises of linguistic skepticism" that evolve from this and that Hofmannsthal knew all too well are not categorically bound to stir an extreme linguistic despair of the sort presented in the "Letter of Lord Chandos"[33]—no, they can also lead to a new love of language, one that assigns value to the muting of language in order to guide silence back to language through new, fruitful, and even magical means. This is what Hofmannsthal had in mind when he said, "Finer and spiritually richer than language critique would be the attempt to wrestle oneself away from language into a magical mode, as is the case with love."[34] For the magic of love is silent communication, and when it speaks, it is a magical construal of the word; it is poetry, music. Does something like this happen to a person who has transformed linguistic skepticism into a love of language? For Lord Chandos, the despairer of language, words have become incoherent; but for someone who nurtures a loving hope for language, they are simply uninterpretable, and the thought he wants to express, to write down, becomes for him a "fore-thought," a "pre-text," whose vocabulary and syntax make sense, yet remain "uninterpretable," so that it remains for the poet, as both text philosopher and word composer, to undertake the interpretive, poetic "musicalization" and "architecturation." Yet is it sufficient to be in a state of linguistic skepticism? Is it sufficient to construct a poetic work symphonically, steeping it with musicality down to the connections of consonants and vowels? Of the many besides Hofmannsthal who did this, Joyce was of the greatest consequence, dissolving words into quarter and even eighth tones; is this sufficient for the execution of the required radical "musicalization"? It is not; linguistic skepticism remains, because a superpoetic, superlinguistic power is necessary to annul it. "True love of language is not possible without denial of language,"[35] and it is precisely with this denial of language (which clearly comes very close to the despairing of language) that the power of music is invoked and called to aid (the only appeal available), so that it may render musical a linguistic composition and undertake the conclusive explanation of the word. Hence the dismissal of the poet and his heroic renunciation. This is the significant step from theater to opera, the step from poet to librettist, a step from linguistic skepticism to linguistic despair and the love of language, yet also one that still includes self-transcendence and for that reason is a final stylistic intensification of the theater. And for that reason Hofmannsthal's concept of style, its Pythagorean, comprehensive sense of order, exacted so radical a conclusion, the musical resolution of language.

Yet doesn't this suggest a highly suspicious proximity to Wagner? Doesn't the *Gesamtkunstwerk* proclaim itself in this final stylistic intensification of the theater, in the intensification of language to music? For Hofmannsthal, just as for Wagner, the artistic life work was an unbroken unity, a product of inner necessity, and for neither one nor the other was the libretto a mere subordinate concern—not for Wagner, because he was a genius of the theater; not for Hofmannsthal, because he was born in the music city of Vienna, and one of the essential elements of his being and art took root in the musical. Nevertheless, this is not one of those frequent cases where two antagonists unknowingly want the same thing. Had fate equipped the poet Hofmannsthal with compositional talent too, he would hardly have become a musical revolutionary. For the value vacuum of the world, affirmed by Wagner and the soil from which he sucked his power, was for Hofmannsthal the most profound anxiety of his life. The fact that he assimilated the style of the Burgtheater can be judged an escape, an escape from style vacuum and freedom of style, and the fact that the intensification of this style enabled him to achieve the architectonic of his life work reveals the anti-Wagnerian traditionalism of his musical conception (a traditionalism universal to Vienna of the time), a traditionalism that held musical structure to be unshakable and scientific, established once and forever. Music like that of Wagner, or exotic folk music, which refuses to fit into the established rules, was considered either foolish or undeveloped. Musical structure appeared as a fixed pole. Much therefore speaks for the fact that Hofmannsthal expected musical structure to overcome the vacuum, to prove the catalyst to a renewed crystallization of value. It was a hope against better judgment, yet one that had to be embraced and held fast to by anyone who had that chilling premonition of what chaotic danger was already germinating in the dissolution of norms effected by the vacuum, of what horrible human misery was yet to develop from the collapse of traditional values and their ethicality. Hofmannsthal's intuition of reality recognized this early on; the anguished, chaos-possessed "Letter of Lord Chandos" dates from the year 1901. He was neither able nor allowed to accept this premonition, nor did he wish to accept it; and for precisely that reason he sought to cling to existing—subsisting—forms, was indeed forced to cling (in both human and artistic respects) to subsisting tradition and its seemingly still curable style, to preserve it by intensifying it, and to encapsulate himself within it and make his conservative position into a permanent and impenetrable fortification. And the greater the dissolution around him, the more important this impenetrability became, the more relentless the conservatism was forced to become. The libretti, though the most brilliant since Da Ponte's and surpassing those in every way, became pure conservatism, a perfect match to the conservative music of their composer—the final luster of a dying epoch.

No doubt Hofmannsthal knew from the very beginning that he was himself ultimately assimilating to the vacuum. But he could do nothing else. The unity of person and work which in the work of Stefan George had degenerated into a mere attitude ran much deeper for Hofmannsthal, was for him the unity of ego and work; accordingly, his person was bound to become a symbol of both, and he was bound to take himself and his life as a symbol, the symbol of his fate. He could not dispute his fate; all he could do was intensify its ultimate meaningfulness—a transcendence of fate was its ultimate meaning—and because it was a final meaning, it was realized in *The Tower*. Yet to that end he had had to pursue his entire experiment in life and death, an experiment into which he was compelled by his heritage every bit as much as by his specific and almost ominous talent, in short his fate, and one which he was thus forced to take upon himself, even though the agonizing insecurity of wisdom would now never leave him. He saw all too clearly that he stood everywhere on desolate ground: there were no prospects for the continued existence of the Austrian monarchy, which he had loved and never stopped loving; there were no prospects for his fondness for a nobility that had become little more than a caricature; there were no prospects for the stylistic integration of a theater whose greatness now rested on the shoulders of a few surviving actors; and there were no prospects of bringing about a renaissance of this entire vanishing legacy of the splendor of the Maria-Theresian eighteenth century, now reduced to a Baroque-tinted grand opera.[36] Hofmannsthal's life was a symbol, a noble symbol of a vanishing Austria, a vanishing nobility, a vanishing theater— symbol within the vacuum, yet not of the vacuum.

This alone—notwithstanding the vacuum, notwithstanding the collapse of the old value system, which dissolved piece by piece and was swallowed by the vacuum, notwithstanding the tragic experimentation with an entire and all too short a life, notwithstanding his struggle against the vacuum and his limitation by the vacuum, both in constant effort toward assimilation— this remains the self-affirmation of a true destiny, Hofmannsthal's existence, his high style and his high art.

# 3

# Hugo von Hofmannsthal's
# Prose Writings

Almost all of Hugo von Hofmannsthal's lyric poetry (the short verse dramas as well as the poems) stems from one decade of his youth, the years 1890–99. The lyrical period is outlasted on one side by the epic, superseded on the other by the dramatic. The former establishes itself with the *Tale of the 672d Night* of 1894 and leads to two highpoints, namely the novel-fragment *Andreas*, which emerged around 1912, and the great symbolic tale *The Woman Without a Shadow*, published in 1919 as a prose successor to the opera of the same name. The dramatic period, however, which may be considered to begin with the first act of *The Mines of Falun* (1899), continues unbroken until the poet's death in 1929.[1] Independent of this poetic achievement, however, runs his essayistic production, never slackening, constantly increasing in dimensionality. It accompanies Hofmannsthal on his entire literary journey, which he embarked on in his seventeenth year, and was his constant means of self-evaluation and self-explanation, the philosophical diary of his existence.

## 1. The Turn Away from Lyricism and the "Letter of Lord Chandos"

For a born dramatist to abandon his narrative production or to confine it to the short story, tied to situations and hence related to drama, is an occurrence substantiated by a whole row of examples—Kleist, Hebbel, Grillparzer, even Shaw and Oscar Wilde. And it is just as understandable, with born storytellers like Zola, Gorki, Hamsun, Thomas Mann, Joyce, for the reverse to occur. Yet there are absolutely no precedents for a born lyricist to abandon the poem totally in favor of prose epic and the stage. Yet such is the case with Hugo von Hofmannsthal. He renounced lyricism when hardly past his twenty-fifth year—the time when poetic power usually achieves its first full efflorescence.

"Precocity spells early death" in a very superficial generalization that explains nothing, though it must be added that Hofmannsthal never, not even in his first poems, wrote truly youthful poetry. What is usually of sole importance to young people, the subjective reaction of their ego, is hardly noticeable in the young Hofmannsthal. From the earliest poems on, aside from the occurrences of the first person, which are in any case very rare, the ego is concealed, the lyrical statement is shifted to the object in an attempt to reclaim it from what is seen, felt, and experienced, while on the other hand all seeing, feeling, and experience, in short every element of subjectivity, is cut off. For with the omission of that typically youthful "poetry of confession," the immediate result is a "poetry of knowledge" of the kind achieved by *normal* poets as a final stage, after a long process of maturation and growth. Of course, even a final stage holds the potential for endless further development; no *goal* was arrived at with the first leap of Hofmannsthal's œuvre; and it was not the leap, allegedly too sudden, still less the exhaustion that followed the leap, but other and essentially more profound causes that inhibited further development. It can be affirmed that inhibition and impulsion are strangely identical in Hofmannsthal's development, and that both must be discerned in the phenomenon of his most striking self-suppression, his ego concealment.[2]

On this point one might recall a sentence, as curious as it is noteworthy, from the *Book of Friends:* "Plasticity develops not through observation, but through identification." This is an instruction to the artist and it implies: as long as things are no more to you than a foil for your ego, you will never, ever grasp their true being, and not even the most intense observation, description, or imitation will help you do so. All the same, you may succeed if you are capable of renouncing your ego by projecting it into the object, so that the object can begin to speak in your place. For you yourself, a single individual in front of a single thing, have only your subjective impressions of it; you therefore, like the mind of an animal, have hardly a language, at best the sounds of terror and rapture, of warning and attracting, at best interjections like "oh" and "ah," whereas real language grasps not only the momentary impressions of things but their lasting essence and thus requires a much richer, subtler, more intimate relation to them than that possessed by animals; and this second immediacy, as one may call it, for knowledge as such springs from it, is achieved solely through the absorption of the ego into the object. Yet whoever remains content with subjective interjections is no artist, no poet; confession is nothing, knowledge is all.

Consequently, knowledge for Hofmannsthal is complete identification with the object. The artist who, as is his task, is able to raise his intuition beyond the everyday toward a complete identification with the world and all it contains hears its specific language; to him it becomes human language as well as the enrichment of human language. Or, more precisely, he senses the preestablished harmony that exists between ego and world, between language, concept-bearing and concept-borne, and the things it describes, so that he grasps them all, whether singly or united, from within, in their essence, for he perceives within them, echolike, their *tat tvam asi*.[3] That is mysticism. And even if it is confined, as with Hofmannsthal, principally to artistic domains, it would be an empty supposition if it did not allow us to inquire after the proof of its evidence. Hofmannsthal gives the answer. Not that he engulfs himself in his historical sources, in the philosophies of India, or Heraclitus, Leibniz, Jakob Böhme—no, his evidence is nothing that comes from reading. He appeals to moments of poetic ecstasy, to those moments he describes as "exaltation," since it is in them that, with one blow, through the extinguishing of the ego, the entirety of being is known or, rather, newly recognized in a wondrous, long-known familiarity, as if in total recall of a previous experience, in a total recollection whose origin (not to be confused with that of physiological generational recall) manifests itself unambiguously as a metaphysical preexistence of man. It is the stage at which man is endowed with the complete identification of the ego with the non-ego (which confronts him as the world), the stage at which he has irrevocably and for all time received the divine gift of harmony of thing and concept and world—in short, the foundation of all world intuition, all knowledge, and all language.

The rediscovery of complete world identification, the rediscovery of preexistence, hence reveals itself—and this is a thoroughly Indian idea—as the highest ecstasy man can attain, probably the very highest attainable life value, and precisely because this complete identification with his object has been posited as the artist's task, indeed as his moral task, his work must be its expression, its image, its symbol; the work itself becomes ecstasizing and thus wins that quality specific to works of art for which the word "beautiful" was coined. Hence knowledge of the nearly insurmountable difficulties that oppose the fulfillment of the task of identification is reserved for the artist. For what constitutes this non-ego, this exterior world with which the ego is supposed to identify? That the world is in constant motion is the slightest of evils; it is far more disturbing that every means of expression (linguistic or otherwise) given to man toward the representation of the world belongs to that world, and most disturbing of all is the fact that with every act of identification a piece of the ego enters into the non-ego, changing and enriching the non-ego so that the process, including its own self, must be immediately repeated. At stake here is not a static object but one that fluctuates to an uncommon degree; and not a single act of identification but an entire chain is required, an entire chain of symbolic constructions, symbol symbolizations which in their initial links may exhibit a certain similarity to primitive metaphor construction, but then reach way beyond that in order to provide by means of an ever closer rapport with reality at least the idea of a total symbol of the world from within the slice of reality it represents—*tat tvam asi* of art.

Yet for this to come about, the chain must ultimately, somewhere, be broken; otherwise there would exist only the "work in progress,"[4] never a completed work of art. When is that completion achieved? It is precisely the lyric poem—in a manner curiously parallel to the joke—that undertakes the most boldly irrational shortenings of the chain, and presumably it is the lyrical content inherent in every work of art that is responsible for its completion. Of course, no objective or even precise criterion is derived from the term "lyric," not even a subjective one, all the less so since what is at stake is not only the secret of concision and economy but also that of artistic intemperance. Where then is the criterion of achieved perfection, since beauty cannot be its own critical authority? It was in connection with music, which already possesses its codified rules, that the criterion of the medium, the criterion of the means of expression, was discovered, in the hope that the latter—provided identification was radically channeled toward it with increasing perfection, somewhat like a correctly constructed fugue—would reveal the completion of a work of art as form in itself, as language in itself. The original mysticism of intuition is joined by a second mysticism, that of form, of language and its perfection. Already suggested by the romantics, yet still hidden by the mysticism of faith and other mysticisms, the new principle emerges unequivocally with Baudelaire, and from there on it dominated the entire poetry of the second half of the nineteenth century, setting the trend for the novel from Flaubert to Proust, becoming absolute dogma for the whole symbolist school through Mallarmé and George, a dogma so absolute and autonomous that one wished in all seriousness to grant it the identity of a new religion for humanity, in the exclusive service of *beauty*.

This is the point where artistic seriousness oversteps the frontier of the ridiculous and art begins to transform its own marble into cardboard imitations. And of this Hofmannsthal's supreme critical mind was thoroughly aware. He had no doubt been convinced from the beginning of the cognitive goal of aesthetic perfection; no doubt the fundamental shock that overcame him at the first flash of preexistential memory and its artistic symbols—with a power it hardly exerted on anyone else—continued to affect him. Yet if there was anyone who considered knowledge not merely the facade but the kernel of aesthetic fulfillment, it was he, to whom it was always the "depths hidden on the surface" that mattered. He recognized the dangers of pan-aestheticism: the idea of a work of art whose universality would by means of symbolic wealth produce an ultimate total knowledge appeared to him condemned in the end to a leap into a void, because the *beautiful*, even when surrounded with the nimbus of religiosity, can never be elevated to the absolute and must therefore remain mute in the transmission of knowledge. In this manner Hofmannsthal renounces pan-aestheticism (and at the same time renounces George), and it is a far more fundamental renunciation than any (so common at the time) based on naturalistic grounds, for it signifies that whoever would supplant genuine with aesthetic religiousness serves a false god and encourages all the aspects of madness and evil which inevitably emerge from all pseudoreligiosity.

The outbreak of madness: just how this is prepared is demonstrated by Hofmannsthal in the "Letter of Lord Chandos."

Lord Chandos, a young, landed nobleman of the Elizabethan epoch, in whom, however, the cultured Oxford graduate and gentleman-aesthete of our own day is not hard to recognize, writes to his paternal friend Lord Chancellor Bacon, the keenest thinker of his time, and describes, of course with the discreet self-suppression imposed by his education and upbringing, an utterly terrifying experience. At one blow he has lost the mystical intuitive unity of ego, expression, and thing, to the extent that his ego is abruptly brought to a hermetic isolation, isolated in a rich world to which he no longer finds access and whose objects, let alone their names, have become meaningless to him. World and things have in a sort of negative way overwhelmed him, for they have withdrawn from him. What reveals itself here is not contrition, not the condition of man thrown into nothingness; no, it is a state of utmost inadequacy and for that very reason utmost disgust—disgust with things because they are unattainable; disgust with the word, which because of all its inconsistencies no longer reaches its object; disgust with one's own being, which has lost both knowledge and consequently all self-fulfillment. Man is defeated by the aggression of things (an aggression dealt with, under a slightly different light, in the essay "The Irony of Things");[5] and the required and now unachievable radical identification with objects, this act of most perfected love, is replaced by the defeat of love, by life impotence itself and its disgust.

Hofmannsthal wisely did not put the Lord Chancellor in the predicament of having to answer the letter. For what could a Bacon, who was no Shakespeare—it would of course have been different if he had been—have made of such an outburst of anguish? To his sober sense of reality, sustained by faith, knowledge was simply knowledge; and that it could ever break down, indeed that this breakdown of the human creative act would also

121

endanger the divine creative act—and this was the ultimate fear expressed in the "Chandos Letter"—he would have considered an absolutely unfathomable blasphemy. In accordance with the ideas of his time he would have seen blasphemy as possession by the devil, hence the inevitable pyre on which both his young friend and the corresponding poet Hofmannsthal would burn. And had he been familiar with modern psychology, he would have spoken of schizophrenia, suggesting that, presumably, every poet is prone to split personality and flees from the threat of it into his work, into which he in turn projects all these splits in order to abreact, by means of such sublimation, his fear of schizophrenia—in any case a somewhat devious reflection for a Lord Chancellor to Queen Elizabeth.

Nevertheless, every human psyche is subject to such splits, the artist's more than most, and the poet's most of all: nowhere is the paradox of the poet's creative process (a genuine paradox of the infinite) as visible as in the phenomenon of the split, through which poetry is as much destroyed as it is made fruitful. The "Chandos Letter" portrays the extreme case of complete destruction, as it portrays man, incapable of identification, incapable of overcoming the tension between knowing and the known, totally at the mercy of unknowable being, its objects, their unassailable hostility, their incomprehensibility, their irony. But the despair over this condition, as the young Lord Chandos expresses it, already reveals the paradox-laden content of the process, namely the identification of the subject with an object capable of identification, the identification with its own opposite, without which it would have been impossible for Hofmannsthal to portray Chandos's despair. Yet this, just this, is the dialectical structure of the poetic process: whether, as here, identification and nonidentification are brought to a synthesis, or whether this occurs with any other pair of opposites, the resulting image is always the primal opposition itself, which (to the displeasure of the Freudian school) is clearly not—or is at best in a very figurative sense—the sexual opposition; it is rather the opposition of ego and non-ego, of the being of the ego and the being of the world, both—thanks to the psychic split—the domicile of man and the source of his poetic creation. For out of the tension between ego and world springs poetic strength, unified at the source and then divided into lyric and dramatic expression, both equally indispensable to it, the former projecting the outer world to the inside, the latter projecting the inside to the outer world, by means of mutual conditioning. All the same this does not yet exhaust the achievement of the psychic split, which not only permits us to experience the contrast to the world, the aggression and irony of the world as well as its objects, so that it all becomes comprehensible and controllable, but which also forms the presupposition for any kind of self-observation. And from the desperate realization of one's own failure emerges that self-irony with which poetry—

no other artistic genre has the same capacity—peers as it were over its own shoulder, relentlessly doubting itself, its truth content, its social earnestness, and expressing that doubt. Poetry is dream, but it is a dream that is constantly reminded of its dreaming and can hence develop into a dream smile. And just because the element of irony is so thoroughly a function as well as an effect of a split, one must assume that it reaches back to the beginnings of poetry, perhaps to the laughter of the gods, and cannot be confined to the romantics in spite of the supreme place they assigned it in their instrumentarium.

As often as the poet succeeds—and to be a poet, he must succeed—in making his splits useful, in clinging to a piece of reality by overcoming all his antinomies, capturing the world, whether in whole or in part, with his symbolic chain, or placing the world under a total symbol that illuminates it as a harmonious unity, he will take part in that *exaltation* which defined for Hofmannsthal the ecstatic moments of highest value fulfillment. And no irony can diminish such ecstatic bliss; it will far sooner be enhanced by ironic knowledge. Nevertheless, what occurs in the "Chandos Letter" is almost beyond irony. A young man is portrayed for whom the ego and non-ego have lost all contact, since for him the symbolic chain was broken even before the first link was forged: nothing remains but the split itself, so that all life values are extinguished. He finds himself in the state diametrically opposed to ecstasy, in the state of panic, in the deepest abyss of man. In presenting and describing this condition, Hofmannsthal must have fully identified with it; he must himself have been in the ultimate stages of life panic. How then could he write at all? How can muteness be abreacted by way of speech, blindness by way of sight? It is conceivable for a poet to invent murders and to identify himself with the murderers in order to work off his own concealed murderous desires, just as it is conceivable that Goethe overcame once and for all his own suicidal intentions after the death of Werther. And it is no less conceivable that any poet who does not succeed in fully incorporating his emotions in his creative work, so that they become a literary residue for him and are, so to speak, neutral in their attitude to life, will assume the fate of his heroes; this is what happened with Strindberg. But it borders on the inconceivable for a poet—and this is the Chandos case—to derive from a panic that has been his own the ecstasy that follows every successful work. Insofar as the work is to be taken seriously, the paradox seems here to have reversed itself into the antinomic.

No doubt the "Chandos Letter" must have been preceded by an exceedingly powerful psychic shock, and it was only natural for that shock to demand an abreaction. It was presumably no less powerful a shock than the one Hofmannsthal had experienced when still practically a boy, at the very beginning of his poetic career, when his poetry revealed to him the wonder of identification between ego and things. Now all of a sudden the reverse had occurred: in his struggle with the problem of symbols he was abruptly faced with the possibility of an inability to identify, which carried within itself the denial of poetic creation. This was a catastrophic discovery, and it would have been no surprise if it had been answered with an immediate silencing of all poetic production. Yet this did not happen; the command to remain silent, for all the accompanying shock, was apparently less imperative than the one which had once impelled him to raise the poetic voice. For if the beginning of poetic activity had taken place as an uncannily beatific and yet overwhelming dream, irrepressible and emerging directly from the darkest depths, the new occurrence was equally uncanny, yet no longer beatific, but somber, taking place in essentially more wakeful and more conscious zones, penetrated by all kinds of rational ideas and reflections. The summons to the renunciation of poetry was no longer a dream command to which the entire person had to submit with every fiber; it was, rather, a moral precept that appealed to the conscience and hence to the free will, and thus one that permits moral confrontation and perhaps even refutation. It was not an unconditional demand; it released every idea of panic but not panic itself, and although this already signified quite enough of a shock, the attempt at its abreaction through creative work could be risked. The attempt was only partially successful, perhaps because a little chamber piece with renaissance ornament—which is what the "Chandos Letter" ultimately is—can hardly encompass such a powerful theme. A compromise was reached: the nonlyric production could be continued; the poetic injunction was limited to lyric poetry.

Even in this compromise, the naming of things, the "christening task" of poetry, is at stake. For of all the branches of literature it is predominantly the one tied to verse that has proved itself suitable to such a name-giving, christening task. Of course this is an assertion to be taken *cum grano salis*, since great prose writers of the caliber of a Cervantes can be set against a Shakespeare, a Dante, or a Goethe (not to mention those of a lesser stature, the not insignificant Hebel, for example); yet as far as the assertion is legitimate, it grants lyricism, the art of verse *pur sang*, a special significance in which popular lyrics do not fail to play a part. Language creation occurs where new layers of reality and knowledge are uncovered, and this can occur only from the ego, from its solitude, from its piety, in short from its lyrical center. Poems that fulfill these conditions—and there are not a few in the long Western tradition from Sappho to Lorca—are swiftly adopted by popular art and transfigured into the anonymous. Yet such honor has to this day never been accorded the works of aestheticism and its decorative art, simply because, for all its high artistic achievement, no verbal splendor suffices to penetrate into the new, and as a result the very reverse holds true:

without the discovery of new planes of reality, whether earthly or extra-earthly, there is no lyricism, or, at best, a derivative lyricism. So it is here that the criteria of aesthetic perfection must constantly be sought, and it is in curiously false humility that the absorption of the subject into the aesthetic object is demanded, whereas popular poetry (in its widest sense) masters the shortening of the symbolic chain so to speak by natural means, with a simplicity of such mystery that, next to it, the entire identification mysticism of aestheticism pales and vanishes. Genuine religiousness versus the adulation of beauty, the search for the essential versus the joy in gesture, the true humility of pride in piety versus arrogance—that is the difference. Hofmannsthal's young nobleman strays into a panic-filled despair because he is an aesthete and is prevented by his own arrogance from finding a way out; were a truly humble and pious man struck by the Chandos catastrophe, he would be made more pious still, and his silence would be contrition and the search for still deeper realities.

All this must have played a highly relevant role in Hofmannsthal's creative work. The "Chandos Letter" may be taken as the first result of his break with aestheticism; the second is the turn to folk art, the search for a genuine instead of a false humility. But can all this be brought about according to a preconceived plan? Hofmannsthal knew very well that folk art permits no imitation and that the imitation of folk lyrics paves the way to triviality. How then to assert himself as a poet? To this end he devised a clever supplementary theory: the return to the popular can be achieved through moral effect on the masses. Consequently, comprehensibility must be required, so that the poem with its inevitably esoteric character is categorically eliminated. But in narrative and above all in the theater, this goal appears to be attainable. And perhaps the success of the theater can be taken as the criterion of perfection toward which aestheticism has vainly striven.

## 2. The Narrative Work

Hofmannsthal's narrative writings encompass two distinctly separate groups of works: on one hand the fairy tales belonging predominantly to his youth, yet taken up again in 1919 with *The Woman Without a Shadow*, and, on the other, the stories in realistic form. This second group contains *A Tale of the Cavalry* (1898), the novellas *Bassompierre* (1900) and *Lucidor* (1910), and the very remarkable attempt *Twilight and Nocturnal Storm*, and it culminates in the unfinished novel *Andreas*, begun in 1912 and continued during the war. The earlier fragment *Contarin* also belongs to this group, as a kind of atmospheric preliminary sketch.[6]

At the time of the First World War, Joyce was working on his *Ulysses*, begun in 1914; *Dubliners* appeared in 1914 and the *Portrait* in 1916. Why mention this contemporaneity? Why not mention the no less contemporary Proust, whom many consider a distant relative of Hofmannsthal? No, surprisingly enough the parallel to Joyce is more illuminating. Why? Because of the tradition-bound character of both men's youthful lyrics? Or because of the similarities between Hofmannsthal's theory of preexistence and the Vichian philosophy of history adopted by Joyce? These are superficial analogies. It is much more important that Joyce too probably had his Chandos experience, for the destruction of expression that he undertook in his prose work in order to create, from its sentence fragments and word particles, a new and more genuine expression of reality points to a positively wild anger and contempt, to a disgust with traditional and impoverished language, with its clichés, petrified in both vocabulary and syntax. And such conjecture is strengthened when one observes how both poets—and scarcely any other—were driven by their common point of departure in the mysticism of art, language, and perfection to the problem of infinite symbolic chains and symbol symbolizations.

Music, in the moments of its highest grace, can sometimes create world symbols out of nothingness; everywhere else they are created out of the reservoir of memory, so that, newly created, they may once again be stored within that memory. Both Joyce and Hofmannsthal graduated to the specific art form of memory, namely to the narrative form, that of the novel. Yet here a fundamental difference appears. Joyce was endowed with a predominantly auditory, Hofmannsthal with a predominantly visual memory, so that symbol chains developed in the former in the form of echo and counterecho, in the latter as a row of images in endless reflection and counterreflection. With Hofmannsthal the novel becomes visual space; with Joyce, sound space. Both methods are legitimate; nevertheless they possess not nearly the same potentialities. For the visual impression can be transposed into the auditory—this too is one of the miracles of world-creating (not world-imitating) great music—whereas the auditory can hardly achieve full expression in the visual. Granted, that is a merely technical impairment, but it was certainly a contributing factor when Hofmannsthal laid aside unfinished his narrative masterpiece *Andreas*. It was given to the far more rational Joyce—the lyrics of his youth show just how much scantier, more contrived, in other words more unpoetic his associations were—to become the master of the modern art of the novel and to inaugurate its entirely new (not only in a technical sense) possibilities of expression. Does this once again bring into view the contrast between the poetry of confession and the poetry of knowledge? Does the former once again prove itself the more productive? If music in its ultimate greatness, perhaps in the work of Bach, can be comprehended as the deepest self-

126

confession, so is painting the ultimate mode of object knowledge, and it would therefore be perfectly justifiable to propose that Joyce the musician strove from the very beginning—most clearly in the *Portrait*—to a poetry of confession.

Does visuality then produce ego suppression, or—and this is more probable—does the ego-suppressing, confession-rejecting man feel impelled toward visuality? To leaf through Hofmannsthal's poetry, to open randomly his diarylike letters, is to be struck at every point with testimony to his visual memory, to be continually surprised by its broad diversity (certainly comparable to the auditory memory of Joyce, trained in twenty languages). Whatever once enraptured the young man's eye, images of the nature through which he wandered, images of cities and villages and their gardens, yet also (and not least) theater scenes and scenery that had profoundly impressed him even as a child—all this is saturated with color and plastically retained. Truly everything is there; only the living human being as such is lacking, and if, as an exception, he is admitted, he will most likely be a actor, denatured to a mere *acteur*, just as if the self-silencing man had to silence his fellow man as well. In the work of one of Hofmannsthal's intellectual predecessors, Adalbert Stifter, unquestionably the greatest prose writer of the Austrian neoclassical period and perhaps the greatest landscape portrayer in all of German literature, this tendency is, if possible, even more pronounced. Whether knowledge or confession, both are rooted here exclusively in the landscape, and man in his relation to the landscape is nothing but an accessory, nothing but—in the truest sense of the word—an optical form, a nonliving creature whose shadow existence follows some kind of abstract-moralizing, idealistically romanticizing conventions and knows no genuinely human desire, and hence (in Freudian terms) is moved only by a kind of superego but never by the id. Two things emerge here: first, that aestheticism is not overcome by moralizing but merely shifted to a sidetrack, and second, that through it the totality of life demanded of the novels of great world literature can never be attained. Hofmannsthal, in his very efforts to free himself from an aestheticizing and hence from a purely visual art, was aware of its deficiencies, aware—his poet in the *Little Theater of the World*[7] proves it—that it breaks down in the face of human essentiality, and in order to overcome these deficiencies he strove to embed his portrayal of man in the immortality of landscape. He created the "man enchanted by landscape," and with his protagonist Andreas he succeeded magnificently. Yet even the most magnificent enchantment has its effect within the bewitched hour only; when the hour has passed and the clock has struck one—and that happens here (with Stifter even more so) so soon as the book is shut—the landscape remains, but the magic creatures disappear, because they possess no human life of their own, to say nothing of that "street existence," as one might call it, with which figures like Robinson Crusoe, Gulliver, Rastignac, Oblomov, Saccard, Alyosha, even Madame Bovary have engraved themselves into the human memory, independent of the books in which they appear and with nearly mythical overtones. All of them approach the totality of the human image, whose multidimensionality encompasses the id as well as the superego, the magical and mystical as well as the fully conscious and the metaphysical. And the very same range is peculiar to Joyce's method, which—growing clear from a certain distance—achieves in a pointillistic and apparently contourless manner, with the help of its auditory particles, the utmost concreteness for Bloom, Dedalus, and Earwicker, yet aims beyond that toward a mythical anchoring, not only by way of the form of the work as a work but, to a greater degree, in that the form, as if to discover the beginnings of language, propels the rows of auditory symbols into the ultimate regions where dream murmurs and, through it, time immemorial.

Nevertheless, neither Bloom nor Dedalus nor Earwicker are mythological figures. For modern mythos, aspired to by so many poets, does not exist. The only thing that exists is what might be described as countermythos. Mythos is in its true sense cosmogony, the description of the primal forces that threaten and destroy man, and against these symbolic figures it opposes no less great, promethean hero symbols, which show how man conquers the seemingly unconquerable and is able to live on earth. None of this applies today; rather, mythological rationality has been supplanted by scientific rationalities, which must now describe with much keener rational symbols the primal forces and the possibilities of conquering them; and though primal fear survives unchanged in the human psyche, even clinging to its traditional forms, the fear-inspiring element has unknowingly shifted and no longer lies within the primeval but—strangely enough—in nature tamed into civilization, in the creations of man, from which the untamed, the untamable emerges anew, once again requiring a mythos, or rather a countermythos. Machine jungle, concrete jungle, civilization jungle: whether they will allow themselves to be tamed with the old heroic means is debatable; at present they form a situation that is as horrible as it is unheroic, and the new heroes with their dictatorial thirst for blood make it all the more unheroic and horrible. It is the situation of utmost helplessness, and Kafka, not Joyce, did it justice. Kafka presents the situation with its countermythos, in whose instrumentarium the hero symbol, the father and mother symbols become nearly or completely superficial, because the concern is the symbolization of helplessness itself, in short, that of the child. Hofmannsthal, however, thanks to a poetic knowledge of the irrational closer to Kafka than to Joyce, sensed this too; had he been able to free himself from the fatal stage-costuming that followed him everywhere with its liveried footmen and the like as a perpetual constriction, the counter-mythical strength of a work like *Twilight and Nocturnal Storm*, written well before Kafka's first publications, would have become clear and fruitful. And the same holds even truer for *Andreas*.

Insofar as one can speak of a Hofmannsthalian myth construction, it stands under the symbol of the voyage, more precisely under that of the river whose waves carry man forth as if in a dream, from birth to death, from the source to the mouth, from the primeval rock accumulated to form mountain ranges and the momentous dynamic of glacial slopes down to the might and the eternal calm of the sea, from beginning to end immutable nature and hence keeping present and visible time immemorial, incomparably more present for the visual man than its manifestation in the murmurs of dream. Yet midway down the path, in the plains transversed by the racing currents, the voyager encounters fortified yet cheerfully decorated towns, well-tilled land, and culture, beauty in itself as well as in its creations, truly rivaling nature in its mystical power of creation, indeed surpassing it, for here in the regions of the spirit, of art, and of human purification, man loses his dullness. Here he is able for the first time to free nature from its primeval danger and to draw it into the circle of newly won beauty, so that he, no longer a creature driven without a will, by virtue of such new receptiveness to nature becomes henceforth the helmsman of his life's voyage, with the last port before him as his home:

| | |
|---|---|
| Water crashes to engulf us, | *Wasser stürzt, uns zu verschlingen,* |
| Boulders roll to strike us dead, | *Rollt der Fels, uns zu erschlagen,* |
| Already the birds come | *Kommen schon auf starken Schwingen* |
| To carry us on their strong pinions. | *Vögel her, uns fortzutragen.* |
| | |
| But below there lies a land, | *Aber unten liegt ein Land,* |
| Mirroring fruits without end | *Früchte spiegelnd ohne Ende* |
| In its ageless lakes. | *In den alterslosen Seen.* |
| | |
| Marble-brow and fountain's edge | *Marmorstirn und Brunnenrand* |
| Rise from the blossoming plains | *Steigt aus blumigen Gelände,* |
| And the light winds blow. | *Und die leichten Winde wehn.*[8] |

This is the poetry of the twenty-four-year-old, striking the theme that would always remain with him, the theme of the mythical voyage, no doubt still trusting in beauty and not yet recognizing that nature, once it had been rendered harmless by culture and elevated to beauty, had, like a Greek bearing gifts, bequeathed to culture the uncanny, the threatening. The beneficiary is the uncreative "civilized" man, the urban "lower classes," estranged from mystery and hostile to it, the rabble of civilization in whose nonbeing the primeval smolders, confused and confounded, a mocking, laughing, terrifying evil. Thus everything is full of polar double meaning, and the mythic journey to the mouth of the river can also become a "bad descent," a desertion of the zones of the superego, a sliding down into the id, an abandonment of the self toward the most anonymous entanglement and hence toward an anonymous shamelessness, to bestial prehumanity, eternal temptation for man, for his mania for throwing off all the human qualities bestowed on him, so that he can fall back into the primal, free of shame, back into the stage of the primordial child.

Alpine landscape as primeval nature, the valley of the Po as the sphere of the most blessed civilization: for Hofmannsthal, who carried in his veins a strong infusion of Austrian peasant and Lombard patrician blood, this was the natural double homeland, and may have been all he had in mind as he began to write *Andreas*. In actuality, however, it became the book of the mythic voyage, and its content is the double descent, on one hand from the nature of the mountains to the culture of the Mediterranean, on the other, from lofty purity to the depths of confusion. It is the story of young Herr von Ferschengelder of Rococo Vienna, who is sent by his parents to Venice to broaden his education and thereby embarks on a trip of increasing enchantment, fraught with ritual danger. The journey leads first into the Carinthian Alps, directly to the first, however brief enchantment with landscape. It embraces Andreas in a beautiful simplicity, for in the old farmstead bearing the coat of arms of the noble peasant family Finazzer, he finds their daughter Romana, a rural Austrian Ophelia, unforgettable, yet only to be abandoned, extinguished in Venice's enchanted oblivion which immediately and inevitably descends on the newcomer. Here, in the endless maze of alleys and canals, in itself a reflection of every possible intrigue, every possible human embroilment, he strays into a net of the most complicated reflections and counterreflections, into a thicket of psychic identifications and antagonisms, into a masquerade of the mind, full of erotic depths and superficialities. What is this water city full of beauty and sludge that he has been transported into? It is salt water and yet not sea—can life's journey, a mix of youth and old age, have already come to its end, flickering in such threatening ambiguity? Here everything is clear-sighted skepticism, yet dream nonetheless; back there, with Romana Finazzer, everything was dreaming illusion, yet it was reality, in the rushing of clear mountain streams. Does Andreas want the one or the other?

The final novel-fragment, describing only the Finazzer adventure and the days of arrival in Venice, does not answer these questions, but the preliminary sketches and notes for the entire plan of the novel clearly indicate that, in Venice, Andreas is moving on forbidden ground. The notes, considerably more extensive than the novel, consist of hundreds of references to situations, cross-sections of dialogue, witty, pointed epigrams, and between them sharp flashes of lightning which illuminate the portraits and contours of the characters, at the same time revealing by their sharpness that these are pseudocontours, for no ego is established. For example: "What is attractive in Andreas is that he is so easily influenced by others, the life of others is in him . . . the geometric locus of strange destinies." And consequently the "lower" forms of life in their vulgarity also gain power over him, first in the person of the servant Gotthilf, whose devilments had forced him to leave the Finazzer estate, and it can be assumed from the drafts that the scintillating city will bring about a repetition of the uncanny, sinister element in an extremely intensified form. Yet is not this convergence of characters, this overflowing of evil into good, an entry into the state of the primeval child? In the notes there is an allusion, though we do not know to whom it refers, to an "Attachment. Solitariness with the child; the child looking up; out of substance, *which I may not seek—for I am it*—are constructed all the heavens and hells of all religions; to cast them away would be darkest night. The child's look binds me . . . to . . . the obvious . . . only the cataclysm reveals the highest ecstasy." These are mystical words; but although they stammer, they are rational in comparison with what they seek to express, in the comparison with the mythical fear that shudders before primal substance and yet longs for it because it is the primal abode of the cataclysm. Mythos cannot endure the rationality lurking in every description; Kafka does not describe, Hofmannsthal cannot get away from it, for no amount of enchantment, however plausibly it may be described, is capable of raising landscape and the visual into the multidimensional. Hofmannsthal knows—however rationally—of the mythical solution ("I would like to die reconciled to my childhood"), but even in regard to the water motif, so important for the mythical journey, which he repeats in the death of the Maltese knight, the noblest figure in the book (he "hears the rushing of water, would have liked to summon up every bit of water he has ever heard flow"), he remains confined to the level of description. And for Andreas himself it is simply determined that he—upstream and without having found "self-knowledge"—is to embark on the return journey, bringing home nothing but one very small addition to his knowledge: "with Romana, it could be his heaven." And even that is a subjunctive.

With the *Andreas* story Hofmannsthal had set for his narrative writing a peak whose height he had underestimated; he abandoned the ascent, because having set out with predominantly visual but not Alpine equipment, he felt all too compelled toward autobiography (the material for which had already accumulated in the preliminary sketches for the novel), and this was incompatible with his ego suppression. More important to him than completion and publication was self-interpretation, self-contemplation, self-education, which had always been the concern of his poetry. He was therefore always able to resign himself to the fragmentary.

Nevertheless a poet never entirely lets go of themes he has not truly mastered, and just as in the phylogenetic total development of poetry, fairy tale emerges from myth, so in Hofmannsthal's ontogenesis the near-mythic *Andreas* is followed by the fairy-tale narrative of *The Woman Without A Shadow*; with the difference that here, contrary to the general rule, the structure of the main theme is not retained but inverted. The theme of the child remains, but it is transposed into the problem of parenthood. A fairy princess, so the story goes, falls passionately in love with the Emperor of the Southeastern Islands, becomes his happy wife, yet stands under a terrible curse, for since she is not really earthly but, having no shadow, is still bound to the realm of spirits, she will have to return there, while the Emperor (oblivious to this and simply in love) is condemned to turn to stone unless within twelve months she feels herself with child and will in this way have earned a human shadow. In the greatest distress, driven by the passing of her appointed time, she absconds from the palace in the guise of a poor woman together with her fairy nurse, whose plan it is to induce the evil, beautiful wife of the dyer Barak by means of promises, money, and magic, to sell her shadow. Yet when they both arrive at the house of the Dyer's Wife, the sale is hampered by one event after another, and the Empress is forced to realize that only by serving mankind can she gain her own humanity, her shadow, her children. She realizes that these ends require the greatest readiness for sacrifice, for death, for renunciation—realizes this even as she is carrying it out and so at once participates in her redemption, her own as well as that of the Emperor, the dyer, and his wife. Despite its oriental pomp this is a simple, almost puritanically moralizing fable—all puritanism, whether Christian or Jewish, allows love and marriage only if blessed with children—and at first no resemblance to the *Andreas* story is to be found. But does not the fairy daughter who wishes to become human find herself in the state of the child? And is not the Emperor, threatened with petrification for his lack of development, in the same position? Indeed, does not the same hold for the dyer and his wife, however kindhearted he, however evil she may be, both of them in a dulled existence? The very problematic of their parenthood makes child symbols of all these characters; their immaturity is just as striking as that of the young Andreas, and if they are ever to rise to that maturity which is the essence of the father symbol and mother symbol, they must strive toward that self-identity which—a recurrence of the Chandos problematic—emerges from identification with being. In the *Andreas* novel it is alluded to (with the mention of a possible solution) as a self-education to love, and seen from this angle the attempts at mythos and fairy tale draw considerably closer together.

In short, whether myth or fairy tale, it is the unfinished and (in contrast to the heroic-childlike Parzival) the childlike-unheroic being to whom a dominating value system is no longer given and who thereby—the most important characteristic of modernity—must obey an endless variety of value systems and becomes to a large extent overwhelmed by commands and hence in an infantile way confused and inactive. Even where heroism is revealed, in the *Tale of the Cavalry*, for example, it is determined by the split and hence conditioned and passive. Hofmannsthal perceived this psychic split as an *evil*, indeed utterly urban enchantment, and with his eye on the popular he contrasted that urban enchantment with the *good*, almost normal enchantment of landscape, almost a flight into a secure normality, which prescribes the bearing of children and permits a simple social life. For that too is enchantment.

All of this—enchantment and moralizing, the longing for the Orient and for pre-Oriental Venice, but side by side with that the longing for a secure bourgeois existence—became as all-encompassing and as permanent as it did because of its clear associations with the first impressions of fairy tales received within the protection of the nursery. The fairy tales of the *Thousand and One Nights* as well as those of the Grimms and Andersen are its godparents. In addition, the form of the fairy tale was especially well suited to Hofmannsthal's talents and limitations, not least to those of visuality and ego suppression. The Oriental fairy tale with its tapestrylike ornamentation is the most visual of all, for its forms are not individualities, not ego-borne, ego-bearing characters but purely visually conceived types; they are *the* caliph, *the* vizier, *the* young son of a merchant, *the* water carrier. They are at once ethereal, transparent, shadowless glass marionettes: they are homunculi; and the hand of the storyteller who picks up their wires can bring them to a most wonderful, so to speak pseudo-visible pseudo-life, yet he cannot overcome the lack of shadow and lack of weight of the floating marionette stage, lit from all sides; the visual method of fairy tales cannot be altered. It is a highly un-Homeric, almost anti-Homeric method, since it recognizes no burden of proof; it thus remains unproved that through her moral and miraculous social conduct and her in no way unbourgeois fairy-integrity the Empress has really won her shadow and her motherhood and fought her way to self-identity. Measured by the logical precision of myth, the form of the fairy tale tends toward a general diffusiveness, toward a general noncommital quality in which the individual statement never goes beyond a vague, empty, at best magical assertion. The tragic path of a character's purification, a fundamental theme of myth and bequeathed by it to all great poetry—we may think of *Faust*, for example—is lost to the fairy tale, perhaps because the latter is a late form; if its imitation purifications are to be convincing, it requires a second means of enchantment, and that is music: the eternal example of *The Magic Flute*.

Hofmannsthal's fairy tales are the final manifestations of a late form. In all the developments of intellectual history there are large and small waves, and the fairy tale, though itself a late form, did once upon a time—as long as it was in the mouths of the people—have its period of youth; at that time it was of beguiling simplicity. Final forms, however, demand the highest technical ability; they are products of late and (like today) final cultures, and their collective impression is like an overcoming of a Chandos experience. The current of symbols has indeed begun to flow once again, but the natural, immediate connection between association, linguistic expression, symbol, and thing has not been reestablished; a certain petrification of symbol has set in, and in order to keep communication comprehensible and flexible, more and more symbols must be brought into play, their very abundance contributing to the process of petrification, since—and this is the transition from symbol to allegory—they would no longer be at all understandable were they not incorporated into a fixed, precisely allegorical canon, the extreme opposite of immediate communicability. And because it is a process of petrification, there is something homunculoid and lifeless inherent in all allegory, exposing it to the danger of petrification as well as evaporation. But is not the Empress too threatened with evaporation, the Emperor with petrification? With one blow, this element in *The Woman Without a Shadow* reveals Hofmannsthal's individual method and its application. In the central chapter of the narrative, the Unborn, the Emperor's future children, appear to him, summoning him to fatherhood, to the act of creation. The scene takes place in the subterranean splendor of a cave, hence (a reminiscence of *The Mines of Falun*) in the womb of the earth. But the Hofmannsthalian symbolism reaches farther than that. For to creative power belongs also the evocation of names, the evocation of essentiality out of the *hic et nun* of things. Thus the little unborn princess, who has spread out in front of her father the world tapestry and on it everything that flies or crawls, comments on her weaving, "I do not see what is and what is not, but rather what always is, and thus, I weave." The entrance to these spheres is of course blocked to the Emperor; his premonitions still slumber in the premonitionless sphere of desire, and though he may be on the threshold of enlightenment, the divine act of creation eludes him, so that he grows mute in the first stages of petrification. In this way Hofmannsthal once again symbolizes (a positively Joycean track) the process of allegorization, symbolized in the content of his own means of representation; and so with continued elegance he breaks through the simply allegorical, the simply elegant, the simply intermediate, and gains for it the second immediacy, the beautiful simplicity without which the fairy tale would not be a fairy tale.

Nevertheless *The Woman Without a Shadow* is an artificial fairy tale, grounded in no kind of popular myth, and as much as Hofmannsthal reckoned it among his most important works—for it was a high peak of his narrative art, a repetition of the mastery over the Chandos experience, and a high technical accomplishment, and so something every artist hangs onto—he knew that he had created a Baroque structure which, in the absence of a preceding Gothic one, floats suspended in the air. Had he not known this so clearly, he would not have felt duty-bound to undertake for a third time the theme of childhood, this time in its final form; he did so in the drama *The Tower*.

### 3. The Turn Away from Epic: The Essayistic Writings

With *The Woman Without a Shadow* Hofmannsthal's creative work takes leave of epic and turns henceforth exclusively to the stage, where already before the First World War he had enjoyed a period of extraordinary fecundity: in an unbelievably short time span there followed *The Mines of Falun, Elektra, Christina's Journey Home, Everyman, Der Rosenkavalier, Ariadne*. Even the prose written during this time has one eye on the theater; the story *Lucidor* (1910) carries the revealing subtitle "characters for an unwritten comedy" and ends with the still more revealing words: "A dialogue like the one that ensued can be created by life and perhaps imitated by comedy but never by a story."

This is a totally incorrect observation, or at least one with no claim to general validity. For Hofmannsthal himself, of course, it held a measure of truth; it is even one of those clues which provide an explanation for the sparseness of his narrative and the fertility of his dramatic production. Indeed, the statement is nothing but an unrestrained admission of his lack of auditivity! Is not the stage therefore the predetermined medium of expression for the visual poet? For him who reduces men to mere show in the total picture, are not the histrionics of the theater the natural or, rather, the necessary medium in which to ground his characters, if not in the earth itself, then at least on the boards that signify the world? But even more, is not the stage the very instrument that is best suited to his penchant for ego suppression, permitting him, or rather positively requiring him to disappear completely behind the performance? The *Book of Friends* contains the remarkable sentence, "The beautiful, even in art, is not thinkable without shame." It is the pronouncement of a man who restrains himself from furnishing a novel with even the slightest autobiographical features, the pronouncement of a discretion which esteems the subjective and the private so highly that they must on the one hand be defended as inviolable and on the other not be imposed on any fellow human being, the pronouncement of a profoundly masculine sense of modesty that shrinks from any of the tempting, shameless exhibitionism that lurks in every artistic manifestation; it is the pronouncement of Hugo von Hofmannsthal. Is it not sheer good luck, then, that the man of theater, the exhibitionist himself par excellence, the authority, as it were, on exhibitionism, stands ready to take over this pronouncement from him? No doubt the vocational exhibitionism of the actor, singer, or dancer (less so the relatively more natural exhibitionism of the actress or the female dancer or singer) has ultimately an effect just as frightening, but it lies beyond the limit of responsibility, and what lies on this side of it—one's own life, voice, and gesture—remains anonymous. All the inhibitions that the desire for ego suppression imposes on a visual poet are taken over by the stage; here his productivity can develop free of inhibitions—does this not make him a born dramatist?

The fallacy in this question is clear. Even if the stage makes concessions to the poet's ego suppression, it does not relieve him of his other difficulties; indeed, it presents him with its own particular difficulties—even the Goethean theater is not exempt from this. By way of example, the landscape painter reduces the human form to a piece of scenery, and this has its scenic analogy in the "character part," hence in that stage figure that lives solely by virtue of its sharp characterization, and not by virtue of its psychological, dramatic, and thus drama-creating conflicts. For the genuine dramatist, the use of the character part is confined to filler and preparation scenes, and to peripheral characters, not uncommonly the servants of the main characters, and most often—Shakespeare's jesters remaining the constant model—members of the "lower classes," colored with dialect and mime. The visual poet, however, knows hardly anything but character roles, and since, therefore, it is hard for him to devise original conflicts, he is inclined to grab at old material, which he then peoples with stock characters, often up to the main protagonists. Exactly this—at least until 1919—was Hofmannsthal's dramatic method; it corresponded to his visuality and he handled it masterfully, occasionally even extending it into narrative (especially in the *Bassompierre* story). His stock characters are full of profound declarations about self and world through which they elucidate their own being and the happenstance in which they are placed, and their wisdom is that of tags and arias, demonstrating, as it were, that their method is operatic and one of situations. For in comedy as much as in opera (especially comic opera), the stock character is sufficient, and on the basis of this insight Hofmannsthal wrote not only the most beautiful modern opera texts—who can forget a Marschallin or a Baron Ochs auf Lerchenau?—but also evolved his own comic style and later guided it, with *The Difficult One*, to a peak of virtuosity, such virtuosity that, in the specific character of Count Kari, ego suppression is made into the center of the play and its inherent masculine modesty is confronted most wittily with the exhibitionism of the stage. Yet, whether opera or comedy, the virtue of both is born from the exigencies of visuality [*Visual-Not*], and that could not have satisfied a Hofmannsthal. Hence, midway through the period of his most light-hearted productivity and easiest successes, not only did he throw himself into the exertions of the *Andreas* project, but, when this too failed to satisfy him, he dared to approach drama once again, this time from an entirely different angle, and with its aid—specifically with *The Tower*—he cast off the method of stock characterizations that he had employed previously and attended to close the gaping antinomy between confessional poetry and ego suppression.

Everything truly human is played out in the realm of the antinomious; the animal, at times the envy of man on that account, knows nothing of it. And the less animal-like man becomes, the more he is torn apart by antinomies, no doubt becoming all the richer thereby, provided he succeeds in reconciling them: human harmony, whose tranquil ecstasy is the ultimate happiness to be found on earth, is composed of antinomies that have been overcome. For that very reason antinomy and harmony are the bedrock on which drama rests; for that very reason drama is able to exercise a more immediate purification effect than any other art form; for that very reason it embodies (especially when its harmonious structure fits into a folk tradition) what is known as national poetry. Goethe, in this narrow sense hardly a national poet, at least not as a dramatist, rose nonetheless to his national position of honor because his control of antinomies—by which his soul was torn apart more terribly than any other—allowed him to attain—to a degree scarcely imagined by anyone else—the most potent and the fullest harmony of being. His ego vanished behind all the worlds of the cosmos in self-confession, and his ego revealed itself in his varied knowledge of the world, there as everywhere gaining self-identity out of fragmentations. It was Goethe, not Schiller (the *real* national poet), on whom Hofmannsthal from his youth had fixed his gaze; it was certainly not on Hölderlin and least of all on Mallarmé or even George; only the Goethean example gave him the hope of a release from his own fundamental antinomy—the symbiosis of the poetry of confession and ego suppression. It was from Goethe too that he learned that poetry, if it is to lead man to purification and self-identification, must hurl itself into the depths of his antinomies, in complete contrast to philosophy, which remains on the edge of the abyss, without risking the leap, satisfying itself with the mere analysis of the observed.

Hofmannsthal was in no way a "nonleaper"; he was an inhibited leaper. He found himself, one might say, in a permanent state of readiness for the

137

leap, a readiness which, however masterful it was in the *Andreas* story, first really prevailed over the instinct to shrink back from the abyss in *The Tower*. The intermediate position at the edge of the abyss was most typical for him, and if, on one hand, it may have oppressed him as a situation of unfulfilled longing for creation, for precisely this reason it awakened him, on the other hand, to a mastery of the philosophical essay hardly equaled in the German language. For everything that inhibited him in pure poetry lost this disturbing quality in the essay, and became totally beneficial. Even the aestheticism of his youth, even the mysticism of language and of perfection, took a positive turn in the essayistic writings, for they were dominated by simple rational statements, and, subordinated to these statements, the inclination to pomposity is sobered into a genuine enrichment. The same holds for the flood of associations and memory-images, whose symbol chains and symbol symbolizations remain in the Hofmannsthalian novel irrepressible to the point of destructiveness, whereas in the essay they work unequivocally as a constructive element. Precisely because Hofmannsthal—in accordance with his entire make-up—had no scientific ambitions, he was permitted to loosen up the essay through the incorporation of these sequences of images, and the result was a previously uncharted, unique form of discourse, essentially closer to lyricism than to philosophy. Are these the harbingers of a new philosophy which draws from poetry the courage to leap into the abyss of antinomies, in order to arrive at the point of hazarding a new knowledge of being? It is quite possible that Hofmannsthal sensed something of all this from the beginning, but here his almost antirevolutionary fear of the leap becomes evident—fear not only of the abyss of antinomies as such, for he shrank also from his own forebodings, the depths of whose abysses he did not even want to be aware of. Nevertheless, the presence of these forebodings was undeniable—one need only read "The Colors," ("Die Farben")[9] an excerpt approaching the ontological; what emerges here is so fearful of overstepping the old familiar limits of philosophy that it is and has every claim to be called confessional prose.

Expressed somewhat paradoxically, if we disregard *The Tower*, it is only outside of poetry that Hofmannsthal achieves confessional poetry. But will this extrapoetic realm permit the poetry to achieve what as confession it intends to achieve, what is expected from it? Can self-identification take place at all when the leap into the abyss of antinomies is foregone? Or can one perhaps expect that the endless flood of images rising from the immense essayistic work will compensate for the leap that never occurred? In their entirety these essays describe that great ellipse of landscape stretching from northern Italy to southern Bohemia, with the Austrian Alps as its nucleus, a region full of heroic culture and heroic nature; with its focal points in Venice and Vienna it provides the mirror, so to speak, for Hofmannsthal's

"Austrianhood" (or rather old-Austrianhood). At first glance this seems to be a solely geographical localization; even so, it doesn't take much to discover that the historicizing bond to the homeland is merely the point of departure for something more essential. For deeply entangled in Austrian culture, open to it with every pore, contributing to it, permanently sharing in its preservation, Hofmannsthal unceasingly experienced the anonymity of culture-forming powers, the anonymity of the folksong, the anonymity of the peasant woodcarvers, the anonymity of the many master builders who shared in making the landscape look the way it did, and the more involved in such development he became, the more this unfurling of culture appeared to him as a natural process: is not poetry also a product of nature, like the language in which it has its place? Is the creation of culture not the innermost nature of man? Does not the way in which human creation—most apparent in architecture—grows into the landscape in order to be reintegrated into it prove that that creation was from the beginning attached to nature? Who can still draw the line that separates the two? The Habsburg empire was the product of wars and acts of state; nevertheless it seems (independent of those auxiliary political mechanisms) to have emerged from a preexistence rooted in its soil, providing it with an eternal, postexistential being. And it is just as incomprehensible that Venice was once upon a time actually built by pile sinkers, masons, and roofers; does not Venice likewise possess a spiritual existence created and protected by nature? The artificial flows into the natural, the natural in turn into the artificial, and whether on the stage or in so-called real life, the planes of reality cut across one another, with the result that man constantly wanders between changing dream sceneries, whose origins are in an anonymous Somewhere but are nevertheless created by man himself. His ego has been discarded, yet he recognizes it everywhere: man's reality lies in the anonymous, and whatever he creates only becomes real when he, like the folk artist, has been submerged in anonymity, returned to the natural, stripped of everything homunculoid and led to the rediscovery of his shadow. Insofar as Hofmannsthal placed the accent of almost the whole of his nonpoetical work on his everlasting attachment to his homeland, it became a confession for him, and the turn to his homeland's folk traditions became for him a conclusive substitute for the leap into the antinomic which he never made.

Plausible as this may sound, however, things are not nearly so simple. A nostalgia-filled 1908 prose piece, "A Memory of Beautiful Days" ("Erinnerung schöner Tage")—the title could stand for Hofmannsthal's entire essayistic work—describes how, after an extended stroll in a receptive state of mind through Venice in late afternoon and evening, the demonically delightful urge to memory and poetry enters him in the night, how the act of poetry springs immediately from the impression of his surroundings, from landscape and qualities of mood, how it entirely fills the ego and yet extinguishes it at the same time, a magical intake and recitation of the seen, a magic that completely dissolves the ego and banishes it to anonymity. Naturally this is essentially more complex than the simple evocation of the homeland and its folk traditions, but it was undoubtedly the scheme (and was so described by Hofmannsthal) by which he attempted to reconcile ego confession and ego suppression. The allusions to the theories of his youth, which demanded the absorption of the subject by the object, are obvious. But what is certainly more striking is the fact that the self-identification that should arise from such ego confession refers to a preparatory stage, to a stage preparatory to the act of confession, indeed to a curiously primitive stage of preparation for the act of poetry (the impression of a stroll and the urge to memory, both psychologically conceived). It was all the more a preparatory stage since the extinguishing of the ego leads only to anonymity; so it comes to a halt at the mystical threshold beyond which not only the terrifying realm of pantheistic chatter but also the more somber one of complete contrition begins, the first justly abhorred by Hofmannsthal, the second unattainable for him.

Hofmannsthal never transcends this preparatory stage, and this is just what his poetry of confession in essay form is, a poetry that reached the highest perfection even in a preparatory stage. Clearly the final identity of world knowledge and ego confession, which Goethe presented to the world on the basis of a universal and therefore ego-revealing confession, appears here merely in an analogical (not imitative) narrowing, in other words within the bounds of a predominantly visual landscape confession, more or less tied to the homeland. But this is precisely the essay's more poetic and, strange as it may sound, more mythical realm, for however and wherever genuine poetry surfaces, there too shimmers a ray of its primal beginning, a ray of mythos.

In fact, several of Hofmannsthal's essays carry this shimmering quality. One of them is the triptych (written around 1910) *Moments in Greece* (*Augenblicke in Griechenland*).[10] The first of the three pieces is a monastery and shepherd idyll, but what an idyll! The passing of clouds is halted, and from the great silence the prehistory of Greece resounds, the imperishable that existed before Homer brought it to language, the heavenly stillness of an eternally awakening soul, the same today as ever and ever. The second piece, called "The Wanderer" ("Der Wanderer"), contains an encounter with a sinister figure on the stony slopes of Parnassus and reveals the true mythological vision of the triptych; this wanderer is an outcast of civilization—a German, significantly enough—a man thrown back into the primeval. For technology and civilization, which have retrogressed to an unfettered natural power, tear society apart at the seams, with the result that he, "wasted away . . . to an animal-like, fear-ridden creature," surrounded by countless mythical threats, pursued by mythical fear, has lost every way out, has become a bewildered child possessed of maturity, full of helpless rage, full of a will to destruction and self-destruction. The cruelest confrontation of ancient and modern! After this climax the third piece, "The Statues" ("Die Statuen"), forms the refrain, no doubt a transfigured and transfiguring one, for the concern here is the mysticism that succeeds all myth and the theology that issues from the latter, the rational revelation: "If the unattainable feeds on my innards and the eternal builds its eternity out of me, then what still stands between the divine and me?" Hofmannsthal achieves his poetic goal of myth more clearly, more concisely, and more intensely here than in his poetry or his novels, and not because he chose a mythological landscape par excellence with this in mind—he achieves the very same effect elsewhere, for example with his fairy-tale description of Fez[11]—but rather because here the difference between landscape and mere scenery completely disappears and the human form is completely dissolved in the landscape, and the landscape in the human form, in their common identity a reduced reflection of that powerful unity which fills mythos when it fuses nature and man to the point of indistinguishability, anticipating the totality of culture, which is man's nature. A mere reduced mirror image, a mere preparatory stage of poetry, and yet—and this is just what the essay becomes with Hofmannsthal—the stage preparatory to mythos or rather to future mythos.

"Everything fictitious in which you participate as a living being is mythical. In myth every thing is borne by a double meaning that is its countermeaning: Death = Life, snakefight = love embrace. For that reason everything in myth is in equilibrium." These words appear in the *Book of Friends*, and they proclaim the constancy of the problematic which gave to Hofmannsthal's life and work an unswerving obstinate direction; his concern with the position of man in the cosmos and with the ethical equilibrium that must be established between ego and being in order that human life may attain some kind of cohesion was unswerving. Hofmannsthal's life (for all his Austrian flexibility) is consistently uniform, and his constant development is decisively so. The essayistic work itself testifies to this; not only does it reveal the cohesion of the symbol groups, which belong to, and themselves conversely make up, the constancy of the problematic; it also shows how they unfold with increasing freedom (hence avoiding all allegorism) and stylistically reflect the growth of the entire personality. As a twenty-three-year-old in 1896, Hofmannsthal wrote of a newly published work (a collection of prose sketches by Peter Altenberg) that the book is "somehow governed by mysterious powers, as the delicate magnet is governed by immense powers dwelling in the Unknown"; and in 1929, in an

141

essay—one of his last and most beautiful—dedicated to the Lessing bicentenary, he uses the same image again and speaks of his subject as "a swinging rod of steel fixed to a granite base: intellect."[12] And if he himself was less granite-like, less rational than the northern German, this statement is an assertion of his own self, confirming his own consistency just as the formulation of 1896 was anticipating it, yet revealing in the stylistic difference between the two statements the entire wealth of maturation of a lifespan that had elapsed between them.

# 4

## The Tower of Babel

It has frequently been remarked that the distinctive cultural phases of modern European history have always lasted for about three generations. The phase that counts specifically as the nineteenth century is no different, and lasted not from 1800 to 1900 but from approximately 1848 to the First World War, and hence corresponds casually to the Victorian-Edwardian reign in England and exactly with the sixty-eight-year reign of Franz Joseph I in Austria. It was to a great extent these long reigns that bound England and Austria so tenaciously to the nineteenth century. Yet whereas England, through the strength of her politico-economic and cultural persistence, upheld the Victorian tradition and is clearly capable of carrying it over evolutionistically into modern times, such persistence was lacking in Austria, especially in Vienna. The sense of decline that had enveloped the Habsburg monarchy for decades had allowed it to ignore death, and all the *mene-tekels* with which the spirit of the twentieth century had proclaimed itself went unheeded. No other place was as unequal to post–World War I modernity as was Vienna.

And Hofmannsthal the Austrian knew less than anyone else how to come to terms with the twentieth century.

### 1. *Fin de siècle, fin d'un millénaire*

At the end of the nineteenth century, from the old-German stylistic mish-mash—in part Renaissance-ish, in part Baroque-ish—a new Rococo developed, which distinguished itself from the genuine by its flattened and narrowed forms, yet which moreover soon assimilated non-Rococo forms and motives—especially the lily and the water lily. Neo-Rococo as such originated in the Parisian furniture shop, but the lilies and water lilies came from England, in particular from English arts and crafts, English book design and illustration, English bookbinding—all of these together influenced by the pre-Raphaelites but also by the Japanese. And whereas the original Louis XVI elements receded more and more into the background (most slowly in France, where they never fully disappeared), the new ornaments became more and more self-sufficient, stereotyped in an increasingly thin-line, expressionless, formal language—or, more precisely, formal idiom—which soon aspired to the honor of having its own title, *Jugendstil*, though basically it was nothing more than a trend and not a true style at all. Nonetheless, it was considered a style, and it reached its climax in Brussels and in Vienna, in Brussels under the aegis of Henri van de Velde, in Vienna under the artistic society of the "Secession," guided principally by the painters Klimt and Orlik and the painter-architect Olbrich,[1] alongside the ubiquitous Hermann Bahr.

No stylistic change in either art or craft, even one associated with a trend, can take hold unless it corresponds to a certain shift in lifestyle. It can truly be said that the bourgeoisie around the turn of the century, without growing disloyal to its hedonism, had lost some of its stodginess, solid ostentation, and compacted stuffiness. Wealth, now frequently in the hands of a second or third generation, had also—where it had not been diminished—become less rural, less binding, less prone to extravagance, in a way less dark; and the dark, carpet-covered splendor with which it had until now been surrounded no longer suited it. That dark splendor suited the new wealth just as little as it suited electric lighting, for which the old bronze gas lamps were being clumsily adapted. Yet it was no better suited to the new paintings that had become worthy of society and capital: not least because of their degree of darkness did the paintings of the romantic period possess a "weight of image" (*"Bildgewicht"*) that allowed them to stand up to the sullen opulence for which they had been painted. The depiction of light and air characteristic of impressionism, however, corresponded in some measure—in its degree of brightness and weight of image—to a Boucher, and was thus simply smothered by all that opulent ponderousness. In short, the fact that cabinetmaking and arts and crafts now reverted to Rococo constituted an eclectic gesture specific to the nineteenth century, which knew of no other way out; yet that fact had a shared origin that signaled modern times. (The painting that contributed to this trend, prematurely as always, attests to this.) The resulting *Jugendstil* was thus by no means as totally absurd and meaningless as it appears today. Although not sustained by a truly new lifestyle and hence a mere arts-and-crafts trend, never able to advance into architecture, and attested to by no edifice of later years, *Jugendstil* nevertheless gave expression to a definite sense of life that reigned in certain spheres of the bourgeoisie and its corresponding bohemia, and hence became—if indirectly—artistically legitimate.

In other words, the hedonistic aestheticism peculiar to the nineteenth century took a new turn, without losing its secondhand eclecticism. In this respect the relation between *Jugendstil* and impressionism is revealing. Faced with the "reality of the medium" that was the great accomplishment of impressionism, all decorativeness, even that of a vacuum, stood helpless, but the impressionistic side-effect of flowing and blurring, which dissolved image contours into little spots—this was comprehensible and adaptable. As an exponent of decorative tendencies, *Jugendstil* literally (i.e. materially) incorporated this "flowing quality," and what was for impressionism a side effect of the method here became coarse, material "water quality" or, if you like, "absinthe quality," decked out with the cheapest symbols of fluidity: water lilies and reeds, sea-anemones and lilies. Where excessive rationality renders the human spirit blind and helpless, able to see only the surfaces of things, its hand can become more deftly independent and even wiser, so that its products combine the meaningful with the meaningless and even become a sort of visual glossolalia. This is very similar to the case of *Jugendstil*, whose very domesticated and weak-voiced glossolalia presents itself to an extent as a "productive misconception," which enabled it to oppose the thoroughly antilinear painterly impressionism with a linear counterform suitable to arts and crafts. It was surely not of parallel significance, yet it was adequate to a new sense of life and for that reason—notwithstanding the empty importance of the vegetable-liquid ornaments—stood nearer to impressionistic painting than the previous ostentatious forms.

Yet this new mood—one might call it that of the buyers of impressionist paintings—encompassed two artistic tendencies, both of which became essentially far more significant than *Jugendstil* itself: so-called musical impressionism, and the new poetic symbolism, both distinguished by commanding names: the first by Debussy, the second by Maeterlinck.

Like *Jugendstil*, musical impressionism owes its origin (or rather its name) to a "productive misconception." Whereas true impressionism is concerned with a world of bodily forms, which are shaped through light and shadow from out of the atmosphere, music believes itself to be impressionistic because it seizes atmospheric moods and thus (like an impressionistic painting) achieves a reillumination of the total sound, unknown in the romantic period, whose degree of luminosity roughly corresponds to Rococo music. This difference of luminosity is revealed, for example, by a comparison with the music of Wagner, which, if only as the orchestral foundation of the onstage happenings and only rarely (perhaps in the *Magic*

*Fire* music) possessing symphonic independence, already contains in its "unending melody" the flowing quality of mood painting, but was too bound by the heavy ostentation of the time to overcome its tonal darkness. It's a long way from beer to absinthe. Yet in the same way, Wagner's music already reveals that the simple melodic line to which music is fundamentally reducible is far less capable than the drawn line (which still possesses the resource of interruption and omission) of expressing qualities of mood and haziness, that to achieve such qualities polyphony must be reenlisted (if not that of the big Wagnerian orchestra then at least that of the piano), and that to all this a rational, elucidating title must be affixed to help the bourgeois, in his absence of thought, to "think about something." In the absence of scenic, visual elucidation, a title must be employed: *Magic Fire, Ride of the Valkyries*, etc., or, in the case of Debussy, *La Mer, Nuages, Fêtes*, or, in the case of Delius, *Over the Hills and Far Away, In a Summer Garden*—in short a title symbolism of vaguely poeticizing, poeticizingly vague situations which, like the symbolic flora of the *Jugendstil*, immediately arouse an impression of blurring, flickering, and fluttering. Where such titles become necessary, the cognitive content of music is impoverished, just as a painting called "Morning Mood" usually expresses nothing painterly; for the musical breadth of expression infinitely surpasses simple qualities of mood. Despite the genius of Debussy, musical impressionism is much farther away from impressionism in painting than from *Jugendstil*, all the more so, it can be affirmed, for the fact that the music of the Debussy school is far less impressionistic than the music of any other school that simply forms its bodies of ideas (its cognitive bodies of ideas, not mere moods) out of its medium—which is precisely what it is—and therefore does what the method of impressionistic painting strives to do with the portrayed object. As productive as the "productive misconception" of musical impressionism was, it remains a misconception.

The case of the new literary symbolism was not much different. Here too, everything focused on "mood"; "moods" were what were symbolized. When blossoms fall, a maiden is reaching womanhood and will sleep on them with her partner; when the sharpening of a scythe resounds, death is not far away; when a bird takes wing, a heart flies away too. But in the end all poetry lives on symbol, and even that of the nineteenth century was not excepted. Wagner was the forerunner not only of musical impressionism but also of symbolism; his monumental symbols, testimonies of the highest theatrical genius, transformed his texts into poetic structures and set them in fundamental contrast to all other operatic romanticism. Conversely—a symbol being one of those instruments which according to dose and method of application can engender as well as cure a disease—naturalism would never have become the romanticizing poetry it did if it had not placed its photographism under the direction of symbols, naturalistic symbols (as for example Zola's work demonstrates). *Das Rheingold* is a monumental symbol for the greed that dominates existence and the gods; the perverse service of the ladylike Madame Renée[2] to the moneygrubber Saccard is a naturalistic symbol for the same; yet Maeterlinck's children of greedy realms eat cake ceaselessly and without hunger, ungrudgingly admired by the beggar children, and this fairy-tale fantasy land itself is here the symbolic mood symbol. For new symbolic combinations spring only from naturalistic inner and outer reality, whereas monumental as well as mood symbols make use of an established, almost allegoresque vocabulary: the first as mythos, the second as fairy tale. If Wagner was the mythos of the vacuum epoch, symbolism is its fairy tale.

That new *Gesamtkunstwerk* in which *Jugendstil*, musical impressionism, and neosymbolism flow into one another in the truest sense of the word stands in the same relation to Wagner: it is no longer grand opera; it is dance, pantomime, ballet. Precisely because they revolve mainly around mood symbols, one corresponding to primitive human feelings—love, gratitude, hate, greed, envy, boredom, etc., one (in its relatively limited scale) thoroughly tied to corporeal expression, yet creating for the third an established vocabulary (which finds nuance and becomes "personal" only in its intersections and fractures)—for these reasons the symbolic is predestined to be assimilated and represented by mutely gesticulating figures, ultimately marionettes. If Hofmannsthal thrust everything onto the stage and its operatic intensification, everything in Maeterlinck thrust itself toward mime, and contrary to the "scenic poetry" of Hofmannsthal's lyrics, Maeterlinck's is "mimic poetry." Its symbolic kernel is nearly always mimic gesture, if often, so to speak, an invisible psychic gesture, and the word—in Maeterlinck full of the most delicately floating nuances—is obliged to make the gesture visible and hence implicitly give direction to the possibilities of its corporeal expression. Practically every one of Maeterlinck's poems can be used as the text for a mimic expressive dance, whereas the theater pieces consistently demand musical support—it is no accident that *Pelléas et Mélisande* was twice set to music—and they come close, especially in the *Féeries*, to an inner relationship with mimic ballet, a relationship that would be unimaginable without impressionistic music.

After Isadora Duncan, a legion of expressive dancers appeared on the stage during the decade 1904–14, and appropriated the entire musical literature of three centuries in order to mold it into mimic lyrics and hence into symbolic *Gesamtkunstwerke* of the smallest dimension, in close relation and yet sharp opposition to their still naturalistic parallel incarnation, the *chanson*, to which Yvette Guilbert gave the last true expression. It is the relation and opposition between impressionism in painting and *Jugendstil*;

Guilbert could have used an impressionistic setting as a background, but none of the expressive dancers, Ruth St. Denis or any other, could have done so. This holds even truer for ballet. For the art of ballet is no creation of the *fin de siècle* and its symbolism, but was merely reawakened through these to its original symbolic tradition. Every folk-mythic element that the theater assimilated and preserved, every representation of gods, spirits, and devils down to the figures of the Harlequinade, all the symbolic forms in which the human world of feeling has for centuries, indeed for millennia, been embodied—all this had experienced its allegory-like fixation in ballet, especially in that of the Baroque, and the mimed emotional language of the dancer had become no less allegorically fixed. The fact that this tradition was most purely maintained in Russia can be traced to three factors: first to the Baroque-like character of the court, second to a sheerly primitive, naturalistic national gift for dance, and closely related to that, to the turn to folk tradition that Russian music had taken since Glinka and that was still formative for the early Stravinsky, hence for the *Firebird*. In the West, however, where the tradition had sunk into oblivion, and the ballet had value only as an operatic sideshow or (disregarding the admirable work of a Delibes) as entertainment for children and old fogeys, its renewed elevation to the level of "serious" music in Debussy's *Prélude à l'après-midi d'un faune*, that surprising product of symbolism, was a revelation of great promise and became all the more so when the work was performed by the Ballet Russe in 1910. The neosymbolism that remained Debussy's lifelong tone was clearly outworn, just as the essentially weaker *Jugendstil* (weaker because of its applicability to arts and crafts) was itself outworn, but the modern ballet was born, surpassing the importance of opera in its grasp of modern music, a sibling to modern painting, with which it would proceed hand in hand. Expressive dance, on the other hand, hardly ever got beyond the peak it reached at that time; it had been the fruit of a mood of the time, and despite the earnest and significant efforts of Mary Wigman and several others, it did not outlive it.

If the ballet tradition of St. Petersburg was revived by national folk music (transmitted, admittedly, by eminent composers), the Viennese ballet tradition was simply destroyed by the waltz, which is operetta and therefore neither folk art nor ballet. The waltz thus stood in the way of artistic expressive dance; in other words, it still allowed the *Biedermeierei* of the Wiesenthal sisters,[3] but nothing beyond that. The Viennese had no time for the symbolic, whether in dance or in literature, and they knew no more what to do with symbolic-impressionistic music than with impressionism in painting or literary naturalism. None of it was in keeping with the spirit of the old Burgtheater, and hence nothing like it took root in Vienna. But how then is it possible that something as thoroughly foreign to the Burgtheater as *Jugendstil* was nonetheless able to rise to such singular, one might almost say unbecoming heights? How is one to explain a Gustav Klimt, who in direct denial of his native Viennese tradition dedicated his supreme talent to a superaestheticizing, superethereal continuation of *Jugendstil*, with the goal of attaining the highest possible decorative effect through paintings crammed with symbolic platitudes? In the end, what fitted into the Viennese tradition was not this decorativeness—decoration is theater—but something beyond Klimt: it was a decorativeness which like *Jugendstil* had its origins in the rococoesque eclecticism of the *fin de siècle*, and this was what was truly sufficient for Vienna—the city of the Baroque. Nevertheless it was an un-Viennese experiment, hence one that was bound to fail in a specifically Viennese fashion. The failure did not result from the fact that the inadequacies of *Jugendstil*, not only in painting but far more in architecture, would cause its demise far more quickly than that of any other style; and it did not result from the sheer dialectical necessity of such a demise; it resulted from the irreconcilability of *Jugendstil* with the Viennese tradition. In painting, Klimt's student Egon Schiele (whose early death cut off a promising development) had left *Jugendstil* behind him, and the same occurred in architecture through the work of Otto Wagner, in his Postal Savings Bank and his metropolitan railway stations (the latter still containing ornamental iron reminiscences of *Jugendstil*), in the residential structures of Joseph Hoffmann (whose geometric patterns sought a new ornamental expression of the time), and in the controversial Michaelerplatz building of Adolph [sic] Loos (whose idea of the modern was the radically unornamented functional structure). Yet for all the correctness, wealth of ideas, and necessity of these endeavors, they remained, by comparison with parallel buildings being done outside Austria—those of Le Corbusier in Switzerland and France, Mies van der Rohe in Holland, Wright in America—almost provincial and inconsequential, condemned to an utterly tragic fate, because the city in which they arose no longer had any place for them. In a purely mystical way, this city was no longer architecturally renewable; what was newly erected in it no longer belonged to it.

In the face of all these phenomena, Hofmannsthal was a typical Viennese. His conservative spirit had little rapport with the modern architectural endeavors; least of all did he want to see them applied to Vienna. As was the case with the old emperor, every further alteration of the traditional city plan, against which the nineteenth century had sinned quite enough, went against his grain. His cool relation to the rest of modern art was no less Viennese. Or, rather, since his eye had grasped and retained an abundance of art which was painted, carved, written, played, and danced to an extent granted only to a few, he was only able to organize this immense mass of artistic phenomena when he considered them in their social context. He is

149

not only the man of the theater who sees the public as an inherent component of the drama; in the face of every other work of art too he is comparable to the historian, who perceives in every document of an epoch, whether artistic or nonartistic, the collective behavior of its corresponding humanity. Seldom does he have an immediate relation to an individual work of art; its value for him is rather as a component within the whole, a component of an epoch, a component of a cultural sphere that is elevated and sustained by his poetic and, as such, extraordinary cultural intuition, and is hence capable of increasing his own ambivalence, as its own "modern" identity itself becomes ambivalent in its rapport with art. (On this subject read the excerpt "The Statues" in *Moments in Greece*, or else, taken broadly, the "Speech in the House of an Art Collector.") Without diminution of perceptiveness, his organizational method of contextualization ["*Einbettung*"] fails, causing him discontent. Thus, for example, the far-reaching significance of the *Prélude à l'après-midi d'un faune* by no means eluded him; yet face to face with that significance, to which he felt duty-bound, he displaced it to a position where its relation to the public would be most unambiguous—to Nijinsky's theatrical execution of the work; here the method of setting things in context could be practiced. Toward this goal (despite Mallarmé, from whom the ballet text is borrowed), Rodin, Gerhart Hauptmann, Moritz Heimann, Horace, Winckelmann, Ingres, Titian, Anselm Feuerbach, Marées, and of course Goethe could be invoked;[4] Debussy, however, is firmly pushed aside: "Next to the stern inner strength of Nijinsky's short scene, Debussy's music seems to me to retreat, to become an element of accompaniment, a 'something' in the atmosphere, not the atmosphere itself."[5] In short, Hofmannsthal clings to a form of the dance which, for all its original ingenuity, is the product of a strict artistic tradition, one which had probably looked much the same in the eighteenth century (Lichtenberg's portrait of the actor Garrick is a sufficient reference).[6] What is new in the ballet, he leaves aside. This leaving aside of the new in favor of the traditional is typical of Hofmannsthal's reflective writings—he writes on D'Annunzio and Barrès but not on Mallarmé, not to mention Valéry, not to mention the neosymbolists; and as for modern painting, with which, as two or three essays reveal, he sought contact as a twenty-year-old, he has given it up completely. In the end, the new was not available to him because the epoch as a whole in which he lived did not form a whole for him and, consequently, not only was unavailable to him, together with all is contents, but represented the all-engulfing, danger-bearing vacuum. In this sense, Hofmannsthal's conservatism borders on the emperor's hatred of innovation. Was it the fear of death? No, it was rather the fear of the end of value, and it was Austrian.

Nevertheless, Hofmannsthal was a child of his time, and he himself produced the new that was appropriate to it. Those properties of the time that he did not absorb into his consciousness grew from within himself, and that was probably another reason why he could not take note of the other. None of the currents of the time left him untouched, and if literary historians describe him as a romantic, an impressionist, and a symbolist, they are all more or less right. This is most striking in his rapport with symbolism. A work as early as *The Tale of the 672d Night* probes into a symbolic realm whose reality would reveal itself to him more deeply with every year of his life. *The Woman Without a Shadow* forms the pinnacle of his voyage of discovery into the primal forest of symbols. But is this primal forest at all penetrable? Baudelaire's primal symbols foreshadow it; they are like screams breaking through into the world of man from the solid impenetrability of an unreachable, faraway jungle. Hofmannsthal enters the jungle, but proves that it is not that of the primal forest; no, it is a symbolic garden and nevertheless a primal garden, perhaps *the* primal garden. For the voyage to the symbolic occurs in dream, and not only are these dreams remarkably refined and even ceremonious; they are totally so—how could it be otherwise with Hofmannsthal?—when they make their appearance as dream within dream and even as a dream transposed to the stage. *The Woman Without a Shadow* was conceived in 1912 for the stage, for Richard Strauss's operatic stage, and commenting upon itself, so to speak, was first converted into a proto–fairy tale after 1914 (with the addition of the hell scene and the unborn children).[7] The poetry was recomposed; the dream within the dream, redreamed. And that is what is extraordinary in this work: although the symbols stem from every possible source, from Oriental as much as from Nordic tales, and although they are used with full knowledge of their mythological significance, that is, rationally and allegorically, the method of combination by which they are made to reflect, illuminate, and obscure each other is so rich (even in the libretto) that the rational is overcome and once again elevated into the magical (especially in the reconversion of the dream to fairy tale). None of the former, rationally applied, inherently symbolic banality is perceptible; and in the same way, side by side with such symbolic poeticism, the simple mood symbolism of the Maeterlinckian style becomes a little scenic gimmick, a poetic instrument of the most paltry structure.

Undoubtedly Hofmannsthal retained—no student first in his class could ever lose it—an uncommonly strong feeling of "I can do better," probably allied to the insecurity of being "singled out," so that he was constantly forced to prove himself through new accomplishments. Yet because his efforts were always successful, he also allowed himself the Viennese narcissism of "leaving aside" everything that failed to content him. And he reacted in just the same way to the symbolically grounded claim of the ballet to represent the new *Gesamtkunstwerk*. Not that he despised ballet—on the contrary, there are two ballet sketches dating from 1901, as well as the Russian-influenced *Josephslegende* of 1914, followed later still by *Achilles on Skyros*.[8] But without the word there was for him no total work of art, and, whether conscious or unconscious, his attempt in *Ariadne* to form an artistic totality by combining a spoken play par excellence (like all the Molière plays) and an opera was an experiment conducted against the new direction. It was just as much a denial of ballet as of the Wagnerian conception of the *Gesamtkunstwerk*, a denial of mood symbolism in the former, of monumental symbolism in the latter, against both of which is posited the symbolism of character and action, a dense allegorical web that is obliged to carry the action and to explan itself through the action. *Der Rosenkavalier*, that refined, elevated Da Ponte comedy, contains only hints of this symbol principle; in *The Woman Without a Shadow* it is conveyed to its utmost; in *The Egyptian Helen* [*Die ägyptische Helena*] it is simplified; and, finally, in *Arabella* it is carried to its perhaps most theatrically felicitous resolution through a very carefully thought-out revival of the Da Ponte tradition. While Hofmannsthal, along with Vienna, rejected everything in art referred to as *fin-de-siècle*, in these operas he presented the city with a farewell festival, in which a *fin d'un millénaire* was represented, for it came at the end of a thousand-year-old Austria.[9]

Yet, any two opposing currents, in art or anywhere else in intellectual history, reveal their common properties when seen retrospectively. If Hofmannsthal's Viennese symbolism coincided with the collapse of Austria, this was hardly an isolated occurrence: a world millennium had expired, and with it a millennium of Western art as well. And one might almost consider it a chance determination that, at its beginning and at its end, art grounded itself in symbol. Roman Christianity of the ninth century excited to stormy motion the value latency (it would not be right to call it value vacuum) of the pagan Germanic and Celtic peoples, and through the new religious existence and lifestyle of the Romanesque awoke in them a symbolic language of such wealth that the Irish monk with his parchments and the stonemason in the French and German cathedrals were hardly able to master and subdue the invading profusion of forms. The nineteenth century, however, which at its close was suddenly becoming aware of the value vacuum into which it had strayed, attempted to dominate that vacuum by inadequate and well-nigh ridiculous means. With a definite sense—at times even a knowledge—that every value system rests on a universally valid symbolic language, with which it is in fact identical, so that in a value vacuum (which is always silent) there can be no communication of language or values between one man and the next, came the intention to overcome this Babylonian condition by putting the cart before the horse and artifically contriving a symbolic language invested with universal validity. Tapped in this fashion, the source spewed absinthe, the absinthe of symbolism and *Jugendstil*.

## 2. *A la recherche des temps perdus*

That the principal contribution to the rise of the new music should have sprung from the city of *Der Rosenkavalier* was one of those pranks of destiny with which it from time to time establishes a sort of poetic justice. Clearly none of it had yet come to light in the decade between 1904 and 1914; Schönberg, the predestined innovator, was already prepared to create the theoretical foundation of his new mode of composition (not without the influence of the great theorist and fellow Viennese Heinrich Schenker), but the early works which he had already published, *Transfigured Night* and the *Gurrelieder*, remained under the romantic influence of Wagner and Hugo Wolf, in part under that of Debussy, and his no less significant pupil Alban Berg had just begun his novitiate. In the same way, Hindemith in Germany had not transcended his romantic beginnings, and Paris was still dominated by the Debussy tradition, upheld by Delius, Fauré, Duparc, Ravel— although the last-named had already detached himself from strict impressionism and was pointing to the rising generation, in particular to Honegger and Milhaud. Yet no matter what form it took, the new was preparing itself, and it was essentially more future-minded than anything Richard Strauss ever intended or created.

Even more future-minded, indeed furiously future-minded, was the course of the visual arts. For the hand that draws, in its unburdened unconsciousness, had forever been the first to lead the way to the future; in this it has surpassed both the thinking and the musical spirits. Even in those times when a value system, whether religious or dominated by a court, inhibited the freedom of movement of painting, there were always portentous breakthroughs—Rembrandt, for example; and when the shackles were broken in the nineteenth century, the impressionist revolution, pioneer of the future, a miracle of unconscious strength of expression, was already at hand. And with an even more vehement strength of unburdened unconsciousness, painting at the beginning of the twentieth century achieved a break with the millennium that had passed and became a harbinger of the new epoch, no matter how long this one might last. That this feel for the new, this affirmation of the new, this will to a new world-epoch was first proclaimed by seemingly mediocre painters in a seemingly mediocre document, the Futurist Manifesto of 1904, and the fact that the manifestants went on to become not good painters but good fascists, is relatively unimportant. (Even a futuristic manifesto can prescribe no artistic, but at most political, attitudes.) What is important is that, perhaps by accident, perhaps enticed by their will to the future, the young Picasso ranked among them, and that, already showing signs of the future antifascist, and not in one single painting having anything in common with the cheap rationalistic stunts of futurism, he soon set out on a course totally different from this pseudorevolutionism. Around 1906 he began to take seriously the overcoming of the nineteenth century initiated by Cézanne, and together with Braque and Léger he began the great experiment of cubism. It was a new vision of reality, but more, it was a segment of unexplored reality, conditioned almost mysteriously by the object as much as by the subject, by the concrete as much as by the abstract, and with one blow it presented the visual arts with completely new tasks. Could the painter still reproduce sensuous impressions? Those structural elements that he reproduced cubistically—were they not largely subjective schemas of apperception, so that artistic integrity would have had only these to fall back on, in order to become the expression of the painter's ego? Artistic expression had a colossal expansion of reality to master, and the process thereby initiated is still far from concluded. For it is precisely as an expansion of reality—how could it be otherwise?—that the new epoch came into the world.

Little or none of this was to be felt in literature. Or, more precisely stated, the avant-garde of painting has always been strong enough to draw, indeed to force, from artistic criticism and especially from the history of art so completely adequate and permanent a reception that, by comparison, the painting of the "salons" has been appropriately consigned to the shadows. Yet just the opposite is true of literature, where just those products which in quality and intention correspond to the painters' "salons" retain all the light and weight in the history of literature, and the avant-garde must be content with a subordinate position, even in subsequent recognition—Büchner, for example. It may seem harsh and even unjust to equate the great majority of literary production along with all its most significant works to the "salon," and even the reference to a good number of respectable paintings that hang there and that likewise should not be condemned with one stroke of the pen does not make the judgment milder; yet it just cannot be denied that the new world-reality that the avant-garde painters scented out was perceived by only a very few poets and writers—Strindberg and, despite the narrow format, one or another of the expressionist poets were among those few. In general, literature knew nothing of the new and wished to know nothing of it.

It is a well-known fact that the great innovators in painting have often come from proletarian and subbourgeois circles, whereas the majority of the great writers have been of bourgeois or higher-than-bourgeois descent. Yet that does not imply that the former were born social revolutionaries and the latter conservatives, but rather that the former, despite the unpropitiousness of their birth and upbringing, found their vocation by way of intractable artistry and were thereby hindered in their revolutionism—the essential revolutionary does not need the detour of art but turns immediately to politics; whereas the other group in opposition to its bourgeois milieu leaped down into the freedom of bohemian life (thus essentially with much more revolutionary, and therefore artistically less vehement, motives). It thus becomes clear that the revolutionism of the artistic avant-garde possesses a radicality which, contrary to Marxist supposition, contains no social or economic revolutionary purpose whatsoever, but rather strives without any such impulse toward the overthrow of a vision of reality, attacking and transforming it in its kernel, in human expression. The revolutionary situation at the turn of the century shows this quite clearly: on one side of the barricade stands the avant-garde of abstract painting, on the other, the "salon," in other words the highly perfected, yet formally conservative psychological-naturalistic novel, and the antagonism between the two, quite apart from the origins of the two groups of artists, cannot be interpreted as class-centered, all the less so since the abstract forms of the first kind of painting were utterly unsuited to the expression of social reality. If there existed a social-revolutionary line of demarcation, it was within the bounds of naturalism itself. For it is only in the naturalistic that the social can be represented, whether visually through caricaturistic overstatement (impressionism was already a hindrance here, since the content dissolved in the medium—as in the *Shooting of Emperor Maximilian*, for example), or in writing, where it can become art with a purpose [*Tendenzkunst*]. Daumier and after him Zola are only imaginable in the naturalistic. Governments that depend on propaganda (and that have in addition, like all governments, a predilection for kitsch) are likewise well aware of this: after abstract art in Russia was for some time erroneously acknowledged as proletarian on account of its radical revolutionism (and in part on account of the proletarian origins of its producers), it is now—only dogmatic idiots take this as a measure of Marxism—branded as "bourgeois," just as in Germany under Hitler it was considered "Jewish degeneracy."

Marxism as a practical politics is like all politics, or rather like all human activities, guided by views which are 90 percent false, oversimplified, or simply stupid; yet when it builds up a worldwide reputation, either despite or because of these qualities, one can always be optimistic enough to ascribe such success to an inherent kernel of justice. And it will be a long time before Marxism is allowed to acknowledge the fact that this kernel of justice is a metaphysical phenomenon that cannot be comprehended materialistically, and it will be just as long before anyone dares to realize that great art and proletarian art, or art representing class struggle, are by no means identical concepts. In production as in reception, art is a function of the class-free human soul, and that is revealed even in a phenomenon as secondary as the novel at the beginning of the twentieth century. If the social novels of Proust, James, or Thomas Mann are considered in the context of economics, so that these almost wistful, nostalgic, lovingly precise portrayals of bourgeois-aristocratic society still reflecting the flickering luster of the European crowns (the Victorian in the West, the Francisco-Josephinian in the East) are interpreted solely in terms of the need of the bourgeois public, which in its fear of the imminent social revolution still clung to existing, or subsisting, forms, and hence demanded the same from its writers (who by their mere production reentered the bourgeoisie)—only a half truth can be drawn, even though and because it sounds so plausible according to a Marxist scheme. In the short time between Zola and Proust, the bourgeoisie had by no means become so socially insecure that it should now suddenly require reassurance from a portrayer of society fundamentally much too complicated for it. Zola continued to be read despite his social intention (and so did the social escapades of Anatole France), and neither can it be protested that Proust, and with him James or Thomas Mann, stood in the grip of a particular social terror. Though no social fighters, they were nonetheless antibourgeois from the beginning, and they portrayed society with that precise, passionless, almost scientific irony which goes back to Flaubert and Stendhal, and which James sharpened further still through the comparison of European and American comportments, and none of them could ever have imagined that their occupation and its significance could be the slightest bit disturbed by a social revolution. For them the bourgeoisie was certainly the class of commerce and success, but it was that for the abstract painters too, and a change in the composition of the buying public or the potential diminution of their buying power made no difference to them, for no economic urgency, even one as great as those endured by Balzac and Dostoevsky, is capable of altering in any way the fundamental attitude of a true artist.

Why then the conspicuous difference between the avant-garde of painting and the writers' "salon"? What is it that blocks the writer from that unconditionality with which painting tracks down new world-realities and their expression? It is primarily language itself that forms the block. For unlike the painter, who can almost create his medium freely (especially since the decline of the conventions of a universally valid value system), and is thus even freer than the musician, the writer remains inseparably bound to language, the most conservative and most venerable, and even more the most rational medium of the human spirit. Through the medium of lan-

156

guage the irrational of simple experience is brought to rational and communicable expression, and is granted by the human spirit the status of knowledge. Every expression of the human spirit, in other words every work of art (no matter how "ornamental"), wants to "say" something, wants to express a "reality" (even if merely that of a "condition"); consequently every work of art is in a final sense a "rationalization of something irrational," and the fact that art always succeeds in raising irrational realities into the rational is the fact of its human miracle. The achievement of painting at the beginning of the twentieth century was the disclosure of a new symbolic language to a new reality, the consequent complete break with the now vacuous symbolic conventions of a millennium, and the introduction of a new epoch—what a difference from the impotence of symbolism. The language of words, however, is not capable of such radically new formations: its rationality is tightly structured and, physically speaking, has an endlessly smaller "degree of freedom" than the language of painting. Hence if the poet, as is his vocation, wants to create in it and from it new irrational realities, he can generally do so only through the unsaid, through the dynamic tension between the words, between the lines, whereas the conservatism of the language system as such allows only the sparsest innovations and decries as mannerism everything that goes beyond the addition or variation of nuance. How then is the writer who has truly grasped the new reality discovered by painting to achieve a break with a thousand-year-old—or indeed even older—convention of language? He can do so only if he renounces the entire petrified language system, if he abandons it and shatters it in its entirety. One man dared to do this, and that was Joyce.

Joyce's masterpiece, the double novel *Ulysses* and *Finnegans Wake*, is still and yet is no longer a novel: it stands between times. As a novel, following the fundamental task of every novel, it develops the totality of life; as a non-novel it uses this totality to probe into its newly inferred inner contours, and hence to feel its way to an intuited new vision of the world, in other words to the new idea of the human essence that stands in its midst. For into the double character of Bloom-Finnegan and its various offshoots like Stephen Dedalus, etc., went everything essential that ever constituted Western man through the long sequence of generations: the destruction by fate in pre-antiquity; Euphrosyne, whose equilibrium taught the Greek to affirm himself against fate and to acquire a feeling for himself as an individual; the mysticism of late antiquity, which let mankind become a limb of an all-encompassing holy community; the Reformation which, summoning man's individual soul anew, returned to him the right to enter into immediate union with God, while the preachers of the Counterreformation sought to restrain him, "skinbag full of phlegm," from such extreme presumption;

157

the bourgeois man of the Enlightenment, in whom everything has paled into romanticism, has paled to such an extent that he no longer has any knowledge of his origins, although he forever carries them with him in the image of himself, in his conception of his fellow beings, in his fundamental attitude toward the world, in his erotic fantasies, in his concepts of morality and beauty—because every phase flows into the next, and remains preserved, anticipating and coercing its return. All this and much more is contained in every moment of human life, in waking and in dreaming, and therefore language, which wishes to be informative of the course of human life, must make possible with every word a sense of such totality, all the more so when the circle closes but does not vanish, so that the course must be charted anew. But this is the present world-moment: man is once again crushed by destiny, he has once again arrived at the sorcery of the beginning, he is once again overcome by the emptiness of helpless extinction. And yet because of what has already been experienced, it is a higher destruction, a higher sorcery, a higher emptiness. This is the image of the new man, and he must be accepted as he is—yet to what moral and aesthetic values will he dedicate his life? What beauty, what love, what language, what poetry is still possible for him?

Clearly, man remains man, and not least because of that he is compelled forever to follow the same circular path; even in Joyce's work he remains the two-legged creature he is, with a nose in the middle of his face. In other words, certain conventions are given the security of reality in such a way that no part of them is amenable to change; even non-Euclidean space is observed from the point of view of Euclidean; $n$-valued logic is expressed with the help of two-valued logic, and the non-novel needs for its representation the basic form of the old-style novel. Nevertheless, the identities of these two-legged creatures wandering through this old-style novel are by no means unambiguous; they are in a perpetual state of form movement, in dreamlike form distortions, at one moment the "skinbag full of phlegm," at another the purest abstract spirit, hardly suggestible in concrete terms, and it is not hard to imagine that at times they carry both eyes in their profile—for in this vision and language everything is present at once. In short, the Joycean atmosphere can be described, and indeed explained, as an analogy to constructivist painting. The soulless, robotlike tube and sphere constructions to which cubism reduces the human form, in order to extract it from the surrounding space recesses and yet at the same time hide it within them, the psychic landscapes of early expressionism, in whose almost pantheistic jungle of color and line dream-ego and dream-space converge, the influence of African primitive art, which first came to the forefront at that time—all this together constitutes a harsh and unrelenting image of the insecurity in which man finds himself, an image of his destruction through fate, and of the exertions verging on the magical with which he confronts it. In contrast to Joyce, none of this was the artistic "purpose" of the painters, and it has absolutely nothing to do with the pictorial content as such. Rather, as true painters they let themselves be guided, as cubism makes clear, exclusively by the technical problems which had found no solution in impressionism and had grown more acute with postimpressionism (particularly in the work of Cézanne). And precisely because the problems and motives that inaugurated the movement were technical, its effect is uncanny, almost demonic; it is as if the technique of art and that of industry—although the word "technique" is about all they have in common—were of the same ruthless unconditionality and had in an identical manner transformed the image of man, so that nothing but his primitive, basic properties, nothing but his two-leggedness, is left; useless all knowledge of man, useless everything he may know about himself.

As little as the writer (the bourgeois writer) was frightened by the prospect of social revolution (or perhaps as little as he was frightened by it at the turn of the century), so much did he, and does he, fear that most profound revolution of the destruction of convention, the revolution of metaphysical unconditionality, which threatens to undermine his innermost existence and production. Clearly bourgeois inhibitions can also be pointed to here, inhibitions in the face of the unconditional, inhibitions generally unknown to the proletarian, even when he wishes, like an artist, to burden himself with no social revolutionary politics whatsoever. For the bourgeoisie, as it was forged in the nineteenth century, is simply unconditional in its Manchesterism; yet when one of its sons, repelled by his origins, turned to art, he brought to it all those private qualities which distinguished the bourgeoisie—conciliatoriness and worldliness, a breadth of education and the tolerance it entails, but of course at the same time the ineradicable reverence for the "beautiful" as well as the penchant for beautiful effect. Even Joyce reveals such bourgeois tendencies in the effects of sound, through whose beauty new symbols are rendered communicable and convincing; and even when the unconditional possesses its own beauty (not least in Joyce), as in the works of Picasso as opposed to the "bourgeois" works of Matisse, it is a beauty that one no longer dares to call beauty. To call a painting like *Guernica* beautiful is to abase human suffering; it is blasphemy against an all-destroying fate, a premonition of which was contained in the new painting of thirty years before. The place of the old aesthetic values, which one can calmly characterize as bourgeois, was taken by something totally different, something unconditional which no longer had anything to do with aesthetically intended beauty and the joy in it, or with human peace, and whoever could not endure such dehumanization was forced to recoil from the unconditionality of the new.

That a man of the sensibility of Proust should not have felt, should not have felt with anxiety, the extraordinary phenomena that were unfolding here (under his eyes, so to speak, in Paris) is hardly an acceptable hypothesis; indeed, one might almost maintain that such anxiety contributed to the aggravation of his illness and to his hermetic seclusion. In the case of Thomas Mann, his *Death in Venice*, which appeared in 1913, testifies to the fact that for all the hopes he placed on the propriety of the Prussian spirit, he had become conscious of the deep insecurity that had the world in its grip. And even Henry James, though nearly a generation older, was aware of Europe's brittle qualities, even if they appeared to him those of a dusty peep show which he observed with loving expertise, and even if he considered them insignificant—because he saw in America's democratic youthfulness a cosmic medicine which was always at hand for such evils, should they ever gain the upper hand. Of the three men, James thus had surely the weakest impulse, Proust probably the strongest, to approach the new with all its threats. But none of the three did so. Joyce at one time began to do so with *Ulysses* (which appeared after the war), and it would be idle to deliberate whether and how the others might have taken a similar route; they were prevented from doing so by a lack of unconditionality, a lack of artistic courage, a lack of profundity of vision. Yet these shortcomings were not only humanly justifiable (that is self-evident) but also artistically justifiable. For unlike the new painting, whose new symbolic language had attained group value, Joyce had most likely conceived a unique experiment. Although, having retained the form of the novel, he had created a hybrid structure, it could hardly be further radicalized; and if it could be radicalized, it would have to become still more subjective in the formation of language and symbol; it would have to flow into a subjective esoteric which no one would be able to resolve. Yet did not the painting of the time already show all the symptoms of such an esoteric? Art, if its radicality and integrity lead to it, certainly cannot evade the esoteric, but does this not mean that art has lost its social function and has become superfluous? Does it not indicate that modern man, the modern generation—a generation without art or with an obsolete art—will fall prey to all the cruelties of dehumanization? Something of these premonitions rises from the last two volumes of the *Recherche*, but the apprehension is never expressed, and the new art is not mentioned. It is as if everything that arouses fear were expressly deleted, as if there were a fear of fear, for if fear had proved itself to be well founded, what sense would there have been in one's own labor?

And it was not mere labor, but slave labor. For the great novelists after the turn of the century, there was no path open that would lead to "natural" narrative as it still appeared in Balzac and the Russians and, to an extent, still in Zola, though no longer in Stendhal. The novel, in its basic conception—think of folk narrative—was a naturalistic structure and had its finest hour in its convergence with nineteenth-century naturalism; at that point, in other words, it developed to a fully conscious art form, the extremely conscious Flaubertian art form, yet seemed thereby to have exhausted its possibilities; and in order to preserve its artistic value, its artistic right to exist, Flaubert's artistic doggedness was forced to be continuously, and downright manically, exaggerated. What in the case of Flaubert was a surprising and even somewhat ridiculous exception now became the rule; the production of a novel became a neurotic cramp which lasted for years, a perfectionism, so to speak, of the totality, in other words an almost mystical effort of faith for the sake of a linguistic structure of expression, which through the precision and economy of its means of representation, through the most precise choice of words, through the most precise architectonic of content and form, through a precise symbolism of psychology and even of sound, strives to achieve the total picture of life prescribed by the novel. In short, Flaubert called to life the "intensive novel," as it might well be called, and Joyce pursued this intensity principle to its extreme (not least because he sought to overcome naturalism through such overradicalization of the naturalistic means); yet even if one leaves aside this one-time experiment, the principle had in this way won a sweeping universal value, to the point where even a narrator as "naturalistic" as Joseph Conrad could not elude it. Thomas Wolfe was the first to break with the intensity principle and to replace it with what appears to be a Balzacian "extensive novel," which strives to achieve totality simply through an immense wealth of content, or rather through a conglomeration of content, yet does so with such radicality (in its own way no less unique than that of Joyce) that the ensuing work of art is measurable not always as a work of art but always as a titanic achievement of labor.

Wherever an especially favorable constellation helps an art form to find its definitive embodiment, it becomes popular art as well as stylistic art. This was the lot of the novel in the naturalistic period of the nineteenth century. After the turn of the century it managed still to maintain its artistic character; yet (apart from the Joycean experiment), since it did not free itself from its naturalistic romanticizing and psychologizing origins, it had to compensate for these by a completely hypertrophied artistic exertion, and even where it succeeded, even where it thereby elevated itself to a near-esoteric level, in comparison with the avant-gardism of painting its art remained the art of the "salon." On the other hand, where this hyper-trophied artistic will is not mustered, the esoteric is no doubt avoided, but the popular product to which the novel is thereby reduced is not that of the former folktale but, like all former folk art, has instead become an industrial product, at best an almost abstract commodity (destined for railway station bookstands), at worst, sheer kitsch. And in film, in its basic structure and attachment to the naturalistic so thoroughly akin to the novel, this state of affairs is repeated. The popular work of art of the twentieth century is a mass commodity of industrial character. And that is repeated in the theater, above all in the form of modern operetta, except that for the sake of its effectiveness onstage modern operetta must retain a specific theatrical element. The theater is never exclusively naturalistic, not even when, in the form of popular comedy—Aristophanes as opposed to Sophocles—it plays off its naturalism against the high style of tragedy; and tragedy in turn (even if it is that of Aeschylus and thus still organized around the purely typical and structural properties of human and godly existence) remains untouched—or it would not be theater. Directed at the people, the theater remains exoterically understandable, not least because it contains for its own part an indelible naturalistic element, namely the presence of the actor, whose human form and voice no mask or cothurnus can totally depersonify. In the theater, which—quite miraculously—has for millennia and through all stylistic change preserved its apparently definitive form, the gap between popular and artistic products is far more organic, in short far more self-evident than in the novel, and for that very reason the playwright has always been spared the hypertrophic cramp with which the early twentieth-century novel was forced to affirm its artistic character—hopelessly, one suspects. The theater may one day, perhaps through film, become just as socially superfluous as the novel already appears to be; until it disappears, however, it will always retain an artistic uninhibitedness that the novel has definitively lost.

Yet is there really no way for the novel to participate in this artistic uninhibitedness of the theater? In his "Imaginary Conversation,"[10] Hofmannsthal has Balzac prove that no fictitious figure, least of all one of Balzac's, is suitable for the stage, because the novel's lot is to show an entire compass of life, with all its ambiguities, all its gradations and blurrings, none of which contain any polar oppositions but where one thing is at the same time another and everything is overshadowed by the phenomenon of predestined existence and events. On the stage, however, catastrophe takes the place of destiny, "catastrophe as symphonic structure," and toward that very end the characters must be contrapuntally simplified and narrowed. But if the transcription of the novel for the stage is impossible (think of how most such experiments in dramatization have miscarried), the reverse route is still open: the narrator cannot forget that his representation and his language are nothing but the prologue or epilogue constantly woven into plays, that he belongs with them among the supernumeraries, and that he must himself be something of an actor, for otherwise there would be no life to his narration. That sounds like modesty, since it brings the novelist down from his esoteric heights and from the significance that he had grown accustomed to arrogate to himself from those heights, and places him on an equal level with imposters and tellers of fairy tales (a problem that has haunted Thomas Mann all his life). On the other hand, the reference back to the histrionic and the theatrical contains a greater and simply unreasonable demand, for it requires that the dream, from which theatrical poetry is woven, be reaccepted, redreamed, in order that the dream within the dream (as it is always present in Hofmannsthal) may be extended to a new dream, in which out of simple narrative (or, if you like, out of the literary), poetry can be recreated, but in which the novel can regain its poetic unselfconsciousness. There are no explicit statements by Hofmannsthal about this; yet not only can a good number of his sayings be interpreted in this sense, and not only is his theatrically oriented fundamental poetic attitude in harmony with it; but he has offered corroboration through deed, a corroboration of the highest perfection, in the form of *The Woman Without a Shadow*, which he created totally in the style of an Oriental storyteller, alongside and from the opera libretto.

Clearly, Hofmannsthal's "scenic epic," as it would be described parallel to his "scenic lyrics," is no more rigid a schema than the latter. On the contrary, his narrative is a continuous process of experimentation, confronting every possible style and mode of expression in order to explore in them the possibilities of new and unique ones. The curve begins in an Oriental style with *The 672d Night* (1894) and *The Golden Apple* and ends with *The Woman Without a Shadow* (1919); in between, a high point of more immediate and hence still more dreamlike representation is reached with the *Tale of the Cavalry* (1898), reminiscent of Kleist; in *Bassompierre* (1900) the dreamlike—in direct imitation of Goethe—undergoes a new modification so that at the same time as the fragment *The Veiled Woman*, which was intended—at least in mood—to be a transposition of the *Falun* play into epic, it could stand side by side with the dreamlike state of the theater.[11] This was the case too with *Lucidor* (1910), which for all its comic structure or precisely because it was thoroughly construed as a source for a textbook, works in sum as an anticipation of surrealistic dream technique. Yet already in 1911 Hofmannsthal had begun work on *Andreas*, that unselfcontained epic masterpiece (the *Contarin* story was its rough draft) in which he tries to unite all the epic means of representation he had achieved, so that by means of such unity he might assemble into the life totality of the novel all the motifs that moved him—the dreamlike and the comic, that of destiny and that of sheer mechanical existence, the Austrian and the cosmopolitan, the Oriental and the Occidental—all in a single setting: the Venetian. With good reason, the novel *Andreas* is subtitled *The United*, for it concerns the unification of all partial visions (even if always symbolized by the union of

163

lovers); and if *The Woman Without a Shadow* through its immediate connection with the stage also achieves an allegoric complexity that *Andreas* lacks and even avoids, it is *Andreas* which, precisely through its reverse dissolution of allegory into symbol, becomes the paradigmatic work of the Hofmannsthalian "scenic epic."

Just as in *The Woman Without a Shadow*, here too everything is called into being in continuous reflections; everything mirrors the mirror and is hence yet another mirror. "Thus his withdrawal becomes lovely, as one who walks into a mirror to be united with his brother":[12] this sentence could have served as the book's epigraph. For it is something quite different if a novelist (more or less autobiographically) simply identifies himself with one of his figures, or if, like Hofmannsthal, he moves among his figures as their creator in order once again to mirror and, to an extent, to make visible as the vision of his vision what he sees on this stage, indeed the manner in which he sees himself there. An extraordinarily subtle splitting of identities is necessary for this, for example the relationship between "Sacramozo and Andreas: the one gradually taking the place of the other," and, more particularly, the relationship between Andreas and the Maltese Knight, who sees in all men "an equal and an opposite" and hence in the end "understands no one," yet for that very reason "feels all the more how Andreas's feeling, intuition, and knowledge are expanding," so that Andreas becomes for him like the *lucerna* or lamp of life, "an alabaster ball, in which through movement and light the blood of a distant and absent one indicates how he fares, bubbles or darkly smolders in misfortune, is extinguished or explodes the vessel in death."[13] Thus in the end is love attained, thus are the unions attained, thus does Hofmannsthal himself come forward from the endless mirror refractions of his work (and it is almost gruesome to think that, the vessel of his existence having exploded, he died two days after the death of his son), magically interreflecting the fortunes of all essences, the living as well as the dead as well as the unborn, and even the fortunes of things. Nothing is isolated, all things are dependent on one another, and hence there is no immediate, "natural" representation: "The natural is the projection of impalpable life onto a very arbitrarily chosen social plain. The maximum of our cosmically moved, time- and space-encompassed human nature cannot be captured through simple naturalness."[14] And it is here that Hofmannsthal's "scenic epic" finds legitimation, as does the "chain of observers," through which he attempts to grasp the essential, as do words like "beautiful" and "pretty" and "ugly," which he employs toward the portrayal of an event, a man, a region—words that would be impermissible in an immediate portrayal because they assume a previous transposition of representation; in short, they are words uttered by spectators upon leaving the theater. Yet here they are allowed. An atmosphere of cool, glassy indirectness is established here—it is the transparent atmosphere of Venice, city of glass and mirrors, and at the same time it is footlights that have been transcended; even the trusted Austrian landscape is submerged in this light, removed to the ends of mediacy, graspable with one's hands yet unreachable, for it is now merely a reflected symbol.

It is somewhat surprising to determine that this complicated method of split characters and opposing symbol reflections possesses certain similarities with the Joycean method; indeed that both symbol methods have a common point of departure—the most radical organization of the Flaubertian "intensity principle"; and, moreover, that both strive, with an extraordinary expense of erudition, toward a common goal—the overcoming of the pedestrian social novel. Of course the differences leap much faster to the eye. Disregarding the fact that *Ulysses* and *Finnegans Wake* despite all their difficulties achieved a monumental self-containment, and that *Andreas*—although Hofmannsthal worked on it even longer—was not completed, apparently because he could not overcome his methodological difficulties, these difficulties lay not least in the indirectness of method, which on top of everything else conceals complexity and feigns a beautiful simplicity. Joyce, however, everywhere of unsparing directness, wants in no way to flatter the reader with simplicity but, just as unsparingly, calmly lays every possible complication before him. Such a thing would have been unthinkable for Hofmannsthal, just as the rationality of the Joycean method would have repelled him; he no doubt took pains to create new forms but could never, not even with the technique of indirectness, totally free himself from poetic tradition. This is what annuls his relation to Joyce, whose pessimistic sense of the future he did not share, and brings him close to the past-obsessed mentality of Proust, so far does he surpass the former in poetic (certainly not in psychological) richness. "A la recherche du temps perdu" was also his fundamental attitude to life, but if in addition to this similarity certain external analogous elements played a role—a closeness of age, high bourgeois extraction, Jewish influence, aestheticism from the parental home, excessive sensibility, fascination with "society," indeed even the plain confusion of society with culture, all of which were significantly absent in Joyce, who was about ten years younger—and if the Viennese milieu contributed no small amount, since with its very concretely grounded, perpetual sense of decline it found itself from the first more than any other major city, above all Paris, within the "temps perdus," the example of Hofmannsthal plainly shows that the fear of the future, which stirred him as it did Proust, can only to the slightest extent be viewed as a social and class fear. The dread of the coming dehumanization, the dread of the coming silence of humanity—the "Letter of Lord Chandos" must again be adduced—the dread of human suffering that proclaimed itself everywhere, this precompassion lay deep within Hofmannsthal and made him more poetic than Joyce, who knew nothing of compassion.

"To be happy without hope," as he says in the speech "Fear":[15] for the sake of this illusion they all, Hofmannsthal first and foremost, clung to the past and created an epic in which yesterday remains a hope for tomorrow, yet because of that persists in its own happiness. They were novels of the present, and even Hofmannsthal's *Andreas* is a novel of the present and not a "historical novel" (which sees "once upon a time" through the eyes of "today"), for like the others, like Proust and James and Thomas Mann, Hofmannsthal wanted to hold on to the being and mood of his young years. Yet that means holding on to Austria, and Austria, inasmuch as it still existed, was Baroque and pre-1848, was still that way, practically unchanged and always as if for the last time. And every year of its continued existence was like a miracle. As miraculous as these prolongations of existence were, Austria's present did not consist in them but embraced a hundred years. Venice, as it took leave of its greatness, had its Guardi and its Canaletto, and the *Andreas* should have become the same for Austria when Hofmannsthal chose to set it in the Austrian Venice of the first half of the century in order to show Austria as a whole, as what it was: the happy country without hope.

Clearly a Pissarro[16] could always stand in as the Canaletto of *fin-de-siècle* Paris, and much of what he initiated is to be found in the "salons" of today; a cubist Canaletto, however, is simply unimaginable. And thus it is only right and natural that those—Hofmannsthal included—who with their novels of the present, which, whether darkly or lightly toned in their writing style, always represented the "salon," held on to their time like Guardi and Canaletto, remained totally unaffected by the new painting, and indeed were forced to reject it.

### 3. Ethical Art

The greatest achievements of painting in the year 1910 were strictly avant-gardist and deeply antinaturalistic; the greatest achievements of the novel in 1910 were conservative and fundamentally naturalistic, indeed belonging to the "salon"; the first explored without hesitation the symbols of the new world-epoch, the second was terrified of them and of their threatening dehumanization: but whether avant-garde or of the salon, they had something in common; they were both pure *l'art pour l'art*.

It was another matter in those instances where the fine arts were incapable of adopting the antinaturalism of the new painting—whether they did not want to or could not. They did not want to in cases where the artist's social temperament resisted the abstract and where he felt compelled to engage actively in the portrayal of human circumstances through his own means of expression. With the growth of journalism, political and social caricature had gained in dimension, and beyond that there existed a social graphics, which in the tradition of Goya led to masterpieces like the drawings of Käthe Kollwitz. Yet there were also neighboring spheres of fine art which could not reconcile themselves to abstraction because of material difficulties. For example, as long as the chief problem of cubism consisted of the two-dimensional representation of space through its own basic forms (cubes, balls, cones), this task, although or because in the end it was "sculpturoid," was not easily transferable to the three-dimensionality of sculpture. For the abstract painter (and especially for the strictly expressionistic one) the object-bearing image counts as a sort of song setting, in contrast to which painting must be raised to the autonomy of absolute music, and the visual symbolization of the three-dimensional through the two-dimensional eases this purpose for him. Yet when the same is demanded of sculpture, which is also concerned, independently of what it represents (its song text), with combinations of simple spatial forms and with equilibrium, in which they are related both to one another and to the total surrounding space, it becomes clear that the aspiration to an absolute spatial music by means of emphasizing and isolating those abstract sculptural elements remains essentially within the naturalistic. In other words, it becomes clear that the forms of nature can indeed be simplified into cubes and balls or lines, and that by rendering these forms independent a possibly even greater variety of combinations may emerge than that found in nature; yet the three-dimensional is still represented by the three-dimensional, so that the overcoming of naturalism and especially the move toward specific non-naturalism in music appears a difficult task. In 1910 such attempts were still far away. Sculpture was what it had always been, more or less stylized naturalism; it had its impressionist influences—Rodin above all— and its *Jugendstil* influences (for which modern dance shared partial responsibility), and from here on a new "earnestness" was searched for. It was found, in accordance with naturalism, in the social, and from it sprang the heroicized workmen and miners of Meunier.

The theater reached an analogous position by an opposite route. Although a predominantly non-naturalistic art, the stage nevertheless inherently contains far too many naturalistic elements ever to become a fully abstract theater. On the other hand, since the eighteenth century it was no longer appropriate to reserve the naturalistic exclusively for popular comedy and clown scenes; it went against social feeling to populate the scenes of the "noble" theater exclusively with kings and noblemen. Hence with the rise of the English middle class, bourgeois comedy emerged from naturalistic popular comedy, in significant proximity to the bourgeois novel. But the theater could not undergo this same development; it needed conflict and tragedy and partiality and could do nothing with a naturalism that culminated in Flaubert's cool scientificality. From the eighteenth century on, bourgeois tragedy was continually modified, and time and again—even in Schiller's *Kabale und Liebe*—the comic and novelistic situations of the bourgeois shone through, patheticized to an unwarranted tragic height and hence prone to parody. This is true even of Ibsen, of whom Hofmannsthal commented with every justification, "What prevented Ibsen from making comedies out of his material was a Nordic-Protestant stiffness and misanthropy."[17] In other words, the burgher is a figure unsuited for tragedy because he is socially bound and consequently can never entirely rise to the level of human destiny as such. The kings of Greek theater, but those of Shakespeare and Racine too, are identical with their destinies: the Greek kings because they live in a sphere in which god and man are indistinguishable and thus both indistinguishably destiny-bound, destiny-possessed, destiny-subjugated; the Shakespearean kings because their characters for all their human qualities exist not for a single moment outside the royal office and bearing which they represent; Racine's kings because they operate in a system of elevated abstractness of a positively Platonic character, and this tightly structured system, though lacking in the unambiguous depth of the Greek system, grants admittance to no secondary motive. None of this can be fathomed from a naturalistic point of view, and no naturalistic character—not even Goethe's Götz or Egmont (if possibly Iphigenie)—reaches that level. For the naturalistic totality of human comprehension rests in the physical, or it would not be naturalistic; and only where destiny seizes upon this physical totality can it once again become tragic. Ibsen's conflicts would to a great extent dissolve into nothing if his characters had to worry about feeding themselves; in this sense his plays are prone to parody. No parody is possible as soon as basic economic worries are put on the stage: the entities of destiny and of the afflicted individual are once again united; and that occurred in plays like Hauptmann's *The Weavers* and Gorki's *A Night's Lodging*. Theatrical naturalism originated in the representation of wretches and after a long detour returned to them, now turned tragic. Alongside the old popular comedy we now have the "poor people play," the new popular tragedy, surely with no narrower an artistic claim.

In this respect the social-ethical capabilities of naturalism introduced a relatively new theme into the art of the nineteenth century. It was not a structural or stylistic novelty but simply a thematic one, nevertheless crucial for the development of the arts. It is connected not least to the (more or less hidden) cognitive tasks of the work of art. For however the symbolic systems of the individual arts may be constituted, they will always express "something," most often a field of objects and events of the external world, but in any case either supplementary to this field or in the case of so-called "objectlessness," autonomously the *n*-dimensional inner objectiveness which can be asserted as the (in the end probably logical) total structure of the human spirit. Structures in which the human spirit sees its own totality reflected, and which in this manner convey to it a piece of self-knowledge, it places under the rubic of art. And this is most clearly manifest in the phenomenon of music, which, in turn, resonates in this very way within the structure of every work of art. All art "develops"; all art is driven forward to new forms by its immanent logic, which is identical to that of the human spirit; all art thus uncovers step by step the inexhaustibility of the human spirit and its transformations, and it is precisely in music that such relentlessness becomes visible, since, even with the finality of a Bach, music could not stand still. According to all traditional conventions, every work of art must renew the entire art, not only because (contrary to the scientific process) the artistic act—or it would not be one—must repeatedly seize upon being in its entirety, as if it were something never seen before, but also because there would be no distinguishable works of art whatever, if each one did not uncover, in the totality which it is, a new reality of being. The fact that there are styles, that they present themselves precisely in the decorative arts, that the Egyptian pyramid (perhaps the closest rapprochement of architecture to sculpture), the Greek temple, the cathedrals of the East as well as the West—that they all reproduce an entirely specific aspect of the human spirit and its structure through the balancing out of the simplest spatial forms, thus through the basic principles of what is today intended by abstract spatial music—testifies to the drive to the "new," yet also to a bond of the three-dimensional symbol to the very cores of material objects, in this case to those of purposes, namely the housing of the god's/king's body, of the godly image, and of the invisible God. (Were abstract spatial music, attempts at which are only now being made, truly to develop to contrapuntal wealth, it might grow to a symbol of a new religious mentality for mankind, a symbol of the radically abstract, radically unhousable God.) No doubt, the social-revolutionary contribution that naturalism made to such development was, relatively speaking, quite small; all the same, it certainly existed.

Naturalistic social art greatly overestimated its achievements—how could it have been otherwise? Above all it fancied itself of immeasurable ethical superiority to *l'art pour l'art*, and was constantly inclined to consider the latter mere kitsch, mannerist in the avant-garde, philistine and reactionary in the social novel, upbraiding this last in addition for providing social appeasement—a goal external to *l'art pour l'art* and one that has for that

169

matter yet to be reached. It does apply to bad *art pour l'art*, but then it is really *l'art pour l'effet*, in short kitsch, which generates pseudonovelty with no new insight into reality, or else does not concern itself at all with the new and produces its effects with more or less academic eclecticism. The same applies of course to bad art with a purpose: notwithstanding the social shudders he wants to inflict upon the bourgeois, and to which the bourgeois is just as impervious as he is to social appeasement, when a Meunier heroicizes miners and workmen into supermen, the result is simply a drive toward an extraartistic effect, of no higher value than a patriotic monument; hence for all its sculptural expertise, it is ultimately kitsch. No amount of social good will can surmount this. Clearly the medieval artist created his holy images within the Christian value system, and the socialist artist is still allowed to seek his themes in the revolutionary, but the moment he takes his brush in hand, there are no more ethical prescriptions for him but only the ethos of art as such, which is that of *l'art pour l'art*. In other words, the artistic value system at any one moment is so radically autonomous that even its own condition of yesterday appears unauthoritative, to say nothing of its ability to accept dogmatic regulations from other value systems. Every one of these foreign systems demands an "effect"—yesterday's system (the academic) a "beautiful" effect, the social system a "revolutionary" effect, or perhaps one of "ethically high value"—whereas for the ethos of genuine art (with the exception of the theatrical arts), it is precisely with effect that sin begins. Only because Van Eyck wanted to deliver a "good" piece of work—in this sense just like every God-fearing craftsman—did his painting turn out to be beautiful and pious painting, and only because Käthe Kollwitz's children of misery sought to prove no social doctrine, yet were therefore master-portraits, were they able to stir the social conscience. Nevertheless, where the ethical incentive is supplanted by the aesthetic, the inevitable result is kitsch. And no social art can surmount this, even if it must be conceded that the social novel is still in more danger of kitsch— Proust of course knew how to escape that danger.

Kitsch is the confusion of the ethical with the aesthetic, and therein lies its relation to the radically evil. Every value system must produce—from dialectical foundations—its countersystem or, rather, its imitative system, in which the infinite value goal—God in religion, truth in science, beauty in art—is reduced to the finite and the earthly and is hence made "value-less": this is the essence of the Antichrist. The ethical attitude with which a man is charged within the framework of these systems and which he must manifest through the "good works" of action, thought, and creation, is an immediate function of the infinite value goal, and for that very reason its earthly residue acquires an aesthetic effect, an aesthetic value—this is particularly visible in artistic creation. If, on the other hand, infinite systems are made finite through imitation, the relevant value goal is likewise pushed back into the finite and the earthly: God becomes an idol, truth dogma, beauty effect; an infinite system becomes a closed one. The imitative system that emerges from art is that of kitsch, and kitsch, accordingly, is not bad art but anti-art, and hence simply occupies the place of evil vis-à-vis the primal system. When the West dissolved the Christian system and knew of no other with which to replace it, the dominion of imitation systems began, and with them began the dominion of "evil." And since the state of the human spirit always expresses itself in its art or non-art, the nineteenth century became that of kitsch par excellence, the century of bourgeois aestheticization and its eclecticism. However insignificant the phenomenon of kitsch may appear, the coming dehumanization of the world first proclaimed itself—mystically speaking—from within it. So was it perceived, as a presentiment, at least by the artists. Of course the artist, then as ever, was solely concerned with his art, indifferent as ever to humanity and its approaching [condition], almost cruelly indifferent, yet since he began to sense the evil inherent in kitsch, he was likewise compelled to sense the coming dehumanized world condition, one that would allow the definitive victory of kitsch. Whether the artist now strove, as he did with the social novel, to flee from such a premonition, or whether he went on, like the avant-garde painters, courageously to master the new symbols summoned by that premonition, both reflected the demand (intensified by *l'art pour l'art*) of kitsch-threatened art, the demand that wished to force a retreat of "evil" (the only way it knew how to fight it) through the "good deed" placed alongside it. What was fought out here on the narrow battlefield of art with specifically artistic weapons was, in the face of the overwhelming events that were to ensue, infinitely insignificant, and was nevertheless an earnest, if as yet unconscious resistance of the humane against the radically evil and its goal of dehumanization.

Under the weight of his premonitions of the future, the artist was bound also to sense the insignificance and ineffectiveness of his efforts. What was the use of placing art alongside kitsch when a time of total artistic blindness was threatening to close in, or had already closed in? What was the use of examples of "good deeds" and, for that matter, art? Had not the artist because of his premonitions been truly appointed a prophet and a seer, forced to address the blind and the deaf, in order to rouse them into action? The life tradition was demolished, and what had remained of it had lost its inner cohesion, was yesterday's form, which had stumbled into today as dogma and cliché, as an empty emotional attitude, in short as kitsch itself; was it not incumbent upon the artist to build the new tradition and once again to invest life with form and its appropriate order? And was this not the single path by which poetry could extend beyond its false domain back into reality and hence into the ethical? This is just what Hofmannsthal expressed in the *Little Theater of the World (Das kleine Welttheater)*:

| | |
|---|---|
| This glow[18] will not hold out for long now, | *Nicht mehr für lange hält dieser Schein,*[18] |
| Already the voices are multiplying, | *Es mehren sich schon die Stimmen,* |
| Which call me to the outside, | *Die mich nach aussen rufen,* |
| . . . I am sent | *. . . ich bin hergeschickt* |
| To put in order, mine is an office | *Zu ordnen, meines ist ein Amt,* |
| Whose name is above all names. | *Des Namen über alle Namen ist.* |
| Yet already the poets | *Es haben aber die Dichter schon* |
| And the builders of royal palaces | *Und die Erbauer der königlichen Paläste* |
| Have sensed something of the ordering of things . . . | *Etwas geahnt vom Ordnen der Dinge . . .* |
| But what are palaces and the poems: | *Was aber sind Paläste und die Gedichte:* |
| Dreamlike likeness of the real! | *Traumhaftes Abbild der Wirklichen!* |
| No web ensnares the real: | *Das Wirkliche fängt kein Gewebe ein:* |
| To lead the *entire* dance, | *Den ganzen Reigen anzuführen,* |
| The real, do you comprehend this office? | *Den wirklichen, begreift ihr dieses Amt?* |

These are the closing verses of the short play, but which of the characters utters them? They are not placed in the mouth of the "Poet," who as the Prologue is the first to enter, but rather into that of the "Madman," implying that the poet, after he has crossed the bridge, must himself be transformed into him. The sequence of Hofmannsthal's "ethical" pieces begins with *Death and the Fool* (1893), in which the purely aesthetic is first condemned, and the meaning of the aestheticized individual, in other words the poet, is that he is "nothing to anyone and no one is anything to him." And it is precisely this motif that is taken up in the *Little Theater of the World* (1897), but why must this turn to the ethical, indeed to the political, now be suddenly expressed by a "madman"? Is the poet only capable of a disposition of madness? A contradiction looms here, all the more conspicuous for the fact that this wish for an establishment of order was not intended for the Apollonian nature of the poet but expressly for the Dionysian—and yet therein already lies the solution of the antinomy as well. There are no Apollonian "premonitions," there are only Dionysian ones, and everything that evolves from them, even in the form of "the establishment of order," is Dionysian identification with the world, with its being and nonbeing, is self-dissolution of man in the material of the world so that the world may be constantly created anew. The leap into life that the poet would dare must be dared as the leap into death; it is the leap from the bridge, was intended as such, yet is inhibited already at its start by the "Doctor" and the "Servant," for both are (like the "Madman") splits in the poetic essence, the one as the principle of the moral intuition, by whose strength the poet recognizes his fellow man with compassion and yields to him, the other, however, as the truly Apollonian, the "healing" principle, to which of course death, the final healer, is likewise no stranger. Of course the ill-intentioned may imagine this to be an unnecessary mythological complication of a self-evident set of circumstances—poets like shoemakers can stick to their last—yet, it is astounding how accurately, indeed how prophetically this twenty-three-year-old knew of the problem of spiritual leadership by the poet—hardly a current one in that seemingly secure period, and how accurately he had already sketched out his own lifelong position toward this: to be a seer, to be able to develop without a guide.

A few years later the problem had become completely current, even for the poets, though it was not their madness that had conjured it up. Throughout Europe the political was becoming more and more intractable; consequently it resembled madness more and more, of course without really being mad, and culminated in the ever more threatening Franco-German schism. The French political tradition, which despite a high-strung facade had always been directed with a sober *bon sens*, continued to be handled appropriately in spite of every concern, and just as appropriate was the metapolitics with which Charles Péguy, perhaps the most vehement poet-thinker of the time, appeared on the scene and, historically penetrating spirit and trained socialist that he was, recalled humanity to concrete Christianity, even to a militant Christianity, so that it might master the moral chaos into whose grip the West was about to fall. Not so in Germany, with its hectic, politically alienated historical development. The dominant mood here was not one of concrete concern but of eschatology, and meta-politics was forced to generate a meta-metapolitics, void of concrete content, in short, a longing for redemption. "The present spiritual confusion contains elements of every German folly since the sixteenth century," wrote Hofmannsthal,[19] and he may well have had in mind Wagner's primitive-mysticizing redeemer posture or—probably to a lesser extent—Stefan George, although the latter had donned the prophet's cloak with far greater aplomb and moreover with that consciousness of rank to which the German poetic vocation, forever overestimated and self-overestimating, had felt duty-bound since Goethe. Whether in poetry, whether in direct address to his apostles, whether in his personal manner of life, conceived and stylized as a model and focused on the lofty, George represented the ethical leader who is obliged to confer on being and above all on German being new

173

discipline and morality. George was far too much his own man to have summoned Wagner to his cause, all the more so as the effect aesthetics of the man of theater must have run deeply counter to his high sensibility; yet he had no more in common with the anti-Wagnerian Nietzsche, whose hatred for rabble philistinism he shared, because his monumentally inclined one-track thinking could find no rapport with the iridescent, leaping thought of Nietzsche. But the redeemer fantasy that dominated them both, and beyond that its aesthetic foundation, ties them both to Wagner. For aestheticism generates superheroism, and if they shunned the Germanomaniac pathos of Wagner and were too far removed from superheroism to offer it to an opera public for its identification and indulgent self-heroification, but wanted on the contrary to have this rabble-public flogged and its philistine spirit broken, so that (to ensure a lasting flogging) a new noble and human elite might arise (equipped with unmistakably German traits), they saw but a single means for such a purifying action—the "purifying steel-bath of war"; already in 1913 George could sing, "Ten thousand must be snatched up by the holy scourge, ten thousand by the holy war," without noticing that, with such brutality, in content as well as in form, which would even have been an emetic as a revolutionary chant, he had arrived in the realm of the gravest political crime. No such words are to be found in Péguy: only where political thought was supplanted by a godless but, for that reason, mystically aestheticizing eschatology, could such a perversion of ethical concepts gain ground.

It had been resolved to redeem the world from evil, and evil had been promoted. The vulgarization that George sensed everywhere and that Nietzsche had already encountered a generation earlier (although at that time in its infancy) was a specifically German phenomenon of decline. In no other country, with the exception of North America, had industrialization and urbanization been initiated so explosively as in Germany, yet whereas in America these phenomena were so to speak *ab ovo* and therefore autonomous—and so assessable neither as good nor as bad and fundamental to the construction of society and tradition—in Germany the masses of shopkeepers that had sprung up so suddenly threw overboard, unthinkingly, a great, profoundly internal cultural tradition. The new German Reich became the most American country on the continent, yet without the American advantages: a country void of individuality yet without democracy, a country of proletarization without revolution; and it was against the philistine who brought this about, against his vulgar commercialization, against his dissipated thought and action, against his sham philosophizing and mercenary production of art (including that of Wagner), but not against the proletarian, who hardly ever caught their eye and was therefore little more than an abstract concept to them, that Nietzsche and George directed their wrath. Yet they forgot what Wagner never forgot: exclusive as they may have been, and little as they wished to be understood by this nation of shopkeepers, their public was recruited from their ranks; and, furthermore, this very kitsch-devoted nation of shopkeepers, not the proletariat, which had its own prejudice and its own kitsch, was, in the contented discontent of its existence, greedy for redemption and full of heroicizing notions, and over its unflinching competence as well as over its exalted merchant spirit (markedly different from the oily-fingered moneygrubbing of other nations), there hovered the kitsch of holiness, in whose name the Wilhelminian nation was constantly ready to set out, whether toward a Nibelung-like world conquest or a Nibelung-like self-immolation in the blaze of the holy flame. At home in bombast, no one felt hurt by the hatred of the philistines; on the contrary, every word of war could and had to have an effect here, had to swell to the most frightful distortion. Not for nothing were Nietzsche as well as George constantly pursued by the image of the Antichrist. They felt that he carried on his terrifying essence through their aestheticism, that he had led them, though cunningly hidden (a cunning of which Wagner had no idea), to a pseudohumanity, an imitative humanity, and hence they too should not have allowed themselves to be surprised that despite the hatred of the philistine, despite the flight from the philistine, despite lonely death, they were in the end (for that matter like Wagner) made into the saints of the now savage rabble, into the saints of the unsaintly par excellence. This is the effect of the imitative system: instead of becoming holy teachers of humanity in accord with their redemption fantasies, they became teachers of dehumanization; they had become able to "lead the *entire* dance," and it was the dance of apocalyptic ruin.

The apocalyptic hovered over the entire world, most hectically over Germany, most gently in the actual center of decline, Austria; for the center of a typhoon is always governed by the vacuum and its stillness. If tension and anxiety were everywhere else, here no one was anxious, for a sense of decline had in any case dominated for a hundred years, and if elsewhere people sought after new means of breaching the threat of ruin, here they were content with the means of conservatism and conservation, because it no longer paid to start new experiments—it was only worth delaying the unavoidable end. And if elsewhere poets were becoming prophets pointing to the future, people knew very little about them here (even if they were called Péguy or George), though they did know that the doings of poets were condemned to eventual failure. The Austrian poet could no longer legitimately appeal to "the outside," and, when that did occur, he had to content himself with the role of counselor and guardian of the status quo, a warning voice who had to confirm the evidence that the mature—only from the mature did Austria together with the Austrian people derive its power to

175

exist—was good and ought to remain good. This role of the poet, the role of guardian, is already sketched out in the *Little Theater of the World*:

| | |
|---|---|
| I wore the crown and the power of the world | *Ich trug den Stirnreif und Gewalt der Welt* |
| And had a hundred noble titles, | *und hatte hundert der erlauchten Namen,* |
| Now my possessions are a basket of bast, | *Nun is ein Korb von Bast mein Eigentum,* |
| A vintner's knife and flower seeds. | *Ein Winzermesser und die Blumensamen.* |
| When from my golden house I saw | *Wenn ich aus meinem goldnen Haus ersah* |
| The flowers being watered, evening and morning, | *Das Blumengiessen abends und am Morgen,* |
| I absorbed the scent of earth and water | *Sog ich den Duft von Erd und Wasser ein* |
| And said: Great consolation lies hidden here. | *Und sprach: Hierin liegt grosser Trost verborgen.* |

Thus speaks the "Gardener," pantheistically equal to the "Madman," yet, turned away from death, a maintainer of life, domesticated to life in the noblest sense of the word and hence free of madness. It is in this sense that *Everyman* is to be understood, which fifteen years later continued the "ethical poetry" begun with the *Little Theater of the World*. Whereas in the intervening Greek plays, *Elektra* and *Oedipus*, tragic guilt is a function of the ancient inexorable fate that has made man into a super- and subhuman double essence, sinful in one half, atoning in the other, yet never reaching a unity which will master fate, in the Christian *Everyman*, that remarkably Austrian restoration of the English *Everyman* of 1490, baptism assures the unity of the human soul from the very beginning. Consquently guilt is no longer thrust upon man by fate but is "freely earned," the guilt of ill-will and of a "fall," which—despite many a good deed or work—drags eternal damnation in its wake, unless the grace of faith is once again earned by the deepest remorse and repentance. That is the simple content of the "play of a rich man" to whom repentance and hence grace come in the lonely hour of his death, so that his few "good works" reemerge and are able to speak for him, and the devil is the loser. At the same time it is the simple, modest profession of the faith of the poet, who appears not as the individual figure of the *Little Theater of the World* but is, rather, personified in the "rich" Everyman. Once again he raises the question of whether his "good works," his good works of art, suffice to assure his salvation; and just like Everyman he is directed to grace, so that the command directed to the "madman" is transformed from an "external" to an "internal" command, the command of God, which alone saves man and artist from madness. As death approaches, Everyman has found the way back to his Christian youth. This was the "great consolation" that should have fallen to the Austrian people in its state's hour of death. But this death proved so full of terror, was so war-bloodied and so apocalyptic, that the earnest-humorous death consolation of *Everyman* was trivial in the face of it, and the World Theater theme had to be taken up again; it became the *Salzburg Great Theater of the World*,[20] a conjuring up of the spirit of Calderón, in the hope that a collapsed Austria and a collapsed world might regain an ethical bearing from its Christianity.

This was the intention of the mystery plays. In reality they were transformed into Reinhardtian spectacles. And even if public success by no means always allows the inference that a work may be kitsch, if on the contrary the public is much more engaged, more primordial, more secure in its judgment in the theater than elsewhere, so that the mystical law of separation of chaff from wheat, of genuine art from sham production applies more readily here than elsewhere, it is nevertheless not to be denied that the one-time theatrical success of the Calderón *Original Ministerias*, achieved with a public of a Christian faith as strong as the poet's, is considerably different from the theatrical victories to which Reinhardt led the Hofmannsthal conversion plays. It was all handled as if the medieval relation to the public could be restored, instead of conceding that what was at hand was a costume play in which, for fun, the public too was dressed in medieval costumes. (Even a transposition of the *Everyman* to the Austrian peasant theater—as it was undertaken with every care by the actor Franz Löser[21]—has the effect of natural honey produced from artificial honey.) And that is the discrepancy. For this is the same public that was despised as rabble by Nietzsche and George and never even noticed it, the same public that could delight in Hauptmann and Gorki's dramas of misery, without its own social conscience being shaken, and the same that could sympathize with the avant-garde painters as easily as with the social novel. It was not aesthetic judgment that this public had lost but ethical judgment, and because no ethical standpoint had any validity for them, they could adopt whichever one they liked, even that of kitsch. In such a state of promiscuity of thought and feeling, in which everything converges and grows hazy, there is no readiness to receive any absolute value. George's aesthetically founded dictate of absolutism inevitably had to tumble into the perverse, and the Christian absolutism in which Hofmannsthal took refuge, after he had recognized the inadequacy of the purely aesthetic sphere, strayed into blasphemy, in other words turned instantly into costume as soon as it was brought to the public as a work of art; and, although this was far less dangerous than George's sin, it was no less sinful.

Such sinfulness is hardly to be found in the ethical art of naturalism. Meunier's figures of workmen were certainly illicit patheticizations, but they neither provided so immediate a foundation for mass murder as the teachings of George, nor were they the occasion for the near-blasphemous displays of philistine rabble as the Hofmannsthal mystery plays were in their Reinhardtian get-up. In short, they did not transgress so immediately against the absolute. And even less was this the case—independent of their social effectiveness or ineffectiveness—with the social-revolutionary art of Zola, Hauptmann, Käthe Kollwitz. In other words it was a morally militant art that wanted to admonish, to educate, and to change, yet appealed to no absolute position because it knew that its artistic and ethical validity was to be found uniquely in the most acute adherence to objects, and that the absolute eluded any sort of naturalistic approximation. Yet how can one venture near an admonition, an education, a process of change, without also possessing the legitimation of an absolute, fundamental position? Was it not this lack that robbed social art of its effectiveness? On the other hand the miscarriage of the aspirations to absoluteness of the sort held by George and Hofmannsthal reveals that only where the absolute's message of grace has already been heard can it be proclaimed also by art; and since the philistine rabble, unlike medieval man, is deaf to such a message of grace, the whole of ethical art seems to collapse under an antinomy and turn into mere chimera. It is almost as if George had guaranteed this bankruptcy when with the aim of purifying the world he demanded the massacre of ten thousand; for when man sets his face against spiritual methods, he is left with only physical methods to force his salvation. The heretic who will not be persuaded must be burned, and for the sake of the conversion of Saxony, Charlemagne executed ten thousand as well. For the sake of admonishment, education, and change, then, it is not necessary to strive unconditionally for the absolute; it is sufficient, especially when there is no alternate course of action, to intensify the naturalistic to a physical power. That sounds paradoxical; yet it explains the appropriateness of naturalism to the social assertion of will: because of its paucity of symbolism—it is always the symbol of the first degree, never symbol of the symbol—it is the most closely related to the "deed"; in its symbolic nature it is sheer "deed in itself," and in a sense that also relieves ethical art of its suspected antinomy.

A deed that would admonish, educate, and change, and thereby meets resistance, physically clears it away; for this purpose the law has equipped itself with the executioner's ax and the prison (the symbolic executioner's ax). The spiritual equivalent of the executioner's ax is mockery (represented by the pillory in medieval justice), the last, so to speak, intellectual means of discussion between two adversaries who because of the total difference of their systems of thought are able neither to persuade nor to refute each

178

other; at the same time mockery is the first symbol of their reciprocal will to destruction. Nevertheless, for all the differences between the two hostile systems of thought, they must possess a certain conformity of language—since otherwise they could not establish their essential divergence, and it is here that mockery strikes root, above all in the imitation of the adversary. And here we are reminded how closely related mockery is to physical attack, for although the physical qualities of the adversary are most often made into the object of imitation as well, it is laughter, physical laughter—that argument almost as powerful as physical blows—with which imitation strives to achieve its intended debasement, especially when in accordance with the essence of laughter it accumulates supporters to its cause in the form of physical witnesses who laugh along. The better mockery imitates, the more exactly it reveals the adversary's physical ugliness, the more documentary the fashion in which it registers its adversary's evil deeds, the more it takes the words out of its adversary's mouth and reproduces them, demonstrating that they are inadequate in themselves and hence spring—consciously or unconsciously—from untruthfulness, all the greater will be the laughter, all the more destructive the effect of the mockery. Amid every kind of subjective attack, mockery is, where it "hits," an objective process, one that achieves its own logical absoluteness when it has revealed the adversary's inner contradictions, thus establishing and condemning his untruthfulness. This alone is the absolute content of mockery, but by the same token it is the process of imitation, forever on the border of physical spheres and hence crassly naturalistic, which, with the intended total destruction of the object of mockery (its symbolic death) as much as with the resulting absolute self-elevation of the mocker becomes a physical mirror of absoluteness. Whatever other instances of absoluteness may be added—for example God, to whose glory medieval art (in a significantly naturalistic manner) mocks the powers of the devil, or a natural law (a godly one at that) in whose name legislation punishes the "convicted" transgressor and delivers him to his shame—all of this is, under the visual angle of mockery, exclusively supplementary legitimation to its strictly naturalistic process, with which it has autonomously produced its claim to absoluteness, its "naturalistic absoluteness."

And this is precisely the absoluteness of satire, which is present in everything that can be called ethical art but is immediately destroyed when the supplementary legitimation of other absolute authorities win the upper hand—the aesthetic, for example, in the case of George, the Christian in the case of Hofmannsthal. Satire is ethical art par excellence. The ethical will to admonish, educate, and change is always aggressive, in other words it is always directed against "evil," always follows the schema of legislation that since the Ten Commandments has been based predominantly on the negation of evil through a "Thou shalt not," and hence seeks to destroy evil, in order that the good can unfold. Even *l'art pour l'art* as an ethical phenomenon originated as a reaction to the evil that had spread rampant in the kitsch of the nineteenth century. But insofar as satire is restricted exclusively to an ethical mission, in other words is not out to force the retreat of "bad works" through its own "good works" but rather—with every right—demands first off their immediate destruction, it develops (all the more so as it can support itself on the naturally naturalistic autonomy and absoluteness of its mockery) into the art of radical attack on everything untruthful, into an art of totality, in contrast to which all the political satire that ever existed with its mockery-with-a-purpose tied to determined empirical standpoints is nothing but a craft. Under the aegis of the visual man's relative freedom of viewpoint, such absolute satire—Goya and Daumier have always to be cited here—is sooner and more often found in drawing than in literature. Swift, Lichtenberg, Lessing, to a lesser extent Voltaire, who was tied to the standpoint of his near-dogmatic anticlericalism, can be counted as the inaugurators of the new absolute satire that may have been predestined to become the central art of the twentieth century. For unlike banal art, the new satire neither conceals the apocalyptic nature of modern existence, nor, like the great majority of ethical artistic endeavors, simply complains without commentary, but, rather, displays in the most immediate way the generating facts of evil and teaches mankind that in their infernal ridiculousness those facts can be cleared away. The removal of evil: that is a beginning which despite the sobriety of satire can well be compared with the beginning of the Old Testament prophets; had it succeeded, indeed had it succeeded even in part, this new ethical art par excellence would have contributed to clearing the way toward a new religious attitude for mankind.

Absolute satire made its first full appearance, necessarily, where the European value vacuum had reached its maximum—in Austria. Karl Kraus grew up in Vienna, a contemporary of Hofmannsthal, and it was in Vienna, or rather against Vienna, that for thirty-five years he executed his satirical work with restless aggressiveness. Thus he was often taken for a local satirist, but what he achieved was absolute satire of universal validity, the prophetic image of world apocalypse, revealed in the Austrian "defects." For even if one had wanted to sanction this specifically Austrian corruption as one of the makeshift apparatuses with which the old monarchy (looked on even by Kraus with a certain malevolent tenderness) held on to life, these were means that had a particularly Austrian quality yet were symptomatic of the epoch and consequently indicated not only the end of Austria but, beyond that, the end of the entire epoch. It was no longer the brittleness of Austria that was at stake, but the brittleness of the world, in which lurked the coming ruin, the coming human sorrow, and this brittleness was contingent on the untruthfulness in which the European—not only the Austrian—philistine riffraff was vegetating. It was an unending net of untruths, an unending predicament of kitsch, incomprehensible as a whole because it consisted of a grid of seemingly isolated, thoroughly insignificant kitsch attitudes and kitsch actions, yet requiring comprehension on the grounds of the pregnant nature of its evil. Kraus took it upon himself to undo this grid of evil, joint by joint, insignificance by insignificance, ridiculousness by ridiculousness, and thereby to identify the evil. He recognized that kitsch extended far beyond the domains of art and of craft, that the untruth and evil inherent in kitsch was evident in all domains of life, in social conventions as well as in vocational structures, in the administration of justice as well as in so-called political persuasions—kitsch, a universally contaminating infection of phraseology, its home the daily press, since it is here that all this non-life is mirrored and at the same time replenished through its phrases. Hence, visible in the daily press, indeed identical to it, the insignificances of the grid of evil must be bundled into satire and "made articulate," and this was just the method of the destruction mockery—never before practiced—that became Kraus's absolute satire. The more he mastered his skill, the sparser his commentaries on the facts became; it was more and more sufficient to let countless little newspaper extracts have their effect simply through characterizing titles and through the architectonic of their juxtaposition, producing a worldwide total picture, in whose ghastly comedy the full horror of the epoch begins to speak with its own words. With this unassailable, sheer photographic naturalism, which exhibits the universal by means of an individual case and proves it to be a universal, Kraus, even in his great satirical essays, held on tightly to ethicality, to justice, and to literature. General ethical prescriptions, especially those that operate with "holy" and "greed," he took to be just as dehumanizing as the ethical delinquencies they battled, and with this intolerance he hit everyone who, like George, imagined himself to be of good will, or, like Hofmannsthal, actually was. Only consummate art is art, only consummate ethics are ethics, and every blank spot, in one or the other, produces kitsch. And in this respect the antipolitical (truly not apolitical) nature of Kraus's absolute satire becomes political, the single valid metapolitics: standing up for those human beings liberated into humanity, appearing against their dehumanization, debasement, and vulgarization, this lie-destroying, phrase-destroying politics had one sole aim—that of plain decency.

Did absolute satire succeed in bringing humanity closer to this goal? Did it succeed in performing a portion of its intended work of removal and diminishing the global effectiveness of evil? Of course one could, might, and should just as well ask for the degree of ethical improvement that the biblical prophets strove for with the Jews, for the answerability of such a question belongs to the essence of a material philosophy of history. Whether it is a religious philosophy and with Augustine interprets history as an increasing concretization of the City of God, or whether it is the pseudoreligious that is to be reached—as in the Marxist classless society (for whose Soviet orthodox church neither Kraus nor, for that matter, the old prophets count as saints, although they were without doubt holy champions of classlessness), or whether one accepts a metareligious historical process that carries humanity to ever higher, ever more valid, ever freer of dogma, yet never definitively final forms of religion—these theories of history, despite their striving for correct logical foundations, are nevertheless in the end one and all doctrines of salvation, and the judgments that can be won from them are apodictic merely in prospect; restrospectively they are quite fickle. The notion can readily be defended that, in the process of de-idolization and de-dogmatization of religious forms, the human breed is increasingly humanized, but that it is (for dialectical reasons) a process that progresses in distinct phases, and in pauses between phases; that is, at the point where one religious value center is dissolved to make room for the next, dehumanization inevitably occurs. Accordingly, if "ethical progress" existed—and ultimately it comes down to this—it would accordingly be of no matter that the prophets had preached mostly to deaf ears, and that, protected by the unending grid of evil, the poor-souled figures that Kraus honored with his destructive mockery were able—as he incidentally foresaw—to pursue their desires unharmed to the peaceful end of their days. The persistence of evil does not negate the good; only seldom can a moving locomotive be stopped by a piece of paper, and war, just like Hitler, was not negation but confirmatory proof of absolute satire. Immediate success is indifferent; what is at stake is ethical progress in its entirety, and that is served by every ethical deed.

This is a mystical perception. And therefore some objection is in order. Did the world in the heyday of Catholicism actually behave more ethically than the polytheistic world in its Athenian heyday? What guarantees that after so deep a reversion to barbarism as the present one there can be any kind of ethical-religious resurgence? And even if it did occur, even if ethical progress were to resume, would not that resumption stem far more from the immense need that brought humanity back to prayer than from long-forgotten individual ethical efforts? All this could be so, and the ethical deed must come to terms with it. And for that very reason, at least for those who carry it out, thrown back on their own resources, it grows into a sort of ethical *art pour l'art*, mystically commanded for the sake of its own ethical content and the *Gloria Dei* (as was clearly the case with Kraus and his language mysticism). Moreover, this relation to artistic *art pour l'art* becomes all the more *éclatant* as the artistic character of absolute satire stands beyond all shadow of doubt; it is ethical art par excellence. Nevertheless, it would be a conceptual confusion and a short-circuiting were one to expect from such a relationship that because of the nonexistence of "artistic progress"—because art contains only further development but no progress to any "higher" plane—ethical progress is also impossible. On the contrary, its mystical possibility and even probability is in itself unassailably at hand and remains so through every good deed—even when it must be practiced for its own sake—as an ever-present secret hope.

Because it is that way, the reverse conclusion may be drawn: artistic *art pour l'art* is at the same time always ethical *art pour l'art*, so that the development of art (not its nonexistent progress) at the same time serves ethical progress and participates in the mystical hope that it may exist and ultimately overcome global disaster. Without this secret faith, the "internal" ethics of art, its demand for an absolute union with reality and its antipathy to every "purpose," of whatever nature or however socially-ethically appealing, cannot be explained. And this creates an uncanny conjunction between the unconditional naturalism of absolute satire and the unconditional antinaturalism of avant-garde painting: that of their common unconditional "faith" in the ethical and hence in the godliness of the humane.

# NOTES

## Translator's Introduction

1. This episode persuaded me to add the subtitle "The European Imagination, 1860–1920," in the interest of giving a clue as to what the book is really about to an English-speaking readership not immediately aware of or interested in Hugo von Hofmannsthal. The Broch citation is from a letter to Daniel Brody, 19 October 1948, no. 501 in *Hermann Broch–Daniel Brody Briefwechsel, 1930–1951*, ed. Bertold Hack and Marietta Kleiss (Frankfurt am Main: Buchhändler Vereinigung, 1971). All translations from German sources, unless otherwise indicated, are my own.

2. *Broch-Brody Briefwechsel*, no. 489.

3. Quoted in Ernestine Schlant, *Hermann Broch* (Boston: Twayne Publishers, 1978), pp. 149–50. The availability of this very fine monograph on Broch was one of the factors that dissuaded me from providing a biographical summary or summary of Broch's entire work in this introduction.

4. *Broch-Brody Briefwechsel*, no. 490. In this letter Broch suggested that the title of the Hofmannsthal study be "Little Intellectual History of the Vacuum (*Kleine Geistesgeschichte des Vakuums*)." Brody responded (no. 500): "Now you've got to choose a good title, since 'Little Intellectual History of the Vacuum' would be very suitable to a vacuum cleaner advertisement, for which the Hoover corporation would surely pay ten thousand dollars."

5. Ibid., no. 498.

6. *Briefe III*, ed. Paul Michael Lützeler (Frankfurt am Main: Suhrkamp, 1981), letter of 6 January 1951, pp. 518–19. This letter was written in English. Whenever possible, all Broch citations will be from the Suhrkamp edition of the complete works, edited by Lützeler (see bibliography).

7. *Hugo von Hofmannsthal: Selected Prose*, trans. Mary Hottinger and Tania & James Stern (New York: Bollingen Foundation, 1952).

8. Hermann Friedrich Broch de Rothermann, in a recent conversation, has corroborated this assumption.

9. "Ein Gedanke, ein Moment, ein Satz." Although this principle is stated in Untermeyer's translator's note, it was written by Broch himself (as was most of the note). See the text of the note and Paul Michael Lützeler's explanation in his edition of *Der Tod des Vergil*, pp. 473–77.

10. "Kultur 1908–1909," in *Philosophische Schriften I*, pp. 11–31.

11. Quoted in Paul Michael Lützeler, *Hermann Broch—Ethik und Politik: Studien zum Frühwerk und zur Romantrilogie "Die Schlafwandler"* (Munich: Winkler Verlag, 1973), pp. 16ff.

12. Karl Kraus, *Die Fackel*, nos. 261/262, p. 1.

13. "Kultur 1908," pp. 11–12. Broch's understanding and use of the term "rationalism" are highly idiosyncratic. "Rationalism" here means for Broch what is usually referred to as its opposite, namely, empiricism, or the thought process gained through experience. See below, note 2 to chapter 1, for an explanation of a slightly different use of the term.

14. See Lützeler, *Hermann Broch*, p. 18.

15. "Kultur 1909," p. 29.

16. "Kultur 1908," p. 21.

17. Ibid., p. 23.

18. Adolf Loos, "Ornament und Verbrechen" (1908), in *Trotzdem* (Innsbruck: Brenner Verlag, 1931) [Vienna: Georg Prachner, 1982]. A third work on a similar theme to appear in 1908 was Wilhelm Worringer's *Abstraktion und Einfühlung* (*Abstraction and Empathy, A Contribution to a Psychology of Style*, trans. Michael Bullock, N.Y.: International Universities Press, 1953.) For a discussion that compares all three, see Mark Bernheim's article "Style: Abstraction and Empathy in Hermann Broch's *Die Schlafwandler*," *Modern Austrian Literature* 13 (1980): 59ff.

19. "Ornamente (Der Fall Loos)," in *Philosophische Schriften I*, pp. 32–33.

20. "Notizen zu einer systematischen Ästhetik," in *Schriften zur Literatur II*, p. 22.

21. Ibid., p. 26.

22. Nietzsche, "David Strauss: Der Bekenner und der Schriftsteller," in Nietzsche, *Werke*, ed. Karl Schlechta (Munich: Hanser Verlag, 1969), 1:140.

23. Quoted in Schlant, *Hermann Broch*, p. 20.

24. Lützeler, *Hermann Broch*, pp. 35ff.

25. "Ethik: Unter Hinweis auf H. St. Chamberlains Buch *Immanuel Kant* (1914)," in *Philosophische Schriften I*, pp. 245–46. (See Chamberlain, *Immanuel Kant: A Study in Comparison with Goethe, Leonardo da Vinci, Bruno, Plato, and Descartes*, trans. Lord Redesdale, [London: John Lane, 1914].) Broch also accuses Nietzsche of having misunderstood Kant. His judgment prefigures the similar accusation Heidegger later leveled against Schopenhauer and Nietzsche for their treatment of Kant's doctrine of the beautiful in the *Critique of Judgment*. See Heidegger, *Nietzsche*, trans. D. F. Krell, vol. 1 (New York: Harper and Row, 1979), pp. 107ff. For a discussion of the Kant-Schopenhauer controversy in fin-de-siècle Vienna, see Allan Janik and Stephen Toulmin, *Wittgenstein's Vienna* (New York: Simon and Schuster, 1973), pp. 146–57.

26. Lützeler, *Hermann Broch*, pp. 37–38.

27. Max Adler, *Marxismus und Ethik: Texte zum neukantianischen Sozialismus*, ed. Rafael de la Vega and Hans-Jörg Sandkühler (Frankfurt am Main, 1970), pp. 178–83.

28. For a discussion of this term, see below, note 9 to chapter 2.

29. Letter to Gina Kraus, quoted by Lützeler, *Hermann Broch*, p. 47.

30. Fritz Stern, *The Politics of Cultural Despair: A Study in the Rise of the Germanic Ideology* (Berkeley: University of California Press, 1961), p. 1.

31. See William J. McGrath, *Dionysian Art and Populist Politics in Austria* (New Haven: Yale University Press, 1974).

32. "Zum Begriff der Geisteswissenschaften," in *Philosophische Schriften I*, pp. 115–30; "Zur Erkenntnis dieser Zeit: Paradigmatische Skizzen zur Geschichtstheorie," in *Philosophische Schriften II*, pp. 11–80.

33. Although Heinrich Rickert asserted that the historian must provide "value-free" analyses of his material, Dilthey never thought this possible. Though this distinction is probably not what Broch had in mind when he somewhat vaguely labeled Dilthey a positivist, it nevertheless provides further evidence for the apositivistic quality of his thought. On this Dilthey/Rickert distinction, see Friedrich Meinecke's essay "Historicism and its Problems," in *The Varieties of History*, ed. Fritz Stern (New York: Vintage Books, 1956 [1973], pp. 267–88. On Dilthey in general see Michael Ermarth, *Wilhelm Dilthey: The Critique of Historical Reason* (Chicago: University of Chicago Press, 1978).

34. Hajo Holborn, "Wilhelm Dilthey and the Critique of Historical Reason," in *European Intellectual History Since Darwin and Marx*, ed. W. Wagar (New York: Harper & Row, 1966), pp. 64ff.

35. *The Sleepwalkers*, book 3, chap. 11, p. 373. All citations from *The Sleepwalkers* are from the translation by Willa and Edwin Muir (Boston: Little Brown, 1932).

36. As was the case with "rationalism," Broch's understanding of the term "naturalism" is highly idiosyncratic. Here he uses it as a synonym for "instinctual" or "immediate." His discussion of naturalism in the section of *Hofmannsthal and His Time* on Van Gogh and Cézanne (chap. 1), however, uses the term in a more standard manner. In that discussion, Broch states that these two painters overcame their naturalist heritage.

37. The first book of *The Sleepwalkers* was actually published in December 1931 but was listed as a 1932 publication.

38. Schlant, *Hermann Broch*, p. 37.

39. "Das Weltbild des Romans," in *Schriften zur Literatur II*, pp. 89–118. It would be very lucrative to compare Broch's essay on the novel to Georg Lukács's *Theory of the Novel*. Most relevant is Lukács's discussion of the lost totality of the tragic cosmos, as well as his assertion that subjectivity on the part of an author precludes the attainment of a totality. "The novel is the epic of an age in which the extensive totality of a life is no longer directly given." *Theory of the Novel*, trans. Anna Bostock (Cambridge, Mass.: MIT Press, 1971), p. 56. Compare Broch's discussion of the late nineteenth-century novel in the first chapter of *Hofmannsthal and His Time*.

40. "Das Weltbild des Romans," *Schriften zur Literatur II*, pp. 97ff.

41. Ibid., p. 116.

42. From "Denkerische und dichterische Erkenntnis (Philosophical and Poetic Knowledge)," in *Schriften zur Literatur II*, p. 43.

43. *Beyond Good and Evil*, Aphorism 14; trans. Walter Kaufmann (New York: Vintage Books, 1966), p. 21.

44. "Autobiography as a Program for Future Work," quoted in Schlant, *Hermann Broch*, p. 39.

45. Letter of 10 April 1930 to G. Meyer of the Rhein-Verlag; reprinted as "Problemkreis, Inhalt, Methode der *Schlafwandler*," appendix to the Suhrkamp edition of *Die Schlafwandler*, pp. 723–25.

46. "Autobiography as a Program for Future Work," quoted in Schlant, *Hermann Broch*, p. 39.

47. "James Joyce und die Gegenwart," in *Schriften zur Literatur I*, p. 76.

48. Ibid.

49. This technique of Goethe's is perhaps best exemplified in *Faust II*, act 3. Faust and Helena's identities and language both reveal the juxtaposition of romantic and classical styles.

50. "James Joyce und die Gegenwart," p. 78. Paul Michael Lützeler, in his edition of this essay, has noted that Broch's idea of the "ideal observer" expounded in this passage has more to do with quantum theory than with the theory of relativity (note 17, p. 92). Joseph Strelka, on the other hand, defends Broch's use of the relativity analogy; see Strelka's article "Broch heute," in the volume of the same title which he edited (Bern, 1978), pp. 16–17.

51. "Realism": *Sachlichkeit*. Unlike *Romantik* or *Anarchie*, this term does not denote a style or even a specific objective state; Broch rather expands the term to encompass both these. The term would be most literally translated as "material reality," or "the way things really are." It denotes a materialist cosmos as distinct from an ethical one—a fundamental polarity in Broch's thought. Huguenau is the embodiment of that cosmos. His personality is one of "matter-of-factness," and hence ethical detachment.

52. *Die Schlafwandler*, pp. 723–24; see note 45 above.

53. Ibid.

54. Ibid.

55. Letter of 19 July 1930 to the Rhein Verlag, reprinted in *Die Schlafwandler*, Suhrkamp edition, as "Ethische Konstruktion in den *Schlafwandler*," pp. 726–27.

56. Dorrit Cohn in her monograph *The Sleepwalkers: Elucidations of Hermann Broch's Trilogy* (The Hague: Mouton & Co., 1966) has observed the same use of the metaphor of sleepwalking as the process of artistic creation in Goethe and Ortega y Gasset. Thus, in *Dichtung und Wahrheit* (book 6) Goethe speaks of having written *Wilhelm Meister* "as a sleepwalker" (*als Nachtwandler*). Ortega y Gasset, in *The Dehumanization of Art*, has written that "a novelist, while he writes his novel, must care more about his imaginary world than about any other possible world. If he does not care, how can he make us care? Somnambulist himself, he must infect us with his divine somnambulism" (p. 88, quoted in Cohn, p. 162n.). Interestingly enough, *The Dehumanization of Art* first appeared in German in 1928, the year Broch began work on *The Sleepwalkers*. Broch admired Ortega and referred to him in several

letters (there is no evidence of any correspondence between them). For more on Broch and Ortega, see Bernheim's article "Style," cited above, note 18.

57. Quoted in Schlant, *Hermann Broch*, p. 73.

58. *The Death of Virgil*, trans. Jean Starr Untermeyer (New York: Pantheon, 1945), p. 482. Untermeyer has "speech" for *Sprache*. Henceforth, all citations from *The Death of Virgil* will refer to this translation and edition.

59. Letter to Hermann Weigand, 12 February 1946, in *Briefe III*, pp. 62ff.

60. Letter to Kurt Wolff, dated "end of 1943" (not included in the *Briefe*); included in *Materialen zu Hermann Broch: "Der Tod des Vergil"* (Frankfurt am Main: Suhrkamp, 1976), p. 216. The phrase "in which the hereafter announced its arrival" reads in German "in der sich das Künftige ankündigte." The use of the word "hereafter" (*das Künftige*) may be read as a pun embracing both cultural death and personal death.

61. Ibid., p. 204.

62. In 1968, Erich Kahler asked Anja Herzog, an old friend of Broch's who had lived in Paris in 1938, to write an account of her efforts to get Broch an exit visa. Her account of her visits to the home of an evasive James Joyce, of his disbelief and naiveté with regard to the political events in Austria, is a highly interesting and moving document. It is, as yet, untranslated from the German and unpublished (Herzog file, Hermann Broch Archive, Beinecke Library of Yale University).

63. Letter to Egon Vietta, 14 September 1947, in *Briefe III*, p. 160f.

64. Schlant, *Hermann Broch*, p. 111.

65. *The Death of Virgil*, p. 255.

66. Ibid., p. 312.

67. Untermeyer translates *Erkenntnis* as "perception." I have translated it as "knowledge," both here and throughout the Hofmannsthal essay.

68. *The Death of Virgil*, p. 320.

69. Ibid., p. 327.

70. Letter to Aldous Huxley, 10 May 1945, in *Briefe II*, pp. 449ff.

71. *The Death of Virgil*, p. 476f.

72. See note 70 above.

73. See Dewey, *Freedom and Culture* (New York: Paragon Books, 1934 [1979]); Isaiah Berlin, *Four Essays on Liberty*, (Oxford: Oxford University Press, 1969); also Bernard Williams's Introduction to Berlin, *Concepts and Categories* (New York: Penguin Books, 1978), p. xi; and Bernard Williams, "Conflicts of Values," in *The Idea of Freedom: Essays in Honour of Isaiah Berlin* (Oxford: Oxford University Press, 1979), pp. 221–32. The other liberal thinker who comes to mind in this context is the Austrian-born Karl Popper, whose *Open Society and Its Enemies*, vol. 1 (Princeton: Princeton University Press, 1966), expressly attacks Platonic social theory for its alleged totalitarian precepts.

74. The old stories were published in magazines and had been "long forgotten," in Broch's words. See *The Guiltless*, trans. Ralph Manheim (Boston: Little Brown, 1974), Broch's afterword "How *The Guiltless* Came into Being," p. 289.

75. Ibid., p. 265. Andreas is also the name of the protagonist in Hofmannsthal's unfinished novel of the same name, discussed at length in chapter 3 of *Hofmannsthal and His Time*.

76. Ibid., p. 288.

77. Nietzsche, *The Use and Abuse of History* (Indianapolis: Bobbs-Merrill, 1949 [1979]), section 6, p. 41: "And if you want biographies, do not look for those with the legend 'Mr. So-and-so and his times,' but for one whose title page might be inscribed 'a fighter against his time.'"

## Chapter 1

1. The terms *Bürger, bürgerlich, Bürgertum* present a common but always exasperating translation problem. They cannot be consistently translated as bourgeois and bourgeoisie. The German word *Bürger* differs in tone and evaluation from the French *bourgeois*; the former connotes "solid citizen," the second, "philistine." In general, where Broch describes a German or Austrian context and merely intends to define the class, I have used the words burgher and *Bürgertum*, terms common to books on central European history. Where his context is pan-European or where his tone is pejorative (and these two most often go together), I have used the word "bourgeois." As far as the adjective is concerned, Broch most often uses the term *bürgerlich* in a pejorative manner, and I was thus able to translate it as "bourgeois." In natural German usage, the adjective *bürgerlich* is more pejorative than the nouns *Bürger* and *Bürgertum*.

2. By "rationalism" Broch refers not to the rationalist tradition in philosophy but to a kind of instrumentalism, and essentially a false system of thought. It is a Nietzschean usage. Thus in "Culture 1909" he had written, "Rationalism is the mode of thought of experience . . . it is a disguise of the spirit, not the spirit itself."

3. "Es entspricht den beiden dialektischen Begriffspolaritäten politisch-sozial und dramatisch, dass das Theater in einem strukturhaft natürlichen Verwandtschaftsverhältnis zum Barock steht, während das 19. Jahrhundert, kraft ähnlicher Verwandtschaft, die Romanform, die es für sich entdeckt hatte, zur Blüte gebracht hat." The way this sentence reads in the German, and the way I have translated it literally into English, the "conceptual polarities" are not identified. They are not the polarities of theater-Baroque and novel–nineteenth century, first because these are identified as the phenomena to which the polarities correspond, and second because each pair is in itself not a polarity. It is very possible that Broch intended the phrase "politically-socially and dramatically" to contain the referents of the "conceptual polarities"; perhaps they should be read as adjectives rather than as adverbs, in other words as "political-social and dramatic-[epic] conceptual polarities." These categories make perfect sense in the context of the discussion of the previous paragraph.

4. Meininger Hoftheater: celebrated German theater under the direction of Duke Georg II of Saxe-Meiningen which toured Europe between 1874 and 1890. See Max Grube, *The Story of the Meininger* (Coral Gables, Fla.: University of Miami Press, 1963).

5. Franz Grillparzer (1791–1872): the most celebrated Austrian classical poet and dramatist, whose 1840 play *Dream as Life* (*Das Traum ein Leben*) was, along with Calderón's *Life is a Dream* (*La Vida es Sueño*), the inspiration for Hofmannsthal's *The Tower*.

6. Friedrich Hebbel (1813–63): northern German playwright who settled in Vienna.

7. Broch seems to be referring to a painting called *A Loge at the Théâtre des Italiennes* by Eva Gonzalès, a pupil of Manet's. It was completed in 1871, exhibited at the Paris Salon of 1874, and currently hangs in the Louvre. I am grateful to Ilene Shaw for this reference.

8. I have translated the term *Mythos* as "mythos" rather than "myth" for two reasons. First, *Mythos*/mythos refers to the quality of myths rather than to the actual stories; second, the English "mythos" retains the positive and poetic connotations of the German word as opposed to the potentially pejorative connotations of "myth." Mythos, especially for Broch, refers to a state of truth rather than to a fabrication.

9. Artistic intellect: *Kunstverstand*. In translating *Verstand* as "intellect" I have followed the example of Hannah Arendt's translation of this Kantian term. For a discussion of that very translation choice, see Mary McCarthy's Editor's Postface to Arendt's *Life of the Mind* (New York: Harcourt Brace Jovanovich, 1978), 2:244–45.

10. Ferdinand von Saar (1833–1906): Austrian social realist who ridiculed Hans Makart in the 1904 novella *Der Hellene*. See Carl E. Schorske, *Fin-de-siècle Vienna: Politics and Culture* (New York: Alfred A. Knopf, 1980), pp. 299ff.

11. Broch's evaluation of Brahms follows the traditional late nineteenth-century dichotomy of Wagner the revolutionary versus Brahms the conservative. This view was first challenged in Arnold Schönberg's groundbreaking essay "Brahms the Progressive" (*Style and Idea*, 1950). For an account of the battle about Brahms, see Peter Gay's essay "Aimez-vous Brahms?" reprinted in *Freud, Jews, and Other Germans* (New York: Oxford University Press, 1978).

12. Gerard van Swieten (1700–1772); Joseph Hyrtl (1829–94); Carl von Rokitansky (1804–78); Theodor Billroth (1829–94): for detailed treatment of these four physicians and the Vienna Medical School they formed and reformed, see Erna Lesky, *The Vienna Medical School of the Nineteenth Century* (Baltimore: Johns Hopkins University Press, 1976), trans. L. Williams and I. S. Levij, M.D.

13. Wilhelm Leibl (1844–1900); Franz von Lenbach (1836–1904); Hugo von Habermann (1849–1929); Paul Heyse (1830–1914).

14. Rudolf Baumbach (1840–1905); Friedrich von Halm (Baron Münch-Bellinghausen, 1806–71), today a forgotten writer, but at one point a competitor of Grillparzer's.

15. August von Pettenkofen (1822–89); Rudolf von Alt (1812–1905); Emil Jakob Schindler (1842–92), father of Alma Mahler-Werfel; Tina Blau (1845–1916).

16. Ferdinand Raimund (1790–1836) and Johann Nepomuk Nestroy (1801–62) are generally referred to together as Austria's most famous popular dramatists.

17. The words *mene, mene, tekel, upharsim*: the "handwriting on the wall," interpreted by Daniel to mean that God had weighed Belshazzar and his kingdom, had found them wanting, and would destroy them (*Daniel* 5:25).

18. "The Political Vacuum": subtitle added by Hannah Arendt (her handwritten insertion of the subtitle appears on the manuscript carbon copy she used to edit the 1955 Rhein-Verlag edition of the essay—Hermann Broch Archive, Beinecke Library of Yale University).

19. Broch's original manuscript had read "Austrian F.B.I." instead of "Austrian state police."

20. Friedrich von Gentz (1764–1832) and Adam Heinrich Müller, Ritter von Nitterdorf (1779–1829), statesmen and political philosophers. Among Gentz's writings translated into English: *Origins and Principles of the American revolution compared with the Origins and Principles of the French revolution*, trans. John Quincy Adams (Delmar, N.Y.: Scholars' Facsimile, 1977); *Reflections on the Liberty of the Press in Great Britain* (London, 1820); *On the State of Europe before and after the French Revolution* (London, 1803). See Golo Mann, *Secretary of Europe: The Life of Friedrich von Gentz, Enemy of Napoleon*, trans. William H. Woglom (London: Oxford University Press, 1946). On Adam Müller, see Desider Vikor, *Economic Romanticism in the Nineteenth Century* (New Delhi: New Book Society of India, 1964). The correspondence between Gentz and Müller is available in German (*Briefwechsel zwischen Friedrich Gentz und Adam Müller* [Stuttgart: J. G. Cotter, 1857]).

21. "Sociology of the Gay Apocalypse": subtitle presumably added by Hannah Arendt as well (see note 18).

22. Broch's use of the terms coachmen (*Fiaker*) and counts (*Grafen*) is an allusion to Hofmannsthal's play *Der Fiaker als Graf* (*The Coachman as Count*).

## Chapter 2

1. Four maxims (my translations) from the *Book of Friends* (*Buch der Freunde*). All four are included in the excerpts translated in the volume Broch edited for the Bollingen Foundation, *Hugo von Hofmannsthal: Selected Prose*, pp. 349–76. This volume will henceforth be referred to as the "Bollingen volume." When citing works of Hofmannsthal, I will cite them as they appear in this volume or in other translations. Untranslated works will be cited as they appear in Hugo von Hofmannsthal, *Gesammelte Werke in Einzelausgaben*, ed. Herbert Steiner (Stockholm: Bermann Fischer; Frankfurt: S. Fischer Verlag): vol. 1, *Gedichte und lyrische Dramen*; vol. 2, *Erzählungen*; vols. 3–6, *Prosa* I–IV; vols. 7–10, *Lustspiele* I–IV; vols. 11–14, Dramen I–IV; vol. 15, *Aufzeichnungen*.

2. There is a factual error in Broch's account of the career of Hofmannsthal's great-grandfather Isaak Löw Hofmann (1759–1840). He was actually granted the noble title of "Edler von Hofmannsthal" in 1835 by Ferdinand I.

3. "Wunderkind, wunderschauendes Kind"; Broch's original title for this section had been "Wunderkind in bürgerlichen Rahmen, trotzdem Wunderkind": "*Wunderkind* in a bourgeois realm, *Wunderkind* nonetheless"—Hermann Broch Archive, Yale University.

4. "Was du ererbt von deinen Vätern hast, erwirb es um es zu besitzen." *Faust I*, lines 682–83.

5. From the *Book of Friends*, Bollingen volume, pp. 349–76.

6. *Hugo von Hofmannsthal: Three Plays (Death and the Fool, Electra, The Tower* (1927 version), translated by Alfred Schwarz (Detroit: Wayne State University Press, 1966).

7. *Death and the Fool*, lyrical drama of 1893; see note 6 above.

8. The emperor's personal bodyguard corps, consisting of honored officers too old to serve on active duty.

9. As mentioned in the translator's introduction, there is a crucial distinction in Broch's thought between the ethical and the moral. The first is a normative term and points to the creation of new value systems; the second is usually used pejoratively to characterize a dogma, as in the sense of "conventional morality." The *ethical* is expressed by two German terms: *ethisch* and *sittlich*. The first is usually used to describe an idea, the second to describe a customary practice, an "ethic." I have translated both adjectives as "ethical," and the troublesome noun *Sittlichkeit* as "ethicality." This last term seems both the most reasonable and the most accurate foil to the term "morality" (*Moralität*).

10. Hofmannsthal was buried in Franciscan garb. The renowned Hofmannsthal scholar Rudolf Hirsch told me that this ritual was a wish of Hofmannsthal's youth, which he would no longer have wished enacted at the time of his death.

11. From the *Book of Friends*.

12. It is unclear which Hofmannsthal text—if any—is being referred to here.

13. One would expect the line to read "Es wird ein *Wien* sein"— "There will be a *Vienna*," but Broch's typescript and all the editions read *"Wein."*

14. *Der Tod des Tizian* (1892), in *Gedichte und lyrische Dramen*, pp. 181–98; *Everyman: The Play of the Death of a Rich Man, revised (Jedermann: Das Spiel vom Sterben des Reichen Mannes, Erneut*, 1911), in *Dramen* II, pp. 7–93.

15. Paraphrase of the maxim from the *Book of Friends* which reads: "Every representation of a being entity (*eines Seienden*) is automatically an indiscretion."

16. Arnold Böcklin (1827–1901): along with Puvis de Chavannes perhaps the most famous nineteenth-century landscape painter, known for romantic, mythological scenes; Hans von Marées (1837–87).

17. *Gespräch über Gedichte, Prosa* II.

18. "Und dennoch sagt er viel, der 'Abend' sagt." 7th stanza, "Ballade des äusseren Lebens," *Gedichte und lyrische Dramen*.

19. "Wie schön ist diese Schlacht": *Das Kleine Welttheater, oder die Glücklichen (The Little Theater of the World, or The Happy Ones), Gedichte und lyrische Dramen*.

20. The initials *k.k.* stand for *kaiserlich, königlich*; imperial, royal. A standard Austrian prefix, in its abbreviated form especially vulnerable to parody, as the letters "k.k." are pronounced "kaka." Robert Musil immortalized that parody and referred to late Habsburg Austria as "Kakania" (*The Man Without Qualities*, book I, chapter 8).

21. Princess Pauline Metternich-Sandor (1836–1921), granddaughter of Klemens von Metternich. She married her uncle, Richard von Metternich, Klemens's son, and became a celebrated hostess in Paris and Vienna.

22. *Der Schwierige*, Lustspiel in Drei Akten; *The Difficult One*, Comedy in Three Acts, in *Lustspiele* II, pp. 145–314. William Johnston has referred to *Der Schwierige* and its theme of language and silence as "the closest parallel that Austrian thought offers to Wittgenstein" (*The Austrian Mind* [Berkeley: University of California Press, 1972], pp. 212–13).

23. "Der Dichter und diese Zeit" (1927) in *Prosa* II, pp. 264–98. Hofmanns-thal's son Raimund considered this essay among his father's most important, and wrote a letter to Broch expressing disappointment that it was not to be included in the Bollingen volume. Hermann Broch Archive, Yale University.

24. Motto after Grillparzer in Hofmannsthal's "Austria's Answer" (*Österreichs Antwort*) in *Gedichte und lyrische Dramen*, p. 95.

25. "Tolstoi" (1910), in *Prosa* II, p. 417.

26. From the *Book of Friends*.

27. "The Development of Poetic Form in Hugo: Style and Expression," part of "Study of the Development of the Poet Victor Hugo" (*Studie über die Entwicklung des Dichters Victor Hugo*), *Prosa* I, pp. 315–98.

28. From the *Book of Friends*.

29. Ibid.

30. Ibid.

31. Letter of 13 September 1912; see *The Correspondence between Richard Strauss and Hugo von Hofmannsthal* (London: William Collins, 1961; reprinted Cambridge University Press, 1980).

32. From the *Book of Friends*.

33. "A Letter," Bollingen volume, pp. 129–41; discussed at length in chapter 3 of *Hofmannsthal and His Time*.

34. From the *Book of Friends*.

35. Ibid.

36. The phrase "nun im Wege einer barock-gefärbten grossen Oper" is painfully ambiguous, and can be alternately read as "*by means* of a baroque-tinted grand opera," i.e., *Der Rosenkavalier*.

## Chapter 3

1. *Märchen der 672. Nacht, Erzählungen*, pp. 7–28; *Andreas, oder Die Vereinigten*, Bollingen volume, pp. 3–128; *Die Frau ohne Schatten*, Bollingen volume (chapter 4 only), pp. 220–46; *Das Bergwerk zu Falun, Gedichte und Lyrische Dramen*.

2. Previously Broch used the term *Ich-Verschweigung*, which I translated as "ego-suppression." Here the terms are *Selbst-Verschweigung* and *Ich-Verschwiegenheit*.

3. Sanskrit *tat tvam asi*: "That art thou," "that" referring to the transcendent godhead ("brahman"), "thou" to the individual soul ("atman"). It is the teaching of the son of Uddalaka Aruni in the sixth book of the Chandogya-Upanishad. Broch most likely got this from Schopenhauer's *Foundation of Morals* (*Grundlage der Moral*); it is mentioned in conjunction with Schopenhauer in Broch's early essays "Culture 1908–1909." I am grateful to Wendy O'Flaherty for the translation of the Sanskrit.

4. The English phrase "work in progress" appears in Broch's original manu-script, presumably as a reference to Joyce's working title for *Finnegans Wake*.

5. "Die Ironie der Dinge," title of the first of "Three Small Reflections (*Drei kleine Betrachtungen*," 1921) in *Prosa* IV, pp. 40–44.

6. *Reitergeschichte*, Bollingen volume, pp. 321–31; *Das Erlebnis des Marschalls*

*von Bassompierre*, Bollingen volume, pp. 309–20; *Lucidor*, Bollingen volume, pp. 332–48; *Dämmerung und Nächtliches Gewitter*, Bollingen volume, pp. 215–19; *The Letter of the Last Contarin* (*Der Brief des letzten Contarin*), in *Erzählungen*.

7. *Das kleine Welttheater* (1897), in *Gedichte und lyrische Dramen*, pp. 297–316.

8. "Song of Voyage" ("Reiselied") (1897), ibid., p. 11.

9. "*Farben*," Bollingen volume, pp. 142–53.

10. *Moments in Greece*, Bollingen volume, pp. 165–90.

11. "Fez": from the essay "Voyage in North Africa ("Reise im nördlichen Afrika")," Bollingen volume, pp. 191–97.

12. "Gotthold Ephraim Lessing," *Prosa* IV, pp. 480–85.

## Chapter 4

1. Emil Orlik (1870–1932): *Jugendstil* painter and graphic artist noted for the Japanese influence on his work; Joseph Maria Olbrich (1867–1908): architect of the "Secession" building in Vienna.

2. The reference is to Madame Renée Saccard, wife of Saccard, a protagonist in Zola's *Rougon-Macquart* novels. Broch's text reads "the ladylike to the moneygrubber Saccard" on the assumption that both "Saccards" will be identified by the reader. P. M. Lützeler, editor of the 1975 Suhrkamp edition, wisely added "[Madame Renée]," and I have followed his example.

3. Elsa, Bertha, Martha, Grete Wiesenthal (born in 1886): Viennese dancers known for their settings of Strauss waltzes.

4. Moritz Heimann (1868–1925); Anselm von Feuerbach (1829–80): nephew of Ludwig Feuerbach; a classicist painter and professor at the Vienna Academy of Fine Arts who ridiculed Hans Markart for his lack of understanding of anatomy.

5. "Nijinsky's *Afternoon of a Faun*" ("Nijinskys *Nachmittag eines Fauns*) in *Prosa* III, p. 146.

6. Georg Christoph Lichtenberg's (1742–99) portrait of Shakespearian actor David Garrick.

7. The story actually dates from 1919; the opera was premiered in the same year.

8. *Josephslegende*, with Harry Graf Kessler, music by Richard Strauss (1914), choreographed by Michel Fokine; *Achilles on Skyros*, ballet in one act (1925).

9. Operas with Richard Strauss after *Elektra* (premiered 1909): *Ariadne auf Naxos* (one-act version 1912; second version with prologue 1916); *Der Rosenkavalier* (1911); *Die Frau ohne Schatten* (1919); *Die ägyptische Helena* (1928), *Arabella* (1933). For a full account of the genesis of these operas, see *The Correspondence Between Richard Strauss and Hugo von Hofmannsthal*, cited above, chapter 2, note 31.

10. "On Character in the Novel and the Drama. Conversation between Balzac and Hammer-Purgstall in a Döbling Garden in the Year 1842," Bollingen volume, pp. 268–84 (under the title "Balzac").

11. *The Golden Apple* (*Der Goldene Apfel*), in *Erzählungen*, pp. 29–48; *The Tale of the Veiled Woman* (*Das Märchen der Verschleierten Frau*, 1900), ibid., pp. 76–86.

12. *Andreas*, Bollingen volume, p. 121 (translation adjusted).

13. Ibid., p. 122 (translation adjusted).

14. Essay on "The Egyptian Helen," in *Prosa* IV, p. 459.

15. "Fear," Bollingen volume, pp. 55–64.
16. Broch's first draft had read "Signac" instead of "Pissarro" here.
17. From the *Book of Friends*.
18. "This glow": "*dieser Schein.*" An untranslatable pun: *Schein* (noun) means glow; *schein* (adjective) means "seeming," "false," "pseudo-."
19. From the *Book of Friends*.
20. *Das Salzburger Grosse Welttheater, Dramen* III, pp. 251–335.
21. Franz Löser (1884–1953): star of the 1922 production of *Jedermann*. As for Broch's account of the Salzburg Festival audience being dressed up as a medieval congregation, I have not found it to be corroborated in any account (or photograph) of the *Jedermann* performances.

# HERMANN BROCH:
# A SELECT BIBLIOGRAPHY

Although Broch's major fiction has been translated into English, his essayistic work has not been. Similarly, most of the secondary literature in English focuses on the novels. What follows here is a listing of Broch's complete works in German as they appear in the Suhrkamp series edited by Lützeler. I have then listed a major selection of the secondary literature in English. A complete Hermann Broch bibliography is currently under preparation by Professor Klaus W. Jonas of the University of Pittsburgh, and I am grateful to him for the references he has contributed to this bibliography. For a complete listing of sources prior to 1971, see Jonas's first Hermann Broch bibliography, included as an appendix to *Hermann Broch–Daniel Brody Briefwechsel, 1930–1951*, edited by Bertold Hack and Mariette Kleiss (Frankfurt am Main: Buchhändler Vereinigung, 1971).

## Broch's Work in German

*Hermann Broch: Kommentierte Werkausgabe*. Edited by Paul Michael Lützeler. Frankfurt am Main: Suhrkamp Verlag, 1974–81. The following volumes have appeared. Creative writings: *Die Schlafwandler; Die Unbekannte Grösse; Die Verzauberung; Der Tod des Vergil; Die Schuldlosen; Novellen, Prosa, Fragmente; Dramen; Gedichte*. Philosophy and Criticism: *Schriften zur Literatur I: Kritik* (includes *Hofmannsthal und seine Zeit*, pp. 111–284, 300–334); *Schriften zur Literatur II: Theorie; Philosophische Schriften I: Kritik; Philosophische Schriften II; Theorie; Politische Schriften; Massenwahntheorie*. Letters: *Briefe I: 1913–1938; Briefe II: 1938–1945; Briefe III: 1945–1951*.

## Broch's Work in English translation

*The Sleepwalkers*. Translated by Willa and Edwin Muir. Boston: Little, Brown, 1932. Reprint, New York: Universal Library, 1971.

*The Unknown Quantity*. Translated by Willa and Edwin Muir. New York: Viking Press, 1935.
*The Death of Virgil*. Translated by Jean Starr Untermeyer. New York: Pantheon, 1945. Reprints: New York: Universal Library, 1965; Gloucester, Mass.: Peter Smith, 1976; San Francisco: North Point Press, 1983.
*Short Stories*. Edited by Eric Herd. London: Oxford University Press, 1966.
*The Guiltless*. Translated by Ralph Manheim. Boston: Little Brown, 1974.

## Works about Broch in English

### Books

Cohn, Dorrit C. *The Sleepwalkers: Elucidations of Hermann Broch's Trilogy*. The Hague: Mouton & Co., 1966.
Schlant, Ernestine. *Hermann Broch*. Boston: Twayne Publishers, 1978.
Ziolkowski, Theodore. *Hermann Broch*. Columbia Essays on Modern Writers. New York: Columbia University Press, 1964.

### Articles

Arendt, Hannah. "The Achievement of Hermann Broch." *Kenyon Review* 11 (1949): 476–83.
———. "Hermann Broch." In *Men in Dark Times*. Translated by Richard and Clara Winston. New York: Harcourt, Brace & Jovanovich, 1968.
———. "A Writer's Conscience." *Times Literary Supplement* 29 (March 1963): 209–10.
Bauke, J. P. "A German Classic: *The Sleepwalkers*." *New York Times Book Review*, 11 October 1964.
Bunzel, Joseph W. "Hermann Broch as a Teacher." *Books Abroad* 26, no. 1 (1952): 31–33.
Casey, Timothy J. "Questioning Broch's *Der Versucher*." *Deutsche Vierteljahrschrift für Literaturwissenschaft und Geistesgeschichte* 47 (1973): 467–507.
Cassirer, Sidonie. "Hermann Broch's Early Writings." *PMLA* 75 (1960): 453–62.
———. "The Short Stories of *Die Schuldlosen*." Yale University, 1957 (dissertation).
Frank, Waldo. "The Novel as Poem: *The Death of Virgil*." *New Republic* 113, no. 8 (20 August 1945): 226–28.
Hanson, W. P. "Hermann Broch's *Unknown Quantity*." *New German Studies* (Hull, England) 2 (1974): 157–70.
Hardin, James. "*Der Versucher* and Hermann Broch's Attitude Toward Positivism." *German Quarterly* 39 (1966): 29–41.
———. "Hermann Broch's Theories on Mass Psychology and *Der Versucher*." *German Quarterly* 47 (1974): 24–33.
———. "The Theme of Salvation in the Novels of Hermann Broch." *PMLA* 85 (1970): 219–77.

Herd, Eric. "Hermann Broch and the Legitimacy of the Novel." *German Life and Letters* 13 (1960): 262-70.

———. "The Guilt of the Hero in the Novels of Hermann Broch." *German Life and Letters* 18 (1964): 30–39.

Huxley, Aldous. "Why Virgil Offered a Sacrifice: Historical Narrative in a Massive and Elaborate Work of Art." *New York Herald Tribune Books*, 8 July 1945, p. 5.

Kahler, Erich. "The Epochal Innovations in Hermann Broch's Narrative." In *The Legacy of the German Refugee Intellectuals*. Edited by Robert Boyers. New York: Schocken Books, 1972. Pp. 186–92.

*Modern Austrian Literature*, vol. 13, no. 4 (1980): Special Hermann Broch Issue. Articles in English: Theodore Ziolkowski, "Broch's Image of Virgil and its Context," pp. 1–30; Mark Bernheim, "Style: Abstraction and Empathy in Hermann Broch's *Die Schlafwandler*," pp. 59–76.

Mueller, Randolph R. "Waiting for the Logos." *Celebration of Life*. New York: Sheed & Ward, 1972. P. 251-72.

Osterle, Heinz D. "Hermann Broch: *Die Schlafwandler*, Revolution and Apocalypse." *PMLA* 86, no. 5 (October 1971): 946–58.

Sammons, Christa. "Hermann Broch Archive—Yale University." *Modern Austrian Literature* 5 (1972): 18–69.

Schlant, Ernestine. "Hermann Broch's Theory of Symbols Exemplified in a Scene from *The Death of Virgil*," *Neophilologus* 54 (1970): 53–64.

———. "Hermann Broch and Modern Physics." *Germanic Review* 53, no. 2 (Spring 1978): 69–75.

Simpson, Malcolm R. *The Novels of Hermann Broch*. Bern, Frankfurt, Las Vegas: European University Papers, 1977.

Sparks, Kim. "A Geometry of Time." Princeton University, 1964 (dissertation).

Strelka, Joseph. "Hermann Broch, Comparatist and Humanist." *Comparative Literature Studies* 12 (1975): 67–79.

Weigand, Hermann J. "Broch's *Death of Virgil*: Program Notes." *PMLA* 62 (1947): 525–54.

———. "*Die Schuldlosen*: An Approach." *PMLA* 68 (1953): 323–34.

White, J. J. "The Identity and Function of Bertrand in Hermann Broch's *Die Schlafwandler*." *German Life and Letters* 24 (1970–71): 135–44.

Winkler, Michael. "The Wanderer in Search of a System." *German Quarterly* 48 (1975): 234–43.

Ziolkowski, Theodore. "Hermann Broch: *The Sleepwalkers*." In *Dimensions of the Modern European Novel: German Texts and European Contexts*. Princeton: Princeton University Press, 1969. Pp. 139–80.

———. "Hermann Broch and Relativity in Fiction." *Wisconsin Studies in Comparative Literature* 3 (1967): 365–76.

## Fin-de-siècle Austria: Selected English Historiography

Boyer, John W. *Political Radicalism in Late Imperial Vienna*. Chicago: University of Chicago Press, 1981.

Janik, Allan, and Stephen Toulmin. *Wittgenstein's Vienna*. New York: Simon and Schuster, 1973.

Jászi, Oscar. *The Dissolution of the Habsburg Monarchy*. Chicago: University of Chicago Press, 1929 (reprinted 1971).

Johnston, William M. *The Austrian Mind: An Intellectual and Social History, 1848–1939*. Berkeley: University of California Press, 1972.

Macartney, C. A. *The Habsburg Empire, 1790–1918*. New York: Macmillan, 1969.

May, Arthur. *The Hapsburg Monarchy, 1867–1914*. Cambridge: Harvard University Press, 1951. Reprint, New York: W. W. Norton, 1968.

———. *The Passing of the Hapsburg Monarchy, 1914–1918*. 2 vols. Philadelphia: University of Pennsylvania Press, 1966.

McGrath, William J. *Dionysian Art and Populist Politics in Austria*. New Haven: Yale University Press, 1974.

Schorske, Carl E. *Fin-de-siècle Vienna: Politics and Culture*. New York: Alfred A. Knopf, 1980.

Williams, C. E. *The Broken Eagle: The Politics of Austrian Literature from Empire to Anschluss*. New York: Harper & Row, 1974.

Zweig, Stefan. *The World of Yesterday*. London: Cassell, 1953.

# INDEX

Adler, Max, 10
Aeschylus, 162
aestheticism, 2, 3, 4, 34, 79, 90, 93–
   95, 100, 101, 121, 124, 126, 127,
   138, 145, 149, 165, 174–75.
Alt, Rudolf von, 60
architecture, 7–8, 33, 110–11, 149.
   *See also* style
Arendt, Hannah, 5, 191 nn. 9 and 18,
   192 n. 21
Aristophanes, 162
*art pour l'art, l'*, 15, 16, 42–46, 51, 58,
   103, 166, 169–71, 180, 182–83
Augustine, 182
Austro-Marxism, 10
avant-garde, 154–56, 161, 166, 171,
   177, 183

Bach, J. S., 126, 169
Bahr, Hermann, 96, 144
ballet, 148, 152
Balzac, Honoré de, 36, 47, 50, 160,
   161, 156, 162
Baroque, 8, 37, 77; Baroque politics,
   37, 62, 64–66, 79
Barrès, Maurice, 150
Barrett, John D., 4

Baudelaire, Charles, 40, 42, 44–47,
   110, 120, 151; *Les Fleurs du mal*, 44
Baumbach, Rudolf, 60
Beer-Hofmann, Richard, 96
Beethoven, Ludwig van, 61, 104
Berg, Alban, 3, 153
Berlin, Isaiah, 27, 189 n. 73
*Bildung*, 87–88, 93, 95, 101, 109–10.
   *See also* aestheticism
Billroth, Theodor, 59
Bismarck, Otto von, 65
Bizet, Georges, 57
Blau, Tina, 60
Böcklin, Arnold, 98
Bollingen Society, 4
Boucher, François, 144
Brahms, Johannes, 17, 57, 86, 191 n.
   11
Braque, Georges, 154
Broch, Hermann: "The Concept of
   the Human Sciences," 12, 13;
   "Culture 1908–1909," 6–7; *The
   Death of Virgil*, 1, 22–27; *The Guilt-
   less*, 20, 27; "James Joyce and the
   Present," 19; *Mass Psychology*, 1, 4,
   19, 26–27; "Notes to a Systematic
   Aesthetic," 8–10; "Ornament, or